COME RIDE
WITH ME

COME RIDE
WITH ME

LORRAINE DUBE

Library of Congress Control Number:		2010917633
ISBN:	Hardcover	978-1-4568-2426-6
	Softcover	978-1-4568-2425-9
	Ebook	978-1-4568-2427-3

This book was printed in the United States of America.

To order additional copies of this book, contact:
Xlibris Corporation
1-888-795-4274
www.Xlibris.com
Orders@Xlibris.com
89260

DEDICATION

This book is dedicated to my super kid, my daughter Melissa
who is also my best friend, mentor, teacher, editor and therapist,
to my three equally super sons, Jerry, Larry and Roger,
who have filled my life with precious memories, to my grandsons
Andrew and Austin, especially, and to all the generations
that will follow them. Last, but not least, it is dedicated to the
memory of my dear Bob.

ACKNOWLEDGEMENTS

First, I thank my dear daughter, Melissa, who planted the seed and encouraged me all the way.

Next, thanks are due to my three sons, Jerry, Larry and Roger for helping in whatever way they could, like tech support, arts and crafts assistance and in doing chores to free my time.

Thanks, for sure, are due my dear daughter-in-law Sheree for her suggestions and for letting me kidnap her husband, Son #1, on his Fridays off, so he could upgrade the memory on my computer and many other things.

I have to also thank my dear son-in-law, Phil, the English bloke, who walked me through many tech problems that I encountered and with such patience with me, a "two-left-feet" amateur.

Others who helped me along the way and must be mentioned are: my sisters, Dee Dee and Lulu, as I picked their brains about memories of our childhood; my cousin Leo, the "official Berube family genealogist," because his very professional work made my work so much easier; my dear cousin Micheline in Amqui, who helped me with my extended Canadian family research and doubled as my French tutor (*ma maîtresse du Français*); my dear cousin, Carmen Dube, (Sister Carmen Dube, of *Les Soeurs de Nôtre-Dame du Perpetuel Secours* in *Québec*), who indirectly helped me. She was the one who really got me started on my genealogy research of the Dube family when she first did her work and sent my Dad a copy of her research, way back in 1982; the New Bedford Free Public Library, who helped me fill in some details along the way and my Jesus Marie Academy friends and classmates who all supplied abundant and endless encouragement.

I may have written this book alone but it was possible only because of all the help I received. THANK YOU ALL!

If I omitted anyone that I should have acknowledged, please forgive me.

FOREWORD

Tapestry of Life*—(from the website of John Mark Ministries)

By Rowland Croucher and others—September 2003

*(Author unknown)

As I faced my Maker at the last judgment, I knelt before the Lord along with all the other souls. Before each of us laid our lives like the squares of a quilt in many piles. An angel sat before each of us sewing our quilt squares together into a tapestry that is our life.

But as my angel took each piece of cloth off the pile, I noticed how ragged and empty each of my squares was. They were filled with giant holes.

Each square was labeled with a part of my life that had been difficult, the challenges and temptations I was faced with every day of my life. I saw hardships that I endured, which were the largest holes of all.

I glanced around me. Nobody else had such squares. Other than a tiny hole here and there, the other tapestries were filled with rich color and the bright hues of worldly fortune. I gazed upon my own life and was disheartened. My Angel was sewing the ragged pieces of cloth together, threadbare and empty, like binding air.

Finally the time came when each life was to be displayed, held up to the light, the scrutiny of truth. The others rose, each in turn, holding up their tapestries. So filled their lives had been. My angel looked upon me, and nodded for me to rise. My gaze dropped to the ground in shame. I hadn't had all the earthly fortunes. I had had love in my life, and laughter.

But there had also been trials of illness, and death, and false accusations that took from me my world as I knew it. I had to start over many times.

I often struggled with the temptation to quit, only to somehow muster the strength to pick up and begin again. I spent many nights on my knees in prayer, asking for help and guidance. In my life I had often been held up to ridicule, which I endured painfully, each time offering it up to the Father in hopes that I would not melt within my skin beneath the judgmental gaze of those who unfairly judged me.

And now, I had to face the truth. My life was what it was, and I had to accept it for what it was. I rose and slowly lifted the combined squares of my life to the light. An awe-filled gasp filled the air. I gazed around at the others who stared at me with wide eyes. Then I looked upon the tapestry before me.

Light flooded through the many holes, creating an image—the face of Christ.

Then our Lord stood before me, with warmth and love in His eyes. He said, *"Every time you gave over your life to Me, it became My life, My hardships, My struggles. Each point of light in your life is when you stepped aside and let Me shine through, until there was more of Me than there was of you."*

"You are the light of the world. A city on a hill cannot be hidden."

"Let your light shine before men in such a way that they may see your good works, and glorify your Father who is in Heaven."—Matthew 5:14,16 (NASB)

INTRODUCTION

"Chacque nation comme chacque individue, à reçu une mission et il doit l'accomplire. Celle du personnage donc j'invoquerai ce soir le souvenir à été accompli à merveille et mérite d'être connue de la nation Franco-Americaine."—Joseph de Maistre

The translation of the above passage is: "Each nation as with each individual, has received a mission which must be accomplished. That of the personage I will recall the *souvenir* of tonight was marvelously accomplished and deserves to be known by the Franco-American nation."

Those were the opening lines of a speech I gave for a French oratorical contest when I was a junior in high school about the life of *Monsigneur* Charles D'Auray, a prominent figure in the Franco-American community of Woonsocket, Rhode Island. That was more than fifty years ago. I have never forgotten those opening lines and could never figure out why.

I think I now know why. My own mission on earth is not yet finished. I have not yet accomplished the mission that God assigned to me when I was born to this life. Never mind the *marvelous* part of it. I do hope He settles for accomplished period, whenever that accomplished part happens.

I think that perhaps part of my mission is to record my life on paper for my grandsons and for the generations that will follow them. Why? Well, I've had a roller-coaster-ride kind of life, as I'm sure many others have. Having never fallen off that roller coaster, and how I was able to hang on to the sometimes more-than-scary rides, *is* the story of my life. I know that the first scary ride, which began in the summer of 1964, was just the beginning.

In retrospect, I think that was my first adult scary ride, the "preparation" one, after having experienced the enjoyable kiddy rides of my idyllic childhood and young adult years. Little did I know that I would experience many interesting rides, challenging rides and even fast rides (like at warp 10 speed)—rides that would continue until I rode the mother-of-all-roller-coaster ride that began in 1997.

What were the events and experiences of my early life from childhood to adulthood that molded my character and prepared me for that roller coaster life? Over the years I've related to my children many stories about my childhood. They all know the story of the mother-of-all-roller-coaster ride because they were all adults by that time, and they rode that scary coaster right by my side. So, my primary purpose is to record for all the generations that will follow me the story of their *Mémère*'s life. My dear daughter, my best friend, Melissa, is the one who suggested to me that I write it all down. This is the result of that effort.

I will strive to write simply and from the heart, always trying to stay true to the facts and not to embellish this tale in any way. "Write simply and don't embellish" were two specific instructions from my daughter. Inserting quips reflecting my sense of humor, when parts of my story become too heavy or depressing, should help to lighten it up.

I will write as if my grandsons were sitting here listening to every word. They may read this story only once, even only when they are well into adulthood, but at least it will all be written down for them. Hopefully, they will glean hope, inspiration and perseverance from my story, along with a few chuckles when they read about their *Mémère*'s *"Freddy Flintstone"* growing-up years, and they will always have something to remember me by.

My life story could give them the courage and determination to ride their own individual roller coasters of life when they happen and serve to guide them to also becoming true survivors like their *Mémère*. I hope it will always remind them all that they came from good, strong Franco-American and French-Canadian stock.

While I am often speaking directly to my grandsons in this story, equally as often I am not. As the roller coaster accelerates, my story takes some twists and turns and I find myself speaking to everyone and no one in particular. While this story was written for my grandchildren, telling it actually became a sort of therapy that helped me deal with my chronic pain—a *souvenir* from my battle with cancer. I believe my story carries a message of survival and hope for everyone. I hope my story brings you the strength to survive your own battles—ones you may have already faced but still struggle with and ones that may still be ahead of you.

I'm Lorraine Dube Barnes and this is the story of my life, which I began writing in May 2005.

Here we go! Hang on!

The roller coaster is taking off. Come ride with me.

With the exception of my primary care physician, all doctors' names have been omitted. All company and product names may be trademarks or service marks of their respective owners.

PART I

CHAPTER 1

"I remember" is the motto of the American-French Genealogy Society of which I am a member. In order for all of us to know who we are we must try to recall our past and especially the history of those who came before us. In these early chapters I will attempt to do so, so that you, my dear grandsons, will better know who I am and then be able to fully understand how it was that I became a true survivor. Here we go! Climb aboard now for some nostalgic roller coaster rides.

I was born on July 23, 1941 at 3:15 a.m., in New Bedford, Massachusetts, five months before Pearl Harbor Day, the event that catapulted the United States into World War II. I was born at home, as most children were in those days, delivered by Dr. George J. Dion who was attended by a nurse, Mrs. D. Latimer. I weighed in at eight pounds, six ounces.

My parents' tenement (apartments were referred to as tenements back then) was on 125 Sylvia Street. I was the second daughter born to Gerard and Imelda (Berube) Dube who had married on July 4, 1939. My older sister Dolores, nicknamed Dee Dee, had been born on the previous July 12, so we were just one year apart. My younger sister Lucille, or Lulu, was born almost eighteen months later on March 11, 1943. As for my nickname, it was "fatso" because I was the chubby one of the three sisters. That was our complete family as no more children were born to my parents. Dad, I'm sure, had wanted a son, but that was not to be.

Of course, no mention of my family would be complete without noting that we were part of a very large French-Canadian family, on both sides. You will hear much more about my family in the coming chapters.

Dad worked at a big factory in New Bedford. The Atlantic Mills or the Hathaway Mills are two that ring a bell, but I am not certain if it was one of them. He had obtained this job through *Oncle* Georges, his godfather, whom he boarded with for a time. While I know he had first been a factory worker, I don't ever recall hearing him say what his exact job was. He rode his bicycle to work on most days and when he couldn't ride that bike because of the weather, he would pay for his ride to work.

Oncle Georges would charge him for those rides. Being thrifty, Dad would pay for a ride only when necessary so as to conserve more of the meager wages he earned.

After the big 1938 Hurricane that hit New England on September 21, 1938, *Oncle* Georges was able to get my Dad promoted to a carpenter's helper at the factory where they both worked. There had been devastating damage from that 1938 hurricane and there was plenty of work to do to restore the factory. *Oncle* Georges had good carpentry skills. He taught these to Dad as they worked side by side replacing windows, flooring, beams and everything else damaged during the horrendous hurricane that went down in history as one of the worst to ever hit the New England area. That hurricane had no name. It happened before they started naming hurricanes. It was just the "Hurricane of 1938," sometimes called the "Long Island Express."

Here are some trivia facts about hurricanes for you, my dear grandsons. Prior to 1950 hurricanes were not named. The first Atlantic coast hurricane officially named was Able in 1950, one of the eight hurricanes that ravaged the Atlantic coastline that year. Women's names were not assigned until 1953. Names of some hurricanes that were so destructive were retired and never used again. Some of these are: Andrew, Betsy, Carol and of course, Katrina. One was named after a famous First Lady. Do you know who that was? That's your quiz question. Look it up on the Internet. The name used the most times (at least with the same spelling) is ARLENE.

An event that was such a misfortune for so many turned out to be a fortuitous event for my Dad and our family. As an immigrant from Canada, it gave him the opportunity to get his piece of the American Pie, to realize the American dream all immigrants from all the various countries dream of and aspire to which was simply a better life.

As a result of that 1938 hurricane and his "promotion," Dad learned the carpentry trade hands on, a trade that would become his lifetime work. Dad eventually became a union carpenter and was in the union, (Carpenter's Union Local 1305), for more than fifty years. When he retired at age 62, he received a good Carpenter's Union pension to supplement his Social Security retirement check. He collected those union pension checks for almost twenty-five years, until he died in 1998 at age 86.

After that promotion to carpenter's helper, Dad earned more money and was able to save more. Before too long he was upgraded to a full carpenter. Later, after he had been introduced to my Mom and had a proper courtship, he was able to get married. My parents were both 27 at the time of their marriage, having both been born in 1911, just one month apart—him in September and her in October.

The story of how they met and married and of their destinies is interesting and will surely make you a believer in fate and destiny. Dad was born in Canada in a small village called *Mont Joli*, in the province of *Québec*, inland but just a few miles from the shores of the St. Lawrence River. He was the third child of Paul Dube and Élise (Smith) Dube. Dad was a fraternal twin. His twin sister Alice died before she reached her second birthday of what they called "*la grippe*" (a pleurisy or pneumonia). When the twins were born, it was my Dad who was weak and sickly. They baptized him right away as they all believed he would not make it through the night. Alice was baptized in the church a few days later, as was the custom back then. Fate, destiny, or was it just God's Master Plan? I know, do you?

Thanks to my dear great-aunt Rose, (Smith-Roy), my grandmother's sister and only sibling, I am able to relate these details to you. She had such a fantastic memory and I recall the detailed recollections she related to us girls whenever we visited her as children and later when I visited her with my own family. Today, I regret not having taken notes of what she told us over the years.

Isn't it curious that Smith, a Scottish name, came to be part of our French-Canadian family? What follows is the story of how that came to be.

Back in the fall of 1750, a British ship traveling up the St. Lawrence River to reach *Québec* City had to transport one of the sailors to dry land, as he had become very sick on board. This beaching of the sailor happened at *l'Ile des Pelerins*, a small island facing *Kamouraska* on the left bank of the St. Lawrence, approximately one hundred miles before *Québec* City.

There, the captain paid a Canadian family to take the sailor in and nurse him back to health. The plan was to retrieve him when they made their return trip down the St. Lawrence coming back from *Québec* City. Well, it seems this Scotsman, John Smith, became smitten with one of the daughters of the family that nursed him back to health. Her name was Charlotte Desjardins. When the captain returned for him, John asked to be released from his maritime contract so he could remain in Canada and marry his new found love. He was born in Glasgow, Scotland on July 15, 1732. That's how the Scottish Smith family name became intertwined with the French-Canadian names in our family genealogy. While he kept his Scottish last name, he changed his first name to Jacques, the French name for John.

In addition to Adrienne, my Dad's older sister, and Paul, his older brother, Dad also had three younger siblings: Bernadette, Jeanne and Joseph. There were six living children from the union of my paternal grandparents. Tragedy struck when Joseph was just an infant and Dad was only five years old. His dear mother Élise died in 1916 at age 28 after catching a draft. According to my Dad, "She got very sick and never recovered." In reality, it must have been pneumonia or a respiratory infection that went untreated. Back in 1916, living on a farm, poor as all the others, doctors were not readily available to the small village population of *Saint Tharsicius* which was a small borough, situated north outside the area of *Amqui, Québec*, in the *Matapédia* Valley area just before the *Gaspée* Peninsula.

Of course, having six children to feed and care for, and a farm to run as the main source of the family's survival, my grandfather Paul had to find a wife and a mother for his orphaned children without any undue delay. He proposed to Clémentine St. Amand, a first cousin to his recently-deceased wife. Clémentine suffered from a bad hip and leg, and limped her whole her life. Handicap aside, she was a strong woman who could withstand the rigorous life on the farm and care for the children. I am sure it was not a marriage of love. Rather, it was a marriage entered into by necessity. I believe this marriage took place in 1917 as Élise, the first child of this union, was born in January of 1918. Also of note is the fact that Clémentine and Paul shared the same birthday, April 26, although he was seven years older than her. He had been born in 1886 and she in 1893.

Clémentine and Paul settled into the routine of life on the farm. Joseph, the baby, had been boarded out to another family for his infant care right after his mother's death, as were Jeanne, who was about four years old, and Bernadette, who was not quite two years old. Jeanne went to live with *Oncle* Pierre and *Tante* Emma (my grandfather's sister) on their farm outside of *Sayabec*. They had no children and were happy to have her to bring up as their own. Jeanne never returned to her father's farm, but Joseph and Bernadette did. Boys were needed to work the farm, so as soon as he was old enough to help, Joseph rejoined the family. As soon as she was old enough, Bernadette also returned to her father's farm to help with chores and contribute to the family's survival. Even though Jeanne never returned to her father's farm to live and was raised by her aunt and uncle, she was never adopted and kept the Dube name.

Less than one year after their marriage, Clémentine gave birth to the first of the eleven children she would bear Paul, a daughter who they baptized Élise, named after Paul's recently deceased wife. She was born on January 15, 1918, on the deceased Élise's paternal great-great-grandfather's birthday (Jacques Smith; Glasgow, Scotland; July 15, 1732). Adrienne, the oldest child of Paul and Élise's union, was about eight years old when her stepmother gave birth to the first of her own children. *Tante* Adrienne told me that she was the one who washed all the diapers for this baby and for most the babies born after that. There was a new baby almost every year. *Tante* Adrienne got married at sixteen. The last four of her siblings would be born after she left the family farm and married. She told me that she "knew her lot in life" and figured she would "wash diapers for her own babies instead of someone else's."

Ten of Clémentine's eleven children survived to adulthood. The seventh child, Adrien, was killed in a horrific farm accident when he was three years old. From the story my father told me, it happened during the haying season. Adrien had accompanied his father and older brothers to ride the thresher. Whatever happened to cause him to fall off was not made clear to me, but apparently he fell right under the cutting blades and both legs were severed at the thighs. He literally bled to death. Remember, this happened in the early 1900s on a remote farm, far from the nearest doctor. The nearest hospital was in *Rimouski* more than fifty miles away. All travel was by horse and buggy. A later-born son was also called Adrien, named after the little one that so tragically died.

My Dad and his brother Paul worked on the farm alongside their father. Being the two oldest sons, they helped their father carry the burden of feeding and providing for the ever-growing family. When Joseph returned to the farm, he, too, worked alongside his father and two older brothers. With a new baby born to Clémentine and Paul every year, the family had sixteen living children by the time my father left the farm around age 20. His little half-sister Anne-Marie, who was born in 1928, the baby of the family, was not quite four when my Dad left his father's farm.

Obviously, there was no television in those days to pass the long evenings. It was early bedtime, no doubt, in part, to save the precious oil for the oil lamps, and plenty of time for lovemaking that naturally resulted in all those children. Besides that, Paul and Clémentine were strict French-Canadian Catholics who followed the teachings of the Church, never using birth control; not that I think they knew anything whatsoever about birth control. That was just not of their time.

Paul first, and later my Dad, left the farm as soon as the opportunity presented itself. They needed to earn and keep their own wages, saving some for the day when they found the right woman, married and started their own respective families. When he left the family farm at 19, Paul married Blanche Cassista, the niece of his stepmother Clémentine. They first lived in *Saint Tharsicius* as Paul hired himself out as a farmer's helper on the Joe Dumais farm. When their third child, a son named Bertrand, was not yet three years of age, they were able to get a small land grant in *Canton Blais*, outside of *Saint Tharsicius*. In English, a Canton simply means a division of territory, usually a square plot for settlement; this was specified in a cadastral which is a public record, survey, or map of ownership used for taxing purposes. They lived in a tent the first year until *Oncle* Paul had cleared enough land and had enough timber to erect the first humble farmhouse along with the necessary barn. They remained there for more than eight years, sold that farm and purchased a larger farm located in the second rank/row, (*le deuxième rang*), two miles north of the village of *Amqui*, which was to the south of *Saint Tharsicius*. *Amqui*, prior to 1889 when it was incorporated into a town, had been named by the Micmac Indians. The word means: "*La, oú l'eau s'amuse*" (where the two rivers play), as the rivers *Humqui* and *Matapédia* met and ran through the area.

I remember as a young child, when we visited them on that farm, my Dad used to say: "We're almost there," in French, of course, when he would turn onto the *rue de l'Église* and climb up the big hill. From the church, it was just a few miles to *Oncle* Paul and *Tante* Blanche's farm.

I also remember the many stories my dear *Tante* Blanche told me about those first early years of her marriage. She collected bottles in the village so she could turn them in for one penny. They saved every penny they could from the wages *Oncle* Paul earned as a farm helper to Mr. Dumais, until they could apply for a land grant and have sufficient funds to buy tools for land clearing, a tent to live in and the bare necessities to survive. When they got the land grant (a square plot of land) they lived in a tent with two young children, Cécile and Bertrand, for the first year, including the winter months. Three children had been born but they lost their dear Gisèle, on December 8, 1935 when she was just about 3 1/2. She had been born on April 5, 1932. Talk about survivors! When I said "strong French-Canadian stock" in my introduction, I was not exaggerating!

Incidentally, Joe Dumais' wife was Marie Cassista, the aunt of Blanche, Dad's sister-in-law.

Everyone was related to someone back then and it follows that today even we are. Those of us that are of French-Canadian ancestry are all related somewhere in our family lineage. It could be a direct relationship or a relationship through a marriage.

We all share a common grandparent somewhere, even if it goes back twelve generations or more.

Deviating a bit from my story here I will comment, especially to my friends and former classmates from ND and JMA, that WE are related. Think about this! We could be seventh cousins, three times removed or thirteenth cousins, twice removed . . . or however those confusing assignations work. But, believe me, WE ARE ALL RELATED SOMEHOW when we backtrack through our individual genealogy trail.

As an aside, and a bit of trivia, I will add that Blanche's father, Octave, was nicknamed "*le petit noire.*" This means the little black one; it was because he was short in stature and was darker complexioned than the others. Blanche also had one brother named Roland who everyone called "*le castor*", which means "the beaver." I remember visiting him, his wife Jeanne and their two daughters, Micheline and Lise when we visited *Québec* City. His wife was a fantastic seamstress. I also remember their tiny "*logement*" (tenement). Their toilet room was so tiny that you opened the door and literally had to back in to sit on the "throne," I believe this was originally a closet that they made into their "throne room." As children, my sisters and I found that to be so comical.

When Dad left his father's farm, he also went to work as a farmhand for *Monsieur* Joseph Dumais, located not far from my grandfather's homestead. Dad was paid a fair wage as a farmhand for Joe Dumais, plus he received room and board. He saved some money, went to the *Quadrilles*, a Canadian version of square dancing that was the center of the social life, and got smitten with one particular young lady named Germaine Lavoie who, incidentally, shared the same birthday as him, although he was a few years older than her. He courted her and wanted to marry her but her parents discouraged that, especially her father. *Monsieur Lavoie* did not think my father would make a suitable husband as Dad had been weakened since his bout of *pleurisy*, a kind of pneumonia, a few years earlier. Germaine's father thought Dad would always be a sickly man and that his daughter's life would surely be too hard with him. She did not go against her father wishes and the two did not marry. Her father further discouraged the courtship by hiring her out as a nanny to a family in *Lauzon, Québec* some 250 miles away. This totally discouraged my father. He was heartbroken.

That bout of *pleurisy* happened when Dad was lumberjacking during the winter months in the area they referred to as "*la Côte Nord*," which means the north coast. This was an area across the St. Lawrence River off the coast of Matane. He also went to "*faire le bois*," which means wood chopping, in New Brunswick outside of the area of "*la Dalhousie*." When he lived on his father's farm, he spent the winter lumberjacking as there was not so much work to be done taking care of the farm during those months. After he got sick, they brought him down from the mountain on a sled. *Tante* Rose, his mother's sister, and Blanche, who was his brother Paul's wife, nursed him night and day, covering him in ice-cold water sheets to reduce the raging fever. After receiving the Last Rites from the priest, Dad survived against all odds.

The sickness had left him weakened and not back up to his prior full capabilities. He could still do farm work but lumberjack work was no longer possible. Lumberjacking was hard, cold, dangerous work. When Dad and his brother Paul worked as lumberjacks in the winter months, they had to turn over their wages to their father when they returned home in the spring. In return, they were given only enough money from their hard-earned wages to buy a new pair of shoes or boots.

His inability to continue lumberjacking, combined with the fact that he was paid no wages to work on his father's farm, were the reasons he left that farm and boarded himself out as a farmhand at Joseph Dumais' farm.

My Dad's uncle and godfather, *Oncle* Georges (my great uncle) was the oldest brother of his father, Paul (my grandfather). *Oncle* Georges had come to America some years earlier and settled in New Bedford, Massachusetts.

In 1937, Dad contacted *Oncle* in the United States and asked if he could board with him if he was able to pay the necessary train fare to reach New Bedford. He also inquired if *Oncle* would assist him in finding work. He was heartbroken over Germaine being shipped off to Lauzon and ready to make a change in his life and try his luck in America, having heard of *Oncle's* success story from his father. *Oncle* already owned his first house on Tankin Hill Road in New Bedford. His first wife, Ferdinanda, had passed away shortly after their little daughter Amanda had died; *Oncle* always referred to her as "Manda." She had died before she was three years old. *Oncle* had returned to Canada and taken as his second wife, his first wife's younger sister named Celine. He had prospered and my Dad figured he could too.

He first contacted the U.S. Department of Labor—Immigration and Naturalization Service in Newport, Vermont in December 1936. They directed him to contact their office in the Drummond Building in *Montréal* to make his application for admission to the U.S. So Dad immigrated to the U.S. sometime in 1937, traveling by train, and boarded with his *Oncle* Georges on Tankin Hill Road.

Dad was brave and without fear, attributes he held on to all through his life. His fearlessness was never more apparent than when, at age 83, he would drive himself down from *Lauzon, Québec* to visit us in the United States, all alone in the car. You will read later on about how it came to pass that he ended up back in Canada and, of all places, in *Lauzon*.

Just imagine him riding that train first from *Amqui* to *Québec City* and then from *Québec City* to Boston back in 1937, debarking that train and having to find the other local train station for the train that would take him to New Bedford where *Oncle* would meet him. Dad spoke no English, not one word. Imagine the challenge it was for him to purchase the food he ate on that trip. He had to order by sight since he could not read a menu in English. *Oncle* had mailed him the train schedule and instructions on where to go to change trains when he reached Boston, along with slips of paper with useful expressions written in English, with the French translation underneath. These were phrases like: Where is the bathroom? Where can I buy food? What time does the train leave?

Imagine the bravery needed to take that trip! My father, who had a third grade education, spoke no English and knew only one person in the United States.

CHAPTER 2

My parents were introduced through the efforts of "*les soeurs*" Gallant. That's the Gallant sisters, much like the Baldwin sisters on the 1970s television series "The Waltons." They were two unmarried sisters who lived in Fall River. My Dad's *Oncle* Georges always advertised for passengers before he took his yearly summer trip to Canada to see his family. He had numerous brothers, sisters, nieces, nephews, uncles and aunts still living in Canada that he visited every year.

He advertised in the New Bedford newspaper, the *Standard Times* and the Fall River *Herald News* to line up two or three paying passengers who wanted to visit their families in the *Québec* province. Those paying riders would absorb the cost of the gas expense and he would make a very good profit on his yearly trips. The Gallant sisters were often the paying passengers on those trips to Canada. When my Dad had saved some money from the carpentry work at the factory (while still boarding with his uncle), he began to seriously look for a suitable wife to begin the next phase of his life. The Gallant sisters were friends of my mother's family, especially of my mother's older sisters Rose and Marieanne.

On one of those paying passenger trips to Canada, conversation turned to my Dad's future and his hope to find a suitable spouse. The Gallant sisters offered to introduce him to Imelda, the younger sister of their good friends the Berube girls. Mom was the baby of twelve children, age 26 then, the same age as Dad. At age 21, she had lost her mother to an early death. Mom had five living brothers and five living sisters. Another sister, Odiana, had died at the quarantine hospital called "The Pest Hospital" during the big smallpox epidemic of 1900, before my mother was even born (reference: *Fall River Globe* newspaper, May 1900).

Mom had a notable fate and destiny also. She was the only one in her family to graduate from high school, Dominican Academy in Fall River. She had entered the convent after graduation. This convent was in the province of *Québec* and was the congregation of the Sisters of Charity, also called the grey nuns. She completed her novitiate and part of her postulant period, but was not yet professed a nun when a typhoid outbreak hit the convent of *Québec*.

She came near to dying but she did survive, although several nuns did succumb to that terrible infection. She was left with lifetime scars from all the needles she had received. As a consequence of that bout of serious illness she was considerably weakened and physically was not able to endure the rigors of the tough convent life in those days. Mother Superior decided that it would be best to send her home. She was 21. Her mother died at age 66 on June 19, 1933 very soon after my mother returned home from the convent. Neither Mom nor Dad had a living mother at the time of their marriage.

She went to work sewing in one of the factories in the Fall River Borden Mills. She had been born while her family lived in the Borden Mill Blocks. That's what the tenement houses built for the mill workers were named.

I'll insert a bit of local history here. Those Borden Blocks were owned by Mr. Borden, also the owner of the Richard Borden Mills, who was a member of the infamous Borden family. Lizzy Borden was accused of bludgeoning her father and stepmother to death with an axe, but was acquitted after a highly publicized trial. There were several made-for-TV movies about this important Fall River mill-town event that made news around the world. The story was immortalized in the little ditty we all learned as children.

"Lizzy Borden took an axe, and gave her mother forty whacks. When she saw what she had done she gave her father forty-one."

Getting back to my story, my Mom's father had eventually prospered after he immigrated to Fall River from *La Baie des Sables* (Sandy Bay) and *St. Ulric, Québec*. These two small boroughs are near *Matane*. In 1915, with his family grown to include eleven living children, her father purchased a two-decker house with a third floor that had bedrooms for his large family. This was on 266 Hamlet Street in the south end of Fall River in St. Anne's Parish. Marie, the oldest daughter was married before the move to Hamlet Street. Alfred, the second oldest son, was married the following year, in 1916.

The first floor tenement had only two bedrooms. One was for the parents; the other was for two of the unmarried girls. Upstairs, on the third floor, the four boys and remaining four girls who were not yet married had four bedrooms to spread out in. The second floor tenement was rented out at that time for income to help pay the taxes, although my mother's oldest sister Marie later took that second floor tenement with her husband and children after they lost their little home on Winthrop Street for non-payment of taxes. Marie's husband eventually deserted the family leaving her with seven living children to bring up alone. She had given birth to eleven, but only seven were living when he deserted his family. He left the state and she never saw him again, until his death nearly fifty years later, when his sisters had his remains brought to Fall River from the New Jersey area for interment in *Nôtre Dame* Cemetery.

My grandfather never had a mortgage on that property because back then there was never a question of getting credit or a mortgage. He had purchased that two-decker house with cash. Yes, it had taken him more than twenty years. The older children who had turned in their wages from the time they each began working at ages 12 to 14 (as was the tradition back then) had contributed a good chunk to this free-and-clear real estate.

He had immigrated to Fall River in 1889. He had come alone, leaving his pregnant wife behind in order to get himself established. He returned to Canada for short trips to see his family. After the birth of their third child, Alfred in 1891, the whole family returned with my grandfather to Fall River and settled in the Borden Blocks. His first three children were born in Canada. Those that followed were all born in the Borden Blocks. My mother was the last one born in those Borden Blocks, at 611 Rodman Street. Before the smallpox epidemic of 1900, when Odiana died, the family had lived at 559 Rodman, another Borden Block tenement. Old records show that their rent was $1 per week. When they moved to the two-decker that *Pépère* Berube bought with cash, my mother was not quite four years old.

Like Dad, Mom also had been discouraged from marrying her first love. Her best friend Gilda, whom she worked with at the sewing factory, had a brother who was smitten with my mother. I regret that I do not recall what my mother told me his first name was, but there is a photo of him with my Mom when they were attendants at Gilda's wedding. I vaguely recall it being Anthony but I can't be absolutely certain of the name. He wanted to marry Mom. When he asked for her father's permission, *Pépère* Berube said no because he was not Canadian or Franco-American. "It was best she married her own kind." He was a nice young man but not the young man for Mom, according to her father's reasoning. Yes, another father who controlled the destiny of his daughter—like my father's first love in Canada who was shipped off to *Lauzon* as a nanny so she would be permanently discouraged from contemplating marriage to my father. It was their fate and destiny, *n'est-ce-pas?* (Wasn't that so?)

When Dad paid that first courtship visit to Mom sometime in 1938, having been properly recommended by the Gallant sisters, *Pépère* Berube loved him on the spot. Dad was from Canada. In fact, *Amqui* was fifty miles south of *La Baie des Sables* where *Pépère* came from. They could have been neighbors in Canada. They would have conversations for hours on end about the areas surrounding *La Baie des Sables, Matane, St. Ulric, Mont Joli* and *Amqui*. In *Pépère* Berube's mind Dad was a fine gentleman who had a trade, carpentry, and was certainly the suitable young man he thought his daughter should marry. There would be no long courtship or "are we truly in love?" period. They were both 26 by now and time was ticking way. They both knew that opportunities for a good marriage would become increasingly less available. They were married less than one year later at age 27 on July 4, 1939 at St. Anne's in Fall River. They lived with *Oncle* Georges and *Tante* Celine for almost a year in order to save money. My Mom became pregnant within a few months and it was at this time that Dad's *Oncle* bought his second three-decker house on North Front Street sometime in early 1940, with the intention of Mom and Dad moving into one of his tenements there. But his plans were not my Mom's plans and she discussed with my Dad her idea of getting their own tenement away from *Oncle* Georges who was, in her opinion, too controlling. This is how it happened that they set up their first household on Sylvia Street where all three of their girls would be born.

Later on in life when we girls were all married, Dad used to tease my Mom by telling us that when she first saw my Dad she immediately deserted the convent and came home to marry him. Of course that was not true. She had left the convent at least five years before she even knew he existed but he'd like to manipulate the facts and tease her. We all had many a laugh when that comment was made.

Getting back to their respective destinies and fate, it is something to note that they both had near death illnesses, both had wanted to marry their first loves, both had lost their mothers at a young age and both their parents were from the same general area of *Conté Matapédia* in Canada.

That's how destiny brought my Mom and Dad together. They were married for forty-one years before my Mom died of bone marrow cancer at age 69. Now, I do have to relate a bit more about fate and destiny as it is relevant to my father in later years.

After my Mom passed on, Dad was lonely living alone in that big house on Hortonville Road in Swansea, Massachusetts. He wasn't too good at cooking and he loved soup. I would make him a big pot of soup on weekends. He'd visit me every Sunday and, when he left my house, he would take the containers of soup home so he'd have good soup to eat every night for the week. *La bonne soupe* he called it. He came to my house every Sunday to fix things and spend the day. He truly was a lost soul without my mother.

My Mom died on January 21, 1981. Right before the second summer after her passing, I suggested to Dad that he go to *Amqui* for a few months to visit with his numerous brothers and sisters and for a much needed change of scenery. He finally agreed it was a good idea and left, leaving me in charge of gathering the mail for him, paying the bills and looking out for the house. His good neighbors, the Costas, really kept a watch on the house, so I did not have to go but once a week to retrieve the mail. My boys kept the lawn mowed weekly that whole summer.

Dad stayed in *Amqui* for two months, at least, and was scheduled to come home the first week in September. Just before his scheduled return, he called and told me he was delaying his return trip for a few more days to attend *Oncle* Wilfrid and *Tante* Jacqueline's 35th wedding anniversary celebration where he would see so many old friends and distant relatives who were going to attend from the *Montréal* and *Québec* City areas. This he did and then, as planned, made the return trip home to Swansea a few days later. After his return, I noticed something different about him. I didn't know exactly what it was, but definitely something was different. I knew, eventually, he would open up to me and I waited.

In late September, on a Sunday night, when we were having some supper at my house before he returned to his house, he finally opened up to me. He began by saying, "You know a funny thing happened to me when I spent that time in Canada." I said to myself that now I was going to find out why I thought something was different about him. He told me that when he attended that wedding celebration, he saw many old friends and cousins from his young days prior to immigrating to the U.S. He told me that he had met up with Germaine, his old girlfriend, who had come for the celebration from *Lauzon*. She, in fact, was the aunt of *Tante* Jacqueline, whose mother was Germaine's oldest sister. Jacqueline was married to Dad's younger half-brother, *Oncle* Wilfrid. They were the couple celebrating their 35th wedding anniversary. Germaine was also a first cousin to Blanche Cassista Dube, the wife of my Dad's oldest brother Paul.

Well, I guess that when they met up again at that anniversary celebration, that old love flame was rekindled from way back when he had first seen her at the *Quadrilles* and been smitten. He proceeded to tell me all about her and her life. She had been widowed more than twenty years earlier and left to raise seven living children all alone. She had never remarried. She had given birth to ten children in all, but only seven were living now, all grown and adults. She lived in a senior citizen apartment in *Lauzon*, right around the corner from St. Joseph's Church. Although she had never told him, he knew from others that she had not had an easy life. Her husband had been an alcoholic and abusive. No wonder she never chose to remarry.

After giving me a good overview of Germaine he said, "What would you say if I told you I was thinking of getting married again?" He said he knew it was not that long since my Mom had died and people would certainly talk. He also said that it would mean him selling his house in Swansea and moving back to Canada. He knew Germaine spoke no English, while he was bi-lingual. He also knew she would never leave her children who were all in the *Lauzon* area. He told me that he realized he would be leaving us girls behind here in the U.S. if he did remarry and move to Canada. Then he asked me what I thought.

In a nutshell, this is what I told him. I said life is for the living and that his marriage vows to my Mom had included the words, "till death do us part." I asked him if he wanted to live the rest of his days alone and lonely. I told him that other people could talk as much as they wanted to but, in the end, he had to do what was best for him and that talk or gossip would eventually burn itself out. I told him *Lauzon* was only one day's ride from where we lived, and we could visit each other several times a year. We could also talk on the telephone every week. I reminded him that we all had our families, and we couldn't be with him every day. Making that change in his life, he certainly would have that much needed companionship in the days and years remaining to him. I reminded him that none of us knows how long we will live and asked if he really wanted to live whatever time he had left as alone and lonely as he had been since my Mom passed away almost two years earlier.

I guess that's what he needed to hear. It's almost as if he wanted my permission. That very night, he called Germaine in *Lauzon*. He had wisely gotten her telephone number before he made that return trip from Canada in September. A long distance telephone courtship began and by early October, he had asked her if she would come to the U.S. to meet his family and see his home, having made pre-arrangements with his brother Paul to make the trip going to *Lauzon* first to pick Germaine up. Remember, Paul's wife Blanche was Germaine's first cousin.

She said yes she would take the trip. They got engaged when she came on that trip. The reason he wanted her to visit him in the U.S. before he asked her to marry him and before offering to uproot himself and move to *Lauzon* was that he wanted her to see his beautiful home, his family and the friends he had here. He wanted to impress upon her that he would give it all up if she agreed to be his wife. She accepted his proposal. She returned to *Lauzon* and began making the plans for the wedding, which was to take place at St. Joseph's church in Lauzon on December 30, 1982.

Her grown children were flabbergasted when, upon their mother's return from that trip to the U.S. in mid-November, she flashed her beautiful engagement ring and announced she would be married before New Year's. Before taking that trip, she had not gone into any details, nor had she recounted to them the story of meeting up with my father in *Amqui* that past summer. They had assumed it was just an opportunity to see the U.S. with her cousin Blanche. They were all in shock, as their mother had been widowed for more than twenty years and they could not recall when she had ever "kept company" with a man in all that time. She proceeded to tell them the story of her youth and of knowing Gerard, of her father's objection to a marriage between them at that time, of her removal to *Lauzon* as a nanny and the reason for that, of my father's eventual decision to try his luck in the U.S., and how each of their paths in life continued separately until that last summer when they were reunited in *Amqui*.

She also told them the story of that beautiful multi-colored candy dish she had. This dish, of bright carnival glass, was always kept on the top shelf of her cupboard, taken down very carefully and used only for special company and Christmas. Her children all said they sure did remember it as she admonished them every time it was used not to break it. Now they understood why she cherished that dish. My Dad was the one who had given it to her for her 17th birthday when they were "keeping company" and in love in their youth more than fifty years earlier. It was a cherished keepsake from her first love.

In the meantime, back in the U.S., I took Dad to the Canadian Consulate office in Boston so he could get his permanent residency status started for domiciling in Canada. As he was 72, he had to undergo numerous medical tests to determine that he was healthy. The Canadian government would never grant residency status if he wasn't, and they also did a financial check to see if he had sufficient income and resources to support him. They didn't want him "on the dole," I guess. He had become a naturalized American citizen after marrying my mother and had given up his Canadian citizenship. In those days, you couldn't hold dual citizenship. After several trips to Boston, they told him he would be granted permanent residency status after he had been there for a year and gave him a temporary residency status document, which he needed for crossing the border.

Back in Swansea, he put the house up for sale and assigned me Power of Attorney to sign the real estate transfer paperwork. He made his preparations to go to *Lauzon* by December 15. The plan was for him to board with Germaine's son Leo and his wife Micheline until they were married a few weeks later on December 30, 1982. He left everything behind, just taking his personal clothes, tools and a few mementos. He walked out of that house where he and my Mom had lived for more than twenty-five years while it still looked just like when she was living. He did not have to endure the agony of dismantling everything. I was the one left to that task after the house was sold in the spring of 1984.

He had seven good years with Germaine before he was left alone again. Sadly and ironically, Germaine also died of cancer in 1990. In a ten-year period of time, my father buried two wives. He never remarried, adjusted to being alone and lived seven years longer in the *Lauzon* and *St. Lambert* areas of *Québec* until he died at age 86 of cancer.

Do you see how fate and destiny, and the Lord's Master Plan, worked in my Dad's life? Germaine, his first love, became his second wife and companion almost fifty years after he was dealt that blow that her father had shipped her off to *Lauzon* to be a nanny to discourage her from marrying him.

CHAPTER 3

We three girls did not have living grandmothers or both grandfathers to dote on us and spoil us a little bit. Our paternal grandmother died when my father was only five years old. My maternal grandmother died when my mother was 21, six years before she married my father. We did have our paternal step-grandmother, Clémentine, who was very loving and doting when we visited her in Canada.

Our paternal grandfather, who lived in Canada, died in 1938 shortly before my parents were married. Our maternal grandfather, *Grand-père* Berube, was 77 years old when I was born. He sat in his rocking chair in the kitchen with his pipe in his mouth, his tobacco stand at his side and his spittoon on his other side. That rocking chair was his. No one ever sat in it but him. It had mahogany wood arms carved like swans, and the upholstery was of very rich-looking damask. He never came outside to play with us, nor did he play indoor games with us. All I can recall is him telling us stories of Canada, in French, because he spoke no English. He also made wooden toys for his numerous younger grandchildren and he built pigeon coops for the older grandsons. His garden was his pride and joy. He grew rhubarb, tomatoes and other vegetables and even some tobacco plants, no doubt to fill his ever-present pipe.

I remember one particular story he told of how one of our great-grandmothers was a Canadian Indian. Later in life, when I researched my mother's family and did the full genealogy line back to France, I did not find this Indian ancestor. I think maybe *Pépère* was just repeating the stories (oral history) he had heard in his childhood. It also could be that one of his ancestral grandparents who had the family surname of Fitzbag (actually, it was Fitzback or Fishback) was the one that had been described as "an Indian" to him and the generations before him. It could be that no one knew the origin of that unusual non-Canadian name, which is actually German, and in the storytelling that was passed on from one generation to another she became the "Indian" grandmother. I don't know all this for certain. I'm only guessing and playing detective here.

Pépère Berube favored my kid sister Lulu, as she was one of the youngest of all his numerous grandchildren. He called her "*Ma Petite Puce*," my little flea.

Pépère died when I was eleven years old. He was 88 years old. *Tante* Emily, my Mom's older, old-maid sister who had cared for her father since the death of her mother, inherited the house upon his death in 1953. A few years later, she moved upstairs into the third floor apartment. It had been converted from the original four bedrooms, with my father doing all the carpentry work, at no cost to *Tante*. She then rented out the first floor to our family. We moved to *Pépère's* house in the summer of 1954 after I graduated from eighth grade.

The second floor apartment was still rented out to *Tante* Marie, Mom's oldest sister, who had lived there for years. This generated the additional income *Tante* Emily needed for taxes and insurance, as she was only receiving a small old-age pension from the city. She lived to be in her early eighties. In her will, she left *Pépère's* rocking chair to "*La Petite Puce*," my sister Lulu, as *Pépère* Berube had stipulated.

*   *   *

While growing up, we always spoke French at home. We also belonged to a French-Canadian parish, *Nôtre Dame de Lourdes*, where Masses and church events were also all held in French in the early years. *Nôtre Dame* School classes ran a half day in English and half day in French.

My mother also subscribed to several French/Catholic magazines. With all this early exposure to the French language, I was able to retain my second language and am still fluent in reading, writing and speaking French to this day. We actually spoke French at home until we started dating. If we forgot, and asked my Mom or Dad a question in English while at home, they would ignore us and not answer. Later on, my parents told us they did this because they wanted us to retain our French. After all, when we visited our relatives in Canada every few years, we had to be able to converse in French, as none of them spoke any English. I remember my little cousins in Canada prodding us to speak some English when we took those trips to visit. They thought we girls were all so dang smart because we could speak two languages.

When we started dating, however, my parents had to relax that rule whenever a non-French-speaking boyfriend came to call. My boyfriend, Bob, was really the only one who spoke and understood French.

I regret that in later years when I had my young children I did not speak French to them regularly. Yes, the circumstances were different than when my parents were raising their girls, but I could have said, "Okay, today is French speaking day" at least once a week. Today only my daughter Melissa can speak French. She started studying while in high school and continued on with her French studies through her four years of college, graduating with French as her second major. Whenever Melissa and I want to tell each other something that we don't want her brothers to hear, we speak in French and the boys do not understand one word of what we are saying.

*   *   *

We have a zillion Canadian relatives since both sets of grandparents were from Canada and had thirty children between them. From there, their progeny has multiplied.

Pépère Dube was one of eighteen children. He was the only one of his siblings that came to the U.S. The names of *Pépère*'s siblings in birth order are: Adrienne, Paul, Alice (who was *Pépère*'s twin), Jeanne, Bernadette, Joseph, and his half-sisters and brothers, Élise, Marie-Louise, Henri, Wilfrid, Adrien (who died very young), Yvain, Maurice, Marie-Ange, Adrien (second child with that name), Roger and Anne-Marie.

Most of *Pépère*'s brothers worked as carpenters during their adult lives with the exception of Joseph, who was the fisherman (salmon).

The oldest sister, Adrienne, who married at age 16, went with her spouse Pierre Dumais to open up new virgin territory 400 miles north of *Montréal* in the area called *l'Abitibi*. She told us many stories of her first years there living in a tent, even during the cold winter months, until they had cleared enough land to raise a small house. She was a true survivor. Adrienne had four sons: Roger, Jean Paul, Lionel and Jean Guy.

Paul married Blanche Cassista and had eight children: Cécile, Gisèle, Bertrand, Monique, Ghislaine, Jean Guy, Yvon and Yolande. *Oncle* Paul was a good practical joker. I recall one time we visited them on his farm when I was about seven. He told us that bubble gum was made from the pink part of the cow's rear end. I believed him and would never chew bubble gum after that. Later on, after he sold the farm, he was the head of the maintenance department at the local hospital.

Alice, *Pépère's* twin, died in infancy. Jeanne married late in life and had no children. She loved to spoil all of us nieces and nephews. Her husband was named Zépherin Gagné. How's that for an odd name?

Bernadette wed Leopold Couturier and had eleven children: Jeanine, Jean-Marie, Lisette, Marguerite, Ghislain, Jean Paul, Nicole, André, Renée, Francine and Sylvie. She had a heart of gold in spite of her tough life.

Joseph was the "Maverick" of the bunch and the non-dancer of them all, yet he married a fantastic dancer, *Tante* Yvette (Ouellet), and all their children are great dancers like their mother. Joseph had twelve children: Marc-André, Lucille, Lucilien, Nicole, Lazare, Gervais, Yvain, Madone-Line, Lynda, Ghislain, Serge and Chantale. *Oncle* Joe was also always so proud of his large garden.

Élise wed Gérard Desrosiers and had four children: Guy, Daniel, Bérangère and Raymond. I remember her as the most reserved and soft-spoken.

Tante Marie-Louise was quiet as a mouse. Her husband Julien Ouelet worked on the railroad. She had three daughters: Ginette, Gisèle and Rita and one son, Joseph.

Henri wed Léa St. Amand and had nine children: Gilbert, Carmen, Denise, Benoit, Raymond, André, Thérèse, Imelda and Normand. He was a master carpenter and constructed many important buildings in *Amqui*.

Wilfrid married Jacqueline Roussel and had seven children: Jean-Ives, Micheline, Lise, Renaud and Renald (twins who died shortly after birth), Rémi and Gisèle. He worked in demolition and in foundation construction. He was very soft-spoken and very active in the local chapter of the Knights of Columbus. My dear *Tante* Jacqueline is my angel on earth, always encouraging me and fortifying my faith.

Marie-Ange wed George-Henri Levesque and had six children: Lorraine, Roger, Jean-Marc, Diane, Lisette and Martine. *Tante* Marie-Ange is the arts and crafts specialist and a carpenter in her own right. When she was raising her family, her husband often spent many months away working in the *chantiers,* or timberlands. One time when he was away she decided to do some remodeling in her little home and she actually changed a staircase going up to the second floor bedrooms, relocating it. She did this all by herself. Her husband thought he was in the wrong house when he returned home.

Maurice wed Cecile Voyer and had no children. He also was an avid fisherman besides working construction, after he sold his farm. He was the son who took over his father's farm when he passed away.

Adrien married Jeannine Morneau and had four children: Line-Christine, Jean-Marie, Sylvie and Guylaine. He is the quiet one of all the boys.

Ivain never married. He loved to dance the *Quadrilles*. He had fallen from a high chair when he was less than two years old, and had some brain damage as a result. Nevertheless, he was the right-hand man to his brother, *Oncle* Wilfrid. He saved *Oncle* Wilfrid's life one time when a wall had collapsed on top of him during a demolition job and had the wind knocked out of him. Yvain, as small as he was, lifted it off of him.

Roger wed Irene Gauthier, the local school teacher, and had three children: Langis, Dany and Jasmine. Uncle Roger is the local pool expert—as in tabletop pool, not the swimming kind. He plays in many tournaments and wins many competitions. He also loves to ride his moped. Jasmine, his daughter, is in the entertainment field. She is a talented singer and performs in many plays and productions. Langis is a deep-sea diver, diving for sunken treasures. Dany is a tour-bus driver in *Montréal*, driving tourists to *l'Oratoire St. Joseph*.

Anne-Marie wed Gérard Ricard and had three children: Denis, Normand and Sylvie. She is the most fun loving of them all and truly full of "piss and vinegar."

All of these are my uncles, aunts and first cousins. Thus, they are my children's great uncles, great aunts and second cousins and your great-great uncles, great-great aunts and third cousins.

*   *   *

Now I'll relate some information on the Berube family.

Alfred married Rose Courcy in 1888 and had twelve children. The first three were all born in Canada (*Baie des Sables*). They were: Marie, Joseph and Alfred. The following were all born in Fall River, Massacusetts: Élise, Rose, Elmire, Odiana (who died in infancy), Marieanne, George, Aimé, Charles and Imelda (my mom and your great-grandmother).

All had numerous children with the exception of Joseph and Elmire, who never married, and Charles and Rose who had no natural children as they married later in life.

Joseph served in the U.S. Army during WWI (Pvt.-MG. co 327th Inf.). George served in the U.S. Army during WWII (Cpl. Aviation Air Crew). Charles served in the U.S. Army during WWII (PFC-3934 Inf. Reg.-2 WIA). Four of Uncle Alfred's sons also served in WWII: Freddie, Leo, Albert and Normand.

Freddie was killed in action in the Pacific. He was a bomber-gunner. More than 60 years later, his remains were found and identified. He was returned to the U.S. and buried in Arlington National Cemetery (reference: Fall River *Herald News* article, October 29, 2006).

Leo was a Master Sergeant in the U.S. Air Corps, 2519 AAFBF. Albert "Allie" was a corporal in the U.S. Army, 8th Field Arty. Ban., and served in the Pacific. Normand, "Norm," served in the U.S. Navy—USS Washington-Sea S/C-301st Construction Battalion, also in the Pacific theatre.

One of *Tante* Marie's sons served in WWII: "Paulie," Navy Sea Bees, 301st Const. Bat., Pacific.

As young children we would refer to *Oncle* Charlie as the "preacher" as he was always discoursing on some religious or theological subject. He married twice, first to Mary Correira and then to Gail Tully.

Oncle Joseph was notorious as the family prankster. Aunt Rose married a widower, Adelard Delphis Sarrasin, and lived in Warren, Rhode Island. She was easy-going and fun-loving and spoiled us nieces and nephews.

Oncle George was the best story teller. He was married to Anne Funk Letella.

Tante Marie, who married Arthur Saucier, was known as the quiet one. She was an expert seamstress.

Tante Elsie (Élise) was the "strange" one. She wore bobby socks with high heels; now that's strange. She, too, married a widower, François Coté.

Tante Emily (Elmire), the spinster, was the one Uncle Joe always played his jokes on. She had no sense of humor and would get so miffed.

She was "the boss" of the household on Hamlet Street after her mother passed away. I recall one time *Oncle* Joe retaliated against "the boss" *Tante* Emily. She had been nagging him to put away his clean laundry. In fact, she had left some of her own clean laundry on the sideboard. When she got up the next day, and then happened to answer the door, she was mortified when the visitor noticed her "bloomers" hanging from the chandelier with a sign attached: "for sale cheap."

Oncle Aimé (who we called *Oncle* Sam) was the happy-go-lucky one, always with a smile. He married Julia White, a licensed practical nurse, who he met in New York. She had immigrated to the U.S. with her sister Peg from Ireland. She told me many stories about her experience upon arriving at Ellis Island.

Oncle Freddie was stern and never believed that TV was for real. He actually believed it was some sort of witchcraft. His wife Eugenie Arcand died before I was born. He never remarried.

Tante Marieanne was the "giggler." She married Armand Lebeau known to us children as "the entertainer" because he played the fiddle with a vengeance.

My Mom (your great-grandmother), Imelda, was the sweetest, most creative and kind-hearted soul of the bunch.

Here's an interesting tidbit for you. My grandparents Alfred Joseph and Marie Rose (Courcy) Berube were married in 1888. The last one of their children to die was Marieanne who died in 1988. That's a span of 100 years. Coincidentally, my grandfather, your great-great grandfather, Alfred died at age 88.

I would be remiss if I did not give you the names of all my first cousins on the Berube side. So, here goes!

Oncle Freddie's children are: Jeanette, born in 1917; Joseph Alfred, born in 1918; Joseph Leo, born in 1920; Albert Noel, born in 1921; and the baby of the family, Normand, born in 1923.

Tante Marie's children are: Albert, born in 1911; Antoinette, born in 1913; George, born in 1914; twins Joseph Alphonse and Joseph Henri, born in 1916; Joseph Ernest, born in 1919; twins Marieanne and Marguerite, born in 1920; Oscar, born in 1922; Paul, born in 1924; and Philippe, born in 1926.

Tante Marieanne's children are: Cecile, born in 1923; Therese, born in 1924; Joseph Raymond, born in 1926 (he died at three weeks old); Bertrand, born in 1926; Jeanne, born in 1932; Claire, born in 1933; Robert, born in 1935; and Raymond, born in 1942.

Oncle Aimé's (*Oncle* Sam to us kids) children are: Richard, born in 1938; Roseanne, born in 1940; Leo, born in 1942; Adrienne, born in 1943; Francis, born in 1945; and George (Pewee), born in 1947.

Oncle George's children are: Rosemary, born in 1951; George, born in 1953; twins Mark and Michael, born in 1955; Georgette, born in 1957; and Pierre, born in 1958. He also had a step-daughter named Anne Marie.

Aunt Elsie had just one son, Joseph, (birth year not known).

CHAPTER 4

I recall a few things from Sylvia Street in New Bedford, Massachusetts where I was born. There was Johnny Baptista who lived next door, whose parents were friends with mine. He was a big boy for his age, about three. We girls were smaller in size, although I was the chubby one. The Baptistas were regular Saturday night card players with my parents. On the rare occasions that my parents went somewhere without us three girls, they had a neighborhood girl who lived up the street baby-sit us. Her name was Celine. Many times, my Mom's niece Cecile came from nearby Fall River to spend some time with our family and she too baby sat for my parents.

I remember my second birthday celebration in the backyard of Sylvia Street, sitting outside on the grass with my birthday cake along with friends and some of the kids of the neighborhood. I know that was a happy day for me. That is the first childhood recollection of a happy time. Many happy times would follow.

I remember Mom pushing the pram (carriages or strollers were referred to as prams back then) with little baby sister Lulu in it to go visit old *Tante* Marie who lived not far away. *Tante* Marie was my Mom's aunt, married to her mother's brother. At the time, she really wasn't that old, but me being not yet three and it being so long ago, I always think "old." I think the name of the street she lived on was Princeton in St. Joseph's Parish. I remember going to Brooklawn Park facing St. Joseph's Church, where all three of us girls had been baptized. I remember the Guisti's bread store where my parents purchased bread direct from where it was made. I remember Sunday visits to *Oncle* Georges, on North Front Street. Often in cold or rainy weather, *Oncle* Georges would pick us all up as this was at least two miles from Sylvia Street. My parents walked everywhere, as they had no automobile at that time. The first automobile came into the picture when I was about seven. There really aren't any other memories of those early years on Sylvia Street.

Sometime shortly just before my third birthday the family moved to 153 Jenkes Street in Fall River, Massachusetts. This was in late spring of 1943 when Lulu was just three or four months old. It was during the early war years. My Dad had secured himself a job as a carpenter at the Shipyard in Providence, Rhode Island, the one off Allens Avenue.

Here are some more trivia facts for you, my dear grandsons. Between 1943 and 1945, the Providence Shipyard built ten Liberty Ships, twenty-one Frigates and thirty-two Combat Loaded Cruise Vessels for the war effort. By June 1943, 14,000 people worked there. There were three shifts; it was operational twenty-four hours a day. At one time, 3,000 women were also employed there. Many of them worked in the production line. They learned skills and performed jobs, donning overalls, working side by side with the men. When you hear the saying "Rosie the Riveter," it refers to these women who did the same jobs as men in all the shipyards across the U.S. during those war years.

Dad became a naturalized American citizen on June 24, 1943. The clerk of the Superior Court in Fall River who signed his naturalization certificate was Charles E. Harrington. Dad had studied for his citizenship test and to learn his English while they still lived in New Bedford. He rode his bicycle to night school to accomplish this. His paperwork came through right after they moved to Fall River, so he was sworn in as a new citizen in the Fall River Superior Court.

That naturalization paper carries the Document No. 6835669. It could be that would be a lucky number for you, my grandsons, later on when you can buy a lottery ticket. Wouldn't it be something if one of you won the lottery playing a combination of that number? Never say never!

I'll have to digress a bit here to mention more on "fate and destiny."

Remember after that big 1938 hurricane my Dad had been promoted to carpenter's helper and caught his first break in realizing the American dream to which all immigrants aspired. Well, my Dad getting that job at the Providence Shipyard, where he made more money and was eventually able to join the Carpenter's Union, was because of World War II. They needed so many experienced carpenters for the war effort. I guess that's what they mean when they say, "along with the bad, comes the good." Two bad events, the hurricane and World War II, resulted in good things for my Dad, the promotion after that hurricane and the better-paying job at the shipyard as a result of the U.S. entering the war.

Okay, now back to the story. My parents moved to Fall River because it was closer to Providence. Dad could more easily get into a car pool to ride to work each day, since he did not yet have his own car. Besides that, Mom had all her family and father in that area, so we were then able to see *Pépère* (my grandfather) and all our aunts, uncles and cousins more often. When we lived in New Bedford, without the benefit of a car, the times were few and far between that Mom could visit with her family in Fall River.

Chapter 5

When I was just a little girl living on Jenkes Street, I remember always being so happy, as all little girls are supposed to be. Looking back on my childhood and the way I was raised makes me appreciate the good things of today and especially to always count my blessings when, at times, the bad days seem to outnumber the good days. Some of the happy memories of my childhood fall in the category of vintage, historical and even "Freddy Flintstone" days, as my children referred to them when I shared a particular reminiscence of mine. These good memories became the foundation blocks of my character. They helped sustain me when the adult roller coaster rides replaced the carefree, happy and early childhood kiddy coaster rides.

I remember the rag man with his horse-drawn cart and the giant scale hanging off the back. He came around the neighborhood on his regular schedule to buy the old clothes and such. Mom would have a bundle of clothes that were old and tattered and certainly could not be of use to anyone. Those items that could be useful to someone were donated to the Salvation Army or the St. Vincent Society for the "really poor" people. These were gathered in a separate bundle, not to be sold to the ragman. We never thought of ourselves as being poor back then. The ragman would weigh Mom's bundle of rags and pay her based on the weight of the bundle. This extra money was not Mom's mad money to be spent on trivial things. This extra money was for her "ace-in-the-hole" fund spent on the little extra and inexpensive treats our parents would indulge us with from time to time. You will read a bit later on in this story about some of those little extra treats we so looked forward to receiving and truly appreciated, as they were indeed treats. I think my Mom's "ace-in-the-hole" fund was the forerunner of my own "ace-in-the-hole" saying.

Many homes were heated with coal. The coal man would deliver the coal through a chute that went down to the cellar coal bin. The egg man would make his weekly treks through each neighborhood. The butcher and grocer would deliver the orders to each family. There were no supermarkets in those days.

I also remember the knife man. That's the knife sharpener man. He, too, had a horse-drawn cart and came on a regular schedule to sharpen the knives and scissors of the ladies of the neighborhood. Mom, of course, never had use for this invaluable service because Dad would sharpen the knives and scissors himself on the big grinding wheel he had set up in the cellar section each tenant had. We kids used to get so excited when we saw the knife man coming down the street. It was a treat to watch him do his work off the back of his wagon with all the big and different knives he was so adept at making as sharp as the first day they were bought. This was truly no-cost entertainment.

The ice man is another one I vividly remember. He, of course, came more often since a good majority of the neighborhood did not have refrigerators. Instead, they had iceboxes. Needless to say, the ice to keep these iceboxes cold had to be replenished very regularly. Buying the ice for the icebox was part of the "utilities" expense of the household budgets. Imagine it; they had to budget for ice. After he had completed his sales in our section of Jenkes Street, and before moving on a bit up the street to his next section, he would give all of the kids a piece of ice; not an ice cube, just slivers or chunks left from what he chopped off the huge ice block and had put aside for just this use. This was the moment all us kids waited for. This was a treat. This made our day. This simple little gift of a chunk of ice made us so happy.

We always anticipated hearing the bell of the waffle-man truck. He usually came around once a week in the warm months but not in the winter months. Yummy! We savored those warm, powdered-sugar waffles, eating them while sitting on the front stoop or steps, relishing each delicious bite. This treat was paid for from Mom's "ace—in-the-hole" fund, no doubt replenished from the latest sale to the rag man. This was another one of the enjoyable treats of my childhood.

Oh, I can't forget to tell you about the pony man. He came around the neighborhood at least once a year. I remember sitting up in the saddle to have my photograph taken. I have a photo of me on that pony somewhere in my old albums.

All of these merchants or peddlers would announce their arrival with their bells, or just by yelling out. Later, when some of them acquired trucks, the horns would be tooted to alert the housewives of their arrival. It certainly was a different lifestyle that is surely unfamiliar to the generation of today.

I remember my first trip to Canada when I was just three or four years old. Little Lulu had been left in the care of *Tante* Emily and just Dolores and I accompanied my parents on the train rides, first to *Québec* and then onto to *Amqui* and *Oncle* Paul's farm. I remember being captivated by the little piglets in the pigpens and how I snuck in under the enclosure and wallowed in the mud trying to capture a tiny piglet. I remember Cousin Cécile taking all the younger girls down to the "*ruisseau*" (brook) that ran behind the farmhouse to clean us up before meals and at bedtime. I remember crying the day we had to leave; I wanted my parents to leave me there. I loved the farm and especially those adorable piglets so much.

I also fondly remember the time spent at Del's summer cottage. *Oncle* Del was married to *Tante* Rose, my godmother. Each summer for about four years, when I was between the ages of five and nine, our family would get to spend a week at the cottage on 20 Evergreen Street in North Dartmouth, Massachusetts. The cottage was just a bit down from Musical Beach where we would go swimming. In the evenings, on weekends, they would have outdoor movies where everyone sat on blankets to watch the double feature.

I clearly recall the big rope swing suspended from the huge tree in the front yard of that cottage, and all the kids taking turns seeing who could reach the highest. This was a very primitive summer cottage. We had to use the outhouse in the daytime and a chamber pot during the night. Some of the cottages had names. I only remember one that was called Old Glory. Those times during the summers spent at *Oncle* Del's cottage were the only vacations our family took, except for the trips to Canada to visit with my Dad's side of the family, which did not happen every year.

CHAPTER 6

Eileen McGee was one of my childhood friends. She lived way down at the end of Jenkes Street. Our tenement was about mid-way down that long street. I recall walking down to her home so we could play a game together. To get there I had to walk past the public school. Not every time, but often enough, I would hear a "whoo-whoo" sound, strange and scary to me. The sounds sure gave me the willies and I imagined that public school was haunted by ghosts. I would walk at a fast pace or even run, past that school to avoid being confronted by the ghosts that I imagined haunted it.

Much later in life a light bulb went off in my head. I don't recall what it was that triggered this light-bulb moment, but I finally figured out that those strange and scary sounds were from the train that ran through Fall River in those days. The tracks were about one-half mile away from that "haunted" school. Of course, all the public school kids knew what those sounds were but we Catholic school kids didn't, and they weren't about to tell us. I never admitted to anyone that I was scared to walk past that school because I thought the ghosts were haunting it. I was not going to be called a "sissy." As I reflect on those memories today, I realize that a lesson was to be learned from that experience. The lesson was to face my fears. Had I faced my fears the very first time I heard those sounds, and confided in my parents about them, surely they would have explained that it was just the train tooting while it ran the tracks a short way from there. I would have spared myself many scary walks to see Eileen.

Getting back to Eileen, the games we played depended on if it was just two of us, or if there were enough of us to have a group play session. Some of the group games were dodge ball, free the box, statues or kick the can. Of course, for us girls, there was the favorite jump rope. With just two of us playing, we could play jacks or pick up sticks, with paper dolls, or with our regular dolls and their little prams, strollers and other doll *accoutrements*. There were no Barbie® dolls or Beanie® Babies in that era. We had coloring books, water painting books, the Monopoly® game and decks of cards to play Rummy or Old Maid. Card games were a favorite pastime for adults too. They mostly played Whist and *les quatre sept* (the four sevens), a French-Canadian card game. This was their Saturday night entertainment, when friends or relatives came over to spend the evening.

An ever-so-favorite-play was when Mom allowed us to take the big Sears and Roebuck catalogue outside. We would sit alone, or with a friend or two, on the long, rear, wooden egress stairs leading up to the second floors. The tenement house we lived in had six tenements, two on each of the three floors. I can picture myself with Jackie Barrett, another friend who was a few years older than me and who lived on the third floor above us.

There, we would go through each of the pages and fantasize about what we would buy with the imaginary $100 we had to spend. I guarantee you we had as much fun with that Sears® catalogue fantasy play as the kids of today have with all their fancy toys from Toys R Us®. That simple, no-cost toy, the Sears catalogue, developed our imaginations and nurtured hope in us. We didn't whine for a new doll, or a new dress, or a new toy; we simply dreamed of these. Somehow we knew our parents would buy these things for us if they could. We truly were satisfied with the little treats they were able to provide for us every now and then and at Christmastime.

Roller skating on the sidewalks was another favorite pastime. Oh, how I remember those cute little metal skates you had to clamp onto your shoes and tightened with your skate key so they wouldn't fall off. Skate keys were guarded like bars of gold. Woe to the one who lost or misplaced that precious skate key. It was possible to borrow a key from others, but everyone was very careful to get theirs right back from the borrower if they let someone use it. The lesson I think I learned back then from that precious skate key was to take special care of things you know you will have a hard time replacing, or that you surely will need again at a future time. Keep important things in a safe place. Don't carelessly ever put things down somewhere where they could "disappear."

The sidewalks were not so smooth. They had many irregularities and bumps that would invariably lead to us falling down somewhere along the line. I recall one particular bad spill I took while roller skating. I badly scraped my right ankle right down to the bone. It bled quite a long time. My Mom called the doctor and he told Mom what to do. He sent the district nurse to check on me and change those bandages until it healed. There were no emergency rooms in those days. I don't remember if I ever told my kids that story or showed them the scar on my right anklebone, a permanent *souvenir* from those childhood roller skating days.

We had more scrapes and bruises along the way. I truly believe that if my parents had invested in Band-Aid® stock back then and held onto it for twenty-five years they would have received a good return on that investment. Bandaids always needed to be on hand with three little girls falling while skating or scraping themselves while trying to reach the box in the free-the-box game, or twisting and falling while dodging the ball.

Of course, buying Band-Aid® stock wasn't really an option for my parents. The wages my Dad earned were enough to support his little family with very little left over. Dad was the breadwinner. Mom was the stay-at-home wife and mother who never really worked outside the home. She cared for neighborhood kids while their mothers went out to work. One of these kids was Charlotte Cabral. She was the youngest of the three girls of Betty and Ernie Cabral who lived upstairs. Her two older sisters were named Betty Ann and Eileen. I remember vividly my Mom bathing Charlotte in the big portable tub that she placed on a towel on the kitchen table. When Charlotte began talking, she called my Mom Mama Dube. Our families remained friends and Charlotte always addressed my Mom as Mama Dube even when she became an adult.

My Dad did not buy his first used car until I was about six or seven. He paid for a ride to work and rode his bike to get to other places. We all walked the few blocks to *Nôtre Dame* Church on Sundays. They took the buses, two each way, with us three girls, to visit her father on Sundays.

Our second family trip to Canada was made right after my Dad had purchased his first used car. I believe it was a green Chrysler, but I can't be sure of that; nor do I recall the year, but it was definitely a used car.

One particular memory of that trip was when my Cousins Ghislaine and Jean Guy took us through the pastures, deliberately leading us through the cow pies. In later years, whenever we would all get together and reminisce about those days they told me they did this because we American cousins were wearing cute little white sandals while they went barefoot all summer. Of course, when those sandals became all caked with cow dung, we had to take them off and then we were all on the same playing field. Weren't they some little mischief makers?

Another memory of that trip is again them leading us through the pastures to go dig up a new supply of potatoes for their mother. They deliberately told us it was okay to cross the field where the bull was grazing. When we did, he charged at us and we ran for our lives. One of us American cousins was wearing a bright red polo shirt which, of course, caught the bull's eye. Those devious cousins knew what would happen and they led us right into their trap. I truly believe, that today, they still roar with laughter whenever they recount those wonderful episodes of our childhood visits to them on the farm.

I recall that it was on the return home from this trip that we stopped in *Mont Joli* to visit my Dad's grandmother, *Grand-mère* Smith, actually my great-grandmother, Anna, your great-great grandmother. Her maiden name was St. Amand. I clearly recall that when we pulled up to the front of her home she was sitting on the porch with her corn cob pipe in her mouth. I also recall her hair was tied into a bun and it was pure white. I have a photo of her taken at the time of that visit.

Mom did work as a checker at the polling places during election years. This extra money was also part of Mom's "ace-in-the-hole" fund. It was used to buy material for new dresses or piano recital dresses that my Mom would sew up or to buy the little Christmas gifts we received each year. My sister Dee Dee and I took piano lessons for a few years from the nuns at Jesus Marie Academy. I have the cutest photo of us in the recital dresses that Mom made.

Since Mom did not work outside the home she had a lot of time to do things with us. I especially recall the Mission parties. A full account of those comes later in this story. I vividly recall making homemade Christmas decorations and helping to create that year's *crèche* (manger) that took up a whole corner of the front room. Christmas was truly the celebration of Jesus' birth back then. It was not the commercial holiday we see celebrated today.

I remember that precious little dish that was placed in front of the crib where Jesus would lay on Christmas morning. During Advent, we would write down little things we had done for Jesus, fold the little slips into tiny squares and place them in the dish. These were our gifts to Jesus for his upcoming birthday. We wrote things like being very attentive at Mass that Sunday, helping Mom with something without being asked or sharing with a sister without her asking. We also wrote that we had recited an extra decade of the rosary or said our prayers more slowly and not rushed through them.

This custom reminded us that it was, after all, Jesus' birthday. It developed the habits of performing good deeds and taught us about not being selfish by sharing with others what we had. I'll write more about the Christmas season and our customs in a later chapter.

Adult recreation time that included us kids was Saturday night piano playing and a sing-along with old Mrs. Adeline Canuel at the piano and everyone else gathered around singing up a storm. She and her husband Ernest lived up the street and were great friends with my parents. They had a daughter, Gloria, who was our sometimes babysitter. She was also Mom's hairdresser, coming over early on Saturday evenings to do my Mom's hair up in pin curls with all those bobby pins.

Getting back to Mrs. Canuel's piano playing, boy she could make that old upright piano rock. Her piano-playing style was a combination of Liberace-style, jazz and "honky tonk." While my Mom played the piano, and even gave lessons to neighborhood kids, her style was more classical.

Yet another favorite entertainment/pastime for the adults and children, too, was playing *Pichenottes* (pronounced peesh-nuts). I'll try to explain this one as best I can.

This was sort of "finger pool." The 31" x 31" game board was like a mini, but square pool table with pockets at each of the four corners. It was on a pedestal base that could be swiveled in front of each player as they took their turn. Each player sat in a chair around the board.

The board was marked with "shooting areas" on each side, labeled 1, 2, 3 and 4 and a large circle on the center of the board. The game pieces, which were little wooden rings about the size of a man's wide wedding band, were red and green. The bonus ring was black. The shooter rings, one for each player, were beige.

The red and green pieces were placed alternately in a circle right on the large circle line in the middle of the board and the black bonus piece was placed in the very center of that ring. The game began with the player in section #1 placing his shooter piece anywhere in his designated section and using his fingers to "shoot" his piece to break that circle in the middle. Shooting was similar to how you use your fingers to shoot marbles, an aggressive flick of the middle finger and thumb.

When a player got the first piece (red or green) into one of the side pockets, the team colors were determined. Players 1 and 3 were partners; players 2 and 4 were partners. The black bonus piece could be sunk at any time but had to be followed by sinking a piece of the shooter's team color, a move that we referred to as "burying it." If the shooter missed "burying" that black piece, it had to be removed and placed back on that center spot on the game board.

The game continued until all the pieces, including the black one, were sunk into those corner pockets. The winning team was the one who had succeeded in doing this before the opposition. We learned early on that it was important to get that black piece "buried" early on, before your team was down to one last team piece to bury it. If that happened, and you were not able to sink the black piece with that one last colored team piece after five tries, the game was declared a draw.

My Dad had made this game board back in the mid-1940s recreating it from memory, as he had played this game as a child growing up in Canada. I have that board along with all the pieces today, more than sixty years later. My children often played this game during their childhood years. I have admonished them to cherish it and to always keep it in the family for future generations to enjoy.

A nostalgic memory of that particular game has to be shared with my readers. My Mom used to buy a big bag of shell peanuts and divide them equally among us three girls and my Dad whenever we were the four players. Whichever team lost the game had to "pay" each winner twenty-five peanuts.

After a few games we all sat, shelled our hoard of peanuts and ate them. Those were simple pleasures, but so pleasurable really. First the game, and trying to beat my Dad, and then enjoying those scrumptious shelled peanuts. I now know that Dad would often let his opposing team win so that they would not lose their stash of peanuts.

Later on, when we were all adults and married, Dad first got a bumper pool table and then a regular pool table for his recreation room. He was an excellent player and so very hard for us to beat.

Sunday was family day. Up until my maternal grandfather died at 88, we always went to *Pépère* Berube's house for Sunday visits. In the warmer months we could play outside in the large backyard. One-fourth of the yard was devoted to *Pépère's* garden. We got his permission to water his tomato plants and proceeded to the big rain barrel attached to the end of a gutter in the back of the house. There, we would scoop out the water with a tin can and water his plants, careful not to step on any of them as he had cautioned us.

That little good deed of watering his tomato plants was kept in the back of our mind, to be written down later and placed in that dish in front of Jesus' manger come Christmastime. Guess we had ulterior motives even at that young age. It did teach us that you had to respect other people's property and that you should render a service to others whenever you could.

After my grandfather died in 1953, we started going to public parks on Sundays for family outings. I especially remember Slater's Park in Pawtucket, Rhode Island. I clearly recall one time when *Oncle* Joe and his girlfriend, Élise Joubert, accompanied us to the outing at Slater's Park. We had been treated to a pony ride in the coral near the carousel. *Oncle* Joe had told us he would pay for a second ride for whichever one of us yelled out "I love the wide open spaces" on that first ride. Of course, I was the one that did as I was never shy. I got that second coveted ride on the Pinto pony and my sisters didn't.

Buttonwoods Park in New Bedford was another favorite park to visit on a Sunday afternoon. Mom would pack a picnic lunch for all of us. Some of the parks had small zoo areas. We enjoyed seeing the beautiful peacocks, polar bears and elephants. We enjoyed watching the ducks and the swans on the little lake. We would also watch the boaters in their row boats. Some parks had a carousel where you could ride for a nickel. Mom would raid her "ace-in-the-hole" stash for this and give us nickels to catch a few rides on those carousels. We never got to take a boat ride. That was too expensive. We never whined about it though. We were satisfied with the little treat of the carousel rides.

On the ride home from Buttonwoods, we would always stop at White's at the Narrows. Yes, the same White's as is there today, except it was just an ice cream store back then. We'd get our big scoop of our favorite ice cream on a regular cone. My favorite flavor was strawberry; maple walnut was my next favorite. There were no chocolate chip or pistachio flavors back then but these are now my favorites too.

Those simple treats of carousel rides and an ice cream cone satisfied us. My mother carefully hoarded her "ace-in-the-hole" stash, raiding it minimally and mindfully, when she felt it was warranted. This surely taught us all to be generous and frugal at the same time. By the way, my dear grandsons, in Canada they say "*bas de laine*" when they refer to our American ace-in-the-hole stash or saying. Literally translated to English, *bas de laine* really means a woolen stocking, but in Québécois French it means a nest egg.

CHAPTER 7

Another childhood memory is one that really must be told. This is a memory which goes back as far as I can first remember Christmas, all the way up until the Christmas when I was 14.

Oncle Georges, Dad's uncle in New Bedford who had given Dad room and board when my Dad first emigrated from Canada, faithfully paid us an annual Christmas visit. Sometimes, after my Dad had purchased his first used car, we made the trek to New Bedford for the annual Christmas visit. Every year, all three of us girls received *exactly* the same thing. It was a box of cherry-filled chocolates. The gift from *Oncle* Georges changed only once in all those years.

We were always polite little ladies. We thanked him for the chocolates and were satisfied with what we were given. When we were older, maybe when Dee was about ten, we began to joke about "our chocolates" from *Oncle* Georges after he left. My parents understood how we felt, but admonished us to always say thank you and never, ever, ever to embarrass them by commenting it was the same box of chocolates as every other Christmas.

Of course, we did as we were told, but we all did have some good laughs after those Christmas visits. To this day I cannot stand eating one of those cherry-filled chocolates. I had my fill of those in my childhood. I love cherries and I love chocolate but NOT those cherry-filled chocolates.

One year, *Oncle* Georges pleasantly surprised us. Instead of the anticipated box of chocolates, we each received a handmade wooden box, a little larger than a shoe box, which had a wooden tray inside. It was stained dark mahogany and had a tiny lock and key. We could keep our embroidery thread and needles in it. That sure was a welcomed change from the chocolates. I don't know what ever happened to my box, but I know I kept it for many years.

Oncle Georges had made the boxes himself from scraps of wood he had salvaged from the factory where he still worked as a carpenter. The only reason we did not get cherry-filled chocolates that year was obviously that the "free" wood he had salvaged would serve him better for Christmas that year. No expenditure was necessary that year on his part for those famous cherry-filled chocolates because of that salvaged free wood he was able to use for the boxes. He was a thrifty one, that's for sure.

Oncle Georges' wife, Celine, was bald and wore a bright red wig. When she was well into her seventies, others suggested to her that she should change to a mixed grey-red wig, more appropriate for her age. *Oncle* Georges, who controlled the purse strings, did not agree. The wig had served her well for more than forty years and was, in his mind, still very serviceable; it would do her just fine. There was no need to waste money on a new wig, just like there was no need to waste money on cherry-filled chocolates that one year, when he had that free wood to make those embroidery boxes for us.

It could be that "thrifty" is not a strong enough description of him. Maybe "tight as a doornail" would be closer to the truth. Right about now I can hear my Mom scolding me from heaven and reminding me to be more charitable in my recollections of dear *Oncle* Georges, a lesson often given to me when I was growing up.

*   *   *

Mr. Monsour's grocery store was at the corner of Jenkes Street. It had outside wooden bins and tables displaying the fresh fruit and vegetables for sale. One day, when my sister Dee and I were about six and seven I think, we were walking past the corner store on our way home from an errand Mom had sent Dee on. I think we had walked to the post office on Pleasant Street for postage stamps. Back in those days you could let your six- and seven-year-old children walk anywhere without fear that they would be harmed or abducted or anything. Dee ran a lot of Mom's errands. She went to the post office, to the cobbler's, to the five-and-dime store for something Mom needed, or to the Chinese restaurant for chow mein take-out on Fridays.

I tagged along whenever I could, as these were all adventures, especially when we went to one of the three five-and-dime stores also on Pleasant Street, which was the main street of the Flint section of Fall River. McClellan's and Woolworth's were two of them. I can't remember the name of the third one. It may have been Kresge's. Oh, did they ever have such great things on display in there. I'd fantasize about when the time would come that I could buy those cute bauble bracelets, the musical jewelry box, that new bigger box of Crayola® crayons, the beautiful ribbons in so many colors or even an extra-special paper doll book.

I got sidetracked, I see. I was telling you about that day my sister and I walked by Mr. Monsour's store on the way back from that errand.

Well, right at the last bin on Pleasant Street, before we took the corner turn onto Jenkes, was the display of big, fat, juicy red apples. I don't recall exactly who said we should take one and go on our merry way. It was probably me. But, yes, we both stole an apple from Mr. Monsour's sidewalk display. We hurried to eat our forbidden fruit before we reached our tenement.

It was delicious. No one saw us, or so we thought. It turns out that Mr. Monsour had seen us take those apples. A week or so later Dad had to go to Mr. Monsour's store on a Saturday to help him repair some shelving or something. Being a carpenter, he was always helping other people out with his talents. He didn't charge Mr. Monsour for this carpentry help. It was just one neighbor helping another. That's how things were back then.

Mr. Monsour knew that my Dad was trying to raise his three little girls to be good, honest, helpful and considerate, qualities he recognized in my Dad. He had to tell my Dad what we had done, not to get us into trouble, but only so that my Dad could "nip things in the bud," and teach us that what we did was wrong.

Well, when Dad returned home from helping out Mr. Monsour, he called both Dee and I over to him and point blank asked us if we had stolen two apples from the store. We could not lie as *we* knew that somehow *he* knew we had taken them. Besides, a lie on top of the "theft" would have resulted in double jeopardy for sure. We admitted our crime.

He said that the next day we would go to the store and each pay Mr. Monsour one nickel for those apples, say we were sorry to him, and promise we would never steal from him or anyone ever again. That was an honest-to-goodness lesson on one of the Ten Commandments: *Thou shall not steal.* He said we had to ask God's forgiveness, too. Besides that, we would have to earn that nickel he gave each of us to pay for those two stolen apples. We would not get our dessert for one night. That really hurt (me, more than Dee) as tapioca pudding was the dessert for that night and it was my favorite.

That apple incident taught me a few things. One is that you may think you can fool people and get away with stealing an apple, but even if Mr. Monsour hadn't seen us, God had. If we hadn't got caught, God still knew we had stolen those apples. We had already been taught in school and at home that God created us to love and to serve Him and to follow his Ten Commandments. In the end, we all have to answer to God for the things we do. None of us really gets away with anything. Two is to always make amends for the wrong we do and ask forgiveness, no matter how humiliated we may feel. Once you have it done and over with, you do feel better. Confession really is good for the soul.

Often when I walk by the big, juicy, red apples displayed in the supermarket today, now more than sixty years later, I recall that "apple caper" of my childhood and the lessons learned from it.

CHAPTER 8

The big walk-in closet on Jenkes Street was our playhouse. It was off the kitchen near the rear entry door and was approximately eight-foot square in size. It was the all-purpose, catch-all closet, a combination broom closet, toy-storage closet, preserving-jar storage closet into which everything imaginable was stored and put out of view. Mom had no linen closet, so the extra bedspreads and blankets were also stored on the very top shelves. In winter, or on rainy days when we couldn't play outside, we were allowed to play in there for hours. Oh, the fun times we had in that closet.

I especially recall the time we all helped Dad paint that closet. He had been given some leftover paint from someone and decided he would use this paint to freshen up that big closet. One Saturday, the closet was emptied and Dad gave each of us a small paint brush to help paint it bright red. After all, we were all big enough to help, and since it was only a closet, our mistakes or sloppy painting would never be noticed. So, that closet got painted in no time, with six little hands helping.

The following Monday when we returned for the beginning of a new school week, all the kids laughed at us. We had so much red paint in our hair that we literally looked like little clowns. It took *forever* before that paint eventually got scrubbed out of our long hair. No matter, we had received a valuable first painting lesson from Dad. We had been his dutiful little helpers.

In our large kitchen there was a huge Glenwood® stove for cooking and heating. It was cream and green, if my memory serves me right. We regularly stoked it with coal and wood from the cellar for cooking and also for our "central" heating in the cold winter months. Off the large kitchen was the tiny panty, with the sink and cupboards for food storage on one side and cupboards that held all the dishes, bowls, platters and glassware on the other side. The lower cupboards held the pots and pans and a variety of items that were needed from time to time. The small bathroom with the claw-foot tub (no shower in those days) was located next to that small pantry. The ice box (that's right, we still did not have a refrigerator) was on the wall in the kitchen and really not too far from that Glenwood stove. The ice needed to keep the icebox cold must have melted pretty quickly. I wonder why that icebox was not placed further away from the stove. It could be that was the only wall space available.

Mom had a long buffet on the wall that separated the two bedroom doorways. This was a maple piece that matched her kitchen table and chairs. She kept her tablecloths, dish towels, sheets and pillow cases in the two large drawers.

There were two fairly large bedrooms, one for my parents and the other for us three girls. Dolores and Lucille slept together in the big double bed, while I slept in a twin bed along the wall to the right of the doorway. This, of course, was when Lucille was a bit older, as she was only about three months old when we moved there from New Bedford. The reason I slept separately from my sisters was that I was the bed wetter. I never got scolded for it or never got embarrassed or shamed by my parents. My father had been a bed wetter and recalled being taken behind the barn and whipped by his father because he wet the bed until he was 13. So, my Dad knew I couldn't help it and he knew that time would change the situation as it had in his case.

The front rooms were the double parlors. The one that you walked in to from the front street entrance of the tenement was also an all-purpose room. There were two rocking chairs, small tables, the floor console radio, Mom's sewing machine and, later on, the little telephone table. I think I was about six when my Mom was able to afford that first phone with our four-party line. This meant four families shared the same telephone line, each one having a distinctive ring. For example, one had one ring, another had two rings etc. This was how you could tell if the incoming call was for your family. If you had to use to phone to call out, you sometimes had to wait until the line was free if it was being used by another on that four-party line. Needless to say, you had to be careful what you said on the phone as eavesdroppers were in abundance.

The formal parlor, off to the right of the all-purpose parlor, held the good parlor furniture set, some floor lamps, the upright piano, the sheet-music cabinet, which also held the large 78 records, and the Philco® gramophone.

I remember listening to those old records. We listened to Caruso, the opera singer. Then there was Roy Rogers, the cowboy singer, with his wife Dale Evans and many others. We also had French-Canadian records. I especially remember listening to a comedic lady singer, who we called "*la Bolduc*" and who sang such funny songs and also told funny jokes and stories. One of the songs she sang was "*La Pitoune.*" She was a French-Canadian folk singer and songwriter. She had died in 1941 but her music lived on. In fact, in later years, I discovered that she had earned the title of "Queen of Canadian Folksingers." I can still picture myself and my sisters laughing so hard our sides hurt.

CHAPTER 9

There was no pre-school or kindergarten back in 1946 when I began school at age five. I was not supposed to start school until the following year. My oldest sister Dee started first grade in September as she had had her sixth birthday on July 12. When she came home from *Nôtre Dame* Parochial School with her papers with stars on them and her coloring creations, I begged my mother to let me go to school with my big sister.

Of course, Mom tried to explain that I had to wait until the following year, after I had celebrated my sixth birthday on July 23. But, at five, I did not understand why I had to wait. I was ready for school *now*. I cried and pestered my dear Mom for almost three months. In her desperate attempt to put an end to this pestering (my stubbornness showed itself early as you can see), she said she would have big sister Dee ask *Mère* Héliodore (Sister Héliodore, who we called Mother), the first grade morning teacher, if I could go to school with my sister Dee. Mom knew, or *thought* she knew, the answer would be no. I would have to wait until I was six. That was, after all, the rule.

Oh, how I recall that day Dee returned from school and announced to Mom that *Mère* Héliodore had said yes; I could go to school with Dee on the condition that "I would be a big girl and not cry or wet my pants or cause any problems." Back in those days parochial schools did not have to strictly adhere to the state law of the child being six years of age to begin school. My Mom must have been in shock I think but I was happy as a lark.

I did not have a school uniform to wear. Those had to be ordered the spring before the start of the school year. So, until a special uniform order could be placed and received, I had to wear regular clothes. Well our regular clothes were hand-me-downs from older cousins and people Mom knew who had daughters older than me. Betty Cabral often passed down clothes from her two older girls, Betty Ann and Eileen. No way was Mom going to send me to school in those hand-me-downs looking like a ragamuffin.

I had one good "Sunday best dress." It was burgundy velvet with a large square lace collar. That's what I wore to school that very first school day in November 1946. I started school three months after all those six-year-old-September-start students, but I never fell back. I kept up with them and continued my Catholic education with the Jesus Mary Order of nuns, first at *Nôtre Dame* then at Jesus Marie Academy (JMA) in Fall River.

Getting back to that first day of school, I recall *Mère* Héliodore pinning brown paper all over the front of my dress so I wouldn't get it dirty or ruin the dress in some way. The other kids laughed at me but I laughed right along with them. After all, I had been told of the rules for my special admission. I had to be a big girl and not cry.

That first day of school for me, I believe now, was yet another stone of the foundation being slowly built that would develop my character and prepare me for life. It taught me a few things, one being that persistence pays off. I nagged my poor Mom for three months, at five years old mind you, but it paid off and I went to school. Then, it taught me to laugh when the world laughs at you. Remember, I had to be a big girl and couldn't cry when walking around that first grade classroom with brown paper pinned all over the front of me with all the class laughing at my attire. Mom had been so worried I'd look like a ragamuffin in the hand-me-down clothes! I think that memorable first day of school awakened the strong sense of humor I have now and that has brought me through many a tough time. I laughed with them. I did not cry.

I remember one particular thing from second grade. This was the little saying *Mère* St. Cléophas always said to us young girls and boys (After sixth grade, the boys all went to Prevost Junior High and High School). She was our teacher for the half-day we had of our English subjects. This *Mère* Cléophas moved up the ladder. She was also my teacher in my first, fourth, sixth and eighth grades. Then she moved further up the ladder and was a one-subject teacher in my sophomore and junior years at JMA.

She used to say to us, "Girls, life is just a bowl of cherries, pits and all." Well, back then, I really didn't understand what she meant, but having heard it from her in the second, fourth, sixth and eighth grades, and then through my sophomore and junior years, I never forgot it.

Much later in life, after experiencing my roller coaster rides, I KNEW what she meant, and especially the part about "pits and all."

*   *   *

As soon as I learned to read, I fell in love with books. I still love to read today. I enjoy good novels, mysteries, biographies and especially history.

I remember reading the Nancy Drew® mysteries. We received books as Christmas gifts from our parents, the Gallant sisters and from our godmothers. These books were cherished. Books would transport us to different places, learning about people, while imagining the scenes we read about. My love of reading was a good part of why I was so successful in my school years.

We read in French too, as my mother subscribed to numerous Catholic magazines. I especially remember "*l'Oratoire St. Joseph*" and the French edition of the *Catholic Messenger*. Some books were read a second and even a third time. I even do that now. I'll enjoy a particular book so much that I will re-read it a year or two later.

Each night at Christmastime, the Fall River *Herald News* would print a chapter or part of the syndicated Christmas story chosen for that year. Mom would faithfully read us this story every night until the final chapter was published on Christmas Eve. We had no television and only listened to the radio, so reading was really considered entertainment. I did so enjoy my Mom reading to us. No doubt this part of my early dose of reading was instrumental in my love of books today.

Another memory of Jenkes Street is the boxing lessons my father gave us three girls. We had little boxing gloves like the real boxers. My Dad was both the teacher and the referee. Mom couldn't understand why Dad wanted his little girls to learn to fight. His answer was it was not to fight, but to learn how to defend ourselves. Believe me, the neighborhood boys and the boys from *Nôtre Dame* School did not try to bully the Dube girls more than once. They learned we could defend ourselves and passed the word to not bother us. Those boxing lessons taught us we could dance around the bullies (use strategy), and if we bided our time (had patience) and, if we were lucky enough to get in the right punch, we could successfully floor our aggressor. Strategy and patience were the two valuable lessons learned.

Later, in the course of my life, if someone would comment to me, "Boy, you sure are one tough lady," my mind would very often drift back to thoughts of those early boxing lessons.

CHAPTER 10

During my childhood, Christmastime and the time leading up to it were very special. Mom would work with us to create new decorations for the tree and for display in the front windows. These decorations were made from scraps saved throughout the year.

Bits of silver foil paper, other pretty paper scraps, cardboard boxes, scraps of cloth, broken costume jewelry, beads, sequins and such, were all carefully saved over the year and transformed into homemade Christmas decorations we all helped to create. Everything that was broken, pretty, or useful in making our decorations was put in a special box for the Christmas ornament and decoration season. The big box was kept in the huge walk-in closet that I described earlier.

Then there was that beautiful *crèche* (manger) display, different every year, which took up a whole corner of the living room. *Oncle* George, Mom's older brother and my godfather, owned a salvage business. They went from store to store cleaning out the obsolete items, outdated store decorations and old display paraphernalia. He came across some great stuff in his work, like those rippled corrugated sheets of cardboard, especially the light blue ones. We tacked them up on the wall behind the *crèche* scene, from the ceiling to a good way down the wall, the perfect "sky" backdrop for the display.

Next came creating the village and the mountains with the sheep pastures. Mom started with a small table in the corner. Then she stacked and arranged boxes of different sizes and books of various thicknesses to create the hills, mountains and the front-and-center platform for the actual *crèche*. When she was satisfied with that layout, she took two clean white sheets and draped them over the foundation she had built, leaving creases and folds to make it look like snow drifts. Many years later when I created my own *crèche* display with my daughter, she pointed out that there was no snow where Jesus was born, asking "Wasn't he born in the desert?" That's when I explained about improvisation, imagination and creativity.

The first thing placed in the *crèche* scene was the actual *crèche* crib for Jesus along with Joseph and Mary, the ox and the donkey and, of course, the two angels. The earliest *crèche* I remember was large and wooden. It had been made for her by her father, my grandfather. Baby Jesus would not lie in his manger crib until Christmas morning. I have that original porcelain Christmas Baby Jesus and I hope my children hang onto it for the generations that follow.

Next, starting from top to bottom, we placed the pine trees with their red stands, and the little cardboard houses representing the village of Bethlehem. Then we placed the shepherds, the flute player, and the common-folk inhabitants. Oh, I almost forgot. Before adding the flocks of sheep, we sporadically placed a few small mirrors on the "snow" to represent the ice ponds the sheep would drink from or have to go around to get to a pasture. (Of course my daughter also questioned the validity of pine trees and ice in the desert, prompting more talk about creativity and imagination.)

We placed the sheep, sheepdogs and reindeer next. I know they didn't have reindeer in Bethlehem but they were a part of our mountain section of that *crèche* scene. (Interestingly, my daughter never questioned the reindeer. I'm not sure if that's because she was tired of the creativity and imagination speech, or because she was such an animal lover that not having them in the scene would have been unthinkable.)

Then, in front of the crib, we placed the three wise men and their camels, with the village folk offering their humble gifts for the child born in the manger. Pine cones were interspersed along the sides of the *crèche* to fill in the "blank" areas. The lights were carefully placed, wires hidden, to light up the scene in various places. The front, where the white sheets hung down, was decorated with stars we had made from those saved scraps, icicles or whatever Mom thought looked good that year. The basic *crèche* scene, of course, never changed from one year to the next, but the foundation and the layout of the display did.

We invited all the neighborhood children to view this beautiful display. Friends and relatives who visited at Christmas would compliment my mother time after time. She always outdid herself and would top the previous year's display.

Of course, there was also that special dish placed in front of the crib for our tiny folded-up slips of paper recording our gifts of good deeds, of prayers faithfully said, or little sacrifices made for Baby Jesus. After all, it was His birthday, and He should receive the most gifts.

My Mom's *crèche* work taught me so many things. One was that you always strive to do better. Another was that you improvise and make do with what you have at hand; no need to go spend money foolishly on store bought stuff. But, I guess the most important thing she taught me was that it was Jesus' birthday and that He should receive the most gifts. On Christmas morning, when we got to open our few gifts, we would be grateful that Jesus shared His birthday with us and that we received some gifts, too. We were taught to appreciate and be thankful for gifts, no matter how meager the gifts were in a particular year. In other words: it doesn't take a lot to make you happy; it's the little things that count.

Christmas Eve meant Midnight Mass for the adults and, when we were older, for us girls too. After Midnight Mass, we would have a *réveillon* feast. The *réveillon* feast is a Canadian tradition. Soda, nuts, chocolates, homemade fudge and, of course, French *tourtières* (meat pies, pronounced *tour-tee-air*), and *cretons*, which we incorrectly pronounced as "cuck-ton," rather than the correct "kra-tun" (a meat spread made of ground pork, resembling "deviled ham" in appearance) filled the table. After we went to bed, Mom placed Baby Jesus in the crib. He was always waiting for us on Christmas morning.

On Christmas morning we ate French toast or pancakes. After the dishes were done and the kitchen cleaned up, we sat and waited to be handed our gifts. On various Christmases I received a new doll. One year, I received an extra doll when *Tante* Rose, my godmother, also bought me a doll.

There were also new coloring books and crayons, a new comb and brush set, new mittens and scarves Mom had crocheted or knitted for us, homemade knitted slippers that we called "*les pichous*" (pronounced *pee-shoes*). My kids grew up calling slippers *pichous*. It always made friends do a double take. "You pee in your shoes?"

There was also at least one new game, new paper dolls and a Christmas stocking filled with fruit and nuts, shell peanuts, licorice and those sweet candy canes. One year I got a cash register with which I could play "store." Another year I received a metal dollhouse with plastic furniture, and there was that beautiful musical jewelry box with the twirling ballerina in a pink tutu that I received another year.

Some years were leaner than others, so we did not always get a special "big gift," but we were satisfied and happy to have new things. We never said, "Oh, I wanted this," or "I wanted that." Oh yes, those special Christmas displays, memories and family customs most definitely taught us many things that served all of us well later on in adulthood.

CHAPTER 11

My Mom gave her mission parties every year, beginning when Dee Dee and I were in the third grade and Lulu was in the first grade. Every spring, the nuns at *Nôtre Dame* School passed out to each student a mission collection card. The card was entitled "For the Missions" and had rows with squares, ten across and ten down, that represented five cents each. The one hundred squares equaled $5 to be collected per card.

The nuns asked each student to collect for the missions using these cards. We asked our neighbors, friends, aunts and uncles to donate a nickel for the missions. Each square was check marked for each nickel we collected. Some aunts donated a quarter or fifty cents, and then we could checkmark five or ten squares or boxes and fill up our mission card even faster. Relatives usually gave more than just one nickel. When the card was filled with the check marks, we had $5 for the missions and would turn the card and money in to our teachers.

Since Dee Dee as and I were in the same class, we each had a card. Then when Lulu began first grade, the three of us collected for the missions. My Mom didn't want friends, neighbors and relatives to be put on the spot, so to speak. Three of us were now collecting, so Mom came up with the idea of having a mission party to fill our cards. The total amount of money needed to fill all three cards was $15.

So, the students in my and Dolores' class, about forty-five total, and the students in Lulu's Class (at least another forty-five) would be invited to our Mom's annual mission party. Actually, there were two separate parties; one for each class held one week apart. Admission to the party was twenty-five cents. Every single student from each of the classes came.

Net proceeds from the mission party admission charge totaled at least $20. This was more than enough to fill all three cards. That meant we could ask the nun for a few extra cards and only had to solicit the nickels from a few people to fill out all the cards we had. My mother felt this was better than us "begging" everyone for a nickel to fill our mission cards. Well, besides filling our three cards, we were able to fill at least two extra ones after that mission party, since my relatives and some friends still donated their nickels, dimes, quarters or fifty-cents for the missions.

The kids returned each and every year after that first one. They had had such a good time for a quarter and everyone went home with a prize. Mom would call out quite a few Bingo games for which there were lots of winners. Then, she'd run a spelling contest in which each round produced three winners. First, second and third place winners received a prize. Then she would have a multiplication table quiz for the older ones. Whoever lasted the longest got the first prize, with two runners-up also receiving prizes.

For the first-graders she had cut out shapes, like a circle, a square, a rectangle and a triangle. She would hold up a shape and ask, "What is this called? The kids would raise their hand to answer. She'd hold up cards with short three-word sentences like: "See Spot run." Whoever's hand went up first and answered correctly would get a prize. Of course, Mom made it easier for the first graders. Everyone got a prize.

Another game was to ask who could recite prayers such as *The Our Father, The Hail Mary, The Credo, The Act of Contrition,* then getting a bit tougher . . . *The Act of Hope,* of *Charity,* etc. Quite a few kids received prizes in this game. There was "pin the tail on the donkey" and bobbing for apples in the gigantic galvanized tub. There were geography quizzes and history questions. Besides all the fun, games and prizes, the kids were served soda and treats like homemade fudge, brownies, cupcakes, puffed-wheat-and-Karo-syrup squares, and the candy dish was passed around several times, too. What a deal for a quarter admission fee!

Now, about the prizes, Mom somehow made sure everyone got a prize. Nobody went home empty-handed. She had a whole year between those mission parties to amass prizes from various sources and to sew some up on her sewing machine. With two classes full of kids in attendance, she had to come up with a minimum of ninety prizes, with a few extras in case there was a tie. She was resourceful and a problem solver and managed to do so each and every year. After all, didn't she come up with that mission party idea?

Her various "prize" sources were her sisters, brothers, some older nieces and nephews, her close friends and neighbors. If someone had an extra box of writing paper with envelopes they generously donated that for the prize cache mom kept in the big closet off the kitchen. There was a big box in there with "MISSIONS" written on the front. We all knew that contained the prizes for the next party.

Relatives, friends and neighbors would donate a candy bar or two and other items that were new that they had received as gifts but chose to donate "for Mrs.

Dube's mission party." Boxes of perfumed talc and toilet water were given as prizes, not that those kids used that kind of stuff. Mom would just tell the winner of those items that it was a nice gift for their mom on Mother's Day or her birthday. Mom also watched for bargains at the McClellan's Five and Dime store, things like coloring books, comic books, watercolor sets and crayon boxes. Whatever she could amass that either cost nothing or cost very little went into the cache for the next mission party. She sewed aprons, pot holders and bean bags. She made sock dolls from old socks and material scraps. She and others knitted mittens, scarves and winter hats.

Prizes for boys were always a real challenge. Somehow, she managed to find these. My Dad did his share, too. One particular thing I recall is the little checkerboards he made using the scrap wood he had accumulated. After constructing these, he would mark them out and paint the squares. For the checker pieces, Mom would have assembled at least fourteen sets of buttons for the checkers. There were fourteen which included two spare checkers for each black and red set. If they weren't all identical they were, at least, all of the same size. Dad painted them red and black. These were not new buttons; rather they were sorted from all the jars of old buttons that everyone saved. These recycled buttons were from old garments that were to be put into the rag bag. Everyone who came to the first party returned year after year so I guess the prizes they ended up with were just fine.

Mom threw these mission parties for five years or more. When I completed eighth grade we moved to St. Anne's Parish, and Mom never gave another mission party. A few years ago when I attended a high school reunion, Claudette (Grillo, later Springer) brought up Mom's mission parties. She expressed her fond memories of those parties and how everyone looked forward to them year after year. Claudette was in my first grade class. We were students together in the same class from first grade until we both graduated high school from JMA.

Thinking back on some of those games, I now realize Mom was killing two birds with one stone. She had a game everyone could participate in, but many served to reinforce what we had learned at home or in school, like reciting a prayer, answering a question about the multiplication tables, identifying a shape, or even playing Bingo which reinforced concentration. Didn't all the kids have to stop chatting and listen attentively to hear the magic number that would give them a Bingo?

Mom was definitely the problem solver. How to get those three mission cards filled without putting financial pressure on others was thoughtful. Using scraps of this and that to make prizes for the mission parties and raiding her "ace-in-the-hole" fund to take advantage of the specials at McClellan's Five and Dime store revealed her creativity and her thriftiness. She sure put into action "killing two birds with one stone" by throwing the best and only mission parties in the whole parish. She got those mission cards filled and provided entertainment for our classmates for a whole afternoon.

The parents of all those kids loved Mom. You see, that party lasted from 1:00 p.m. until 5:00 p.m., so all those parents didn't have to worry about where their kids were for one whole Saturday afternoon. On top of that, it gave them all some respite from at least one child for a whole half-day. They could get their shopping or errands done without having to tote around their child, or at least one less child than usual. Every little bit helps!

Dad was also a problem solver and improviser. He constructed those checker boards that became some of prizes for the boys. He was thrifty, too, using that scrap wood he had accumulated.

Do you see how my parents' examples taught me problem solving, improvising and thriftiness? Those precious lessons learned from my Mom's mission parties, without a doubt, served me throughout my life.

I also know now that my Mom earned a special place in Heaven when she was called home to God as the Lord never forgot her mission parties. They helped indirectly to spread His teachings all over the missionary world.

I also know my Mom still watches over me now, more than thirty years after her death. All her family was by her bedside when she passed. After she had taken in her last breath, my Dad kissed her and my two sisters, in turn, did the same. I was the last one to kiss her goodbye. When I did, the last breath that she had taken (and held) came out in a "whoosh." It brushed my cheek and I jumped as I was so startled. My dear Aunt Julie, a retired nurse, was with us and she explained to me how that last breath upon dying is held for a few minutes before it is expelled. She told me I was given a precious gift from my mother, her last dying breath.

I never forgot that or my dear aunt for being with us at that time. I used to tell her she was my favorite Irish aunt and she always replied: "You dang fool; I am your ONLY Irish aunt." I loved her dearly.

CHAPTER 12

Before I began fifth grade, we moved to Arizona Street. This was a "we're-moving-on-up" move for us. This street faced Lafayette Park and was off of Eastern Avenue. Dad had heard about a second-floor tenement about to be vacated, and he knew the Poitras family who lived across the street from there. With Gene Poitras' recommendation, the Rheaume family rented the tenement to our family. Gene Poitras was a carpenter like Dad, and they often worked on jobs together. See, even back then, there was "networking" to get a foot in the door, whether it was for a job or a tenement.

Memories of those four years on Arizona Street, up until I graduated from eighth grade at *Nôtre Dame* School, are also happy memories. Our best friends were the Canuel family. Albert was the same age as our Lulu. Cecile and Rita were a bit younger. We played together, especially in the empty lot right next to where we lived and that we always referred to as "the dump."

It wasn't a real dump. It was just an empty, undeveloped, unleveled lot of land. It had various small and medium mounds of dirt and plenty of wild scrub brush. It really was a perfect western landscape for when we played cowboys and Indians. Then there was the big wooden swing Dad had helped Mr. Rheaume build for our backyard. It was huge and could easily seat six adults. The driveway from the street led to the large back yard area, in which three cars could be parked. That swing was off to the side where the cars were parked. The kids all enjoyed that swing so much, as did the adults in the evenings after supper.

Arizona Street had a big hilly section which really began right in front of our tenement house. In the winter, when the snowfall had been heavy, the street was closed to traffic and designated as a sledding street. Oh, the fun we had sledding down that big hill over and over again! In the winter we could skate on the ice pond in Lafayette Park. In the summer, there were "carriage days." These were days when the girls decorated their doll carriages with crêpe paper according to a theme, like the "Red Cross," to enter the contest for the best-decorated carriage.

Madeleine Boas was another good friend of mine in that time period. She lived on the next street, Gagnon Street. I remember baking potatoes in hot rocks in her yard and having ourselves a treat. Oh the ever-so-simple enjoyments we had. As we got older, in our seventh and eighth grades, Madeleine and I used to cut out movie star pictures for our movie star scrapbooks. Of course, we also had our autograph books. Oh, we didn't get autographs of famous people. No, we asked special people, adults and children alike, to write a short line or poem and autograph our little book.

Returning to our best friends the Canuels, I recall going over to their house to watch Uncle Milty (Milton Berle, known as the first and most influential salesman for television sets in the 1950s), Howdy Doody Time, Gene Autry and, of course, Hopalong Cassidy on their television. We didn't get our first television for a few more years. Before we got our first television, at home we listened to the radio many nights. I remember programs like Mr. Keene, The Shadow and Amos and Andy.

During summer school breaks, my Dad would arrange for a ride to his job, leaving the car for Mrs. Canuel (Rose) to drive. My mother did not drive. All six kids and the two Moms would pile into the car and go blueberry picking, or to a special treat of an outing to Lincoln Park. These simple little things brought us so much joy. Of course, after the blueberry picking, all of us enjoyed the blueberry pies and muffins our Moms made.

Our two families remained friends over the years and I especially fondly remember playing cribbage with Mrs. Canuel up until a few years before her death at age 99. Albert, Cecile and Rita all keep in touch via e-mails and calls and we still get together from time to time to reminisce about our childhoods.

Another memory I have of summer during school breaks is that of the "scrapbooks" we put together. Mom used to save all of the Catholic magazines she subscribed to. She encouraged us to cut out photos of the missionaries in their far away places doing the work of the Lord and to write our own narratives of the missions. This activity helped pass the time, especially on rainy days when we couldn't play outside. It also was Mom's gentle nudging for us to consider a vocation. I often say I wished I had listened to my Mom back then and at least tried the convent, but that wasn't to be my destiny.

I remember learning to do our own hand washing. The laundry man used to pick up the big laundry bag on Monday morning and return it later that day. We had to shake out all those wet items and hang the clothes on the clothesline. The nice delicate things we had that couldn't be washed in those harsh commercial laundries were all washed by hand. As soon as we were old enough, we had to take over our share of hand washing. My sister Dee Dee got up the earliest, so she would have all hers done before me, giving her the use of the clothesline first. That taught me the lesson of "the early bird gets the worm." To this day I am still an early riser never "sleeping in" as they say.

We also all had chores to do on Saturday mornings. Some of these were washing and waxing the kitchen linoleum, sweeping and washing down the stairway from the second floor to the first floor of our tenement, and cleaning the old claw-footed tub and bathroom. All of these chores had to be done before we could go out to play on Saturdays.

I remember a friend, Ruthie Quinn, who came over to help me get my chore for that week done quicker so we could go out. It was my week to wash and wax the kitchen floor. Well, apparently Ruthie never had to do chores at her house, because she soaped up the floor real good and kept going, never rinsing as she went. She had started on one side and me on the other and by the time I noticed she didn't know how to wash a floor, half of it was dried up with the soap she had liberally applied, but that she didn't know she had to rinse before it dried. So, in reality it took longer to get the chore done that day and Ruthie and I didn't get outside to play until much, much later.

We got our first television when I was about ten. I remember watching Kate Smith, Liberace and Bishop Sheen. I remember Hopalong Cassidy and The Lone Ranger with Tonto and, of course, Ted Mack's Amateur Hour. There definitely were plenty of good clean family-oriented programs back then.

On Saturdays, we would sometimes go to the Strand Theatre on Pleasant Street for a treat. The admission was fifty cents. We saw the newsreel, the cartoons and coming attractions first, then two whole movies, a double feature they called it. It was at least four hours at the theater for that fifty-cent admission charge. I remember helping Mrs. Forcier, who lived up the street from us, to wash her storm windows to earn some quarters for the movies. My, how times have changed since my *Freddy Flintstone* theater/movie days.

Minou and Minoune were the names of our two cats when we lived on Arizona Street. Minou, the male, was naughty and very mean. Minoune, his sister, was so sweet and docile. They were a lot of fun to watch. Minoune loved to sit in our laps and she purred when we petted her. Her naughty brother did not like to be in our lap. He preferred to get into mischief. When my mother was crocheting or knitting, he would harass her by getting entangled in the yarn or crochet thread. Minou was the official mouse catcher. These mice would get into the cellar from the empty lot next door. Next to that lot were the garages and chicken coops that the "old maid" who lived up the street owned. This was the source of the mice. From our cellar, they would sneak up the pipes that led to the pantry where Minou caught his prey.

CHAPTER 13

Freshman year at Jesus Marie Academy was 1954-55. The previous summer we had moved to 266 Hamlet Street, my grandfather's house in St. Anne's Parish that *Tante* Elmire (Emily) had inherited after *Pépère* Berube died in 1953. She moved to that third floor where my dad had converted the four bedrooms into a small apartment and we occupied the first floor. My kid sister Lou now attended St. Anne's School. Later, she attended Dominican Academy. I wanted to continue with all my friends from *Nôtre Dame* School who were starting freshman year at Jesus Marie Academy (JMA). My older sister Dee Dee also continued with me at JMA. She quit after our sophomore year to go to work in a sewing mill.

I remember freshman initiation quite vividly. We had to wear our school uniforms inside out, wear a vegetable corsage, have either bobby pin curls or rollers in our hair and carry an open umbrella to and from classes. We had to do this for a whole week prior to initiation night. We sure looked silly. That "get-up" had to be worn to and from school, for the whole day, and on the bus for those of us who came from other parishes. These were public transportation buses. We certainly got some weird stares and lots of chuckles from the riders.

On initiation night we all gathered in the auditorium for the official welcome to the academy by the senior class. To pass our initiation, we all had to do what the seniors had cooked up for us. My assigned task was to push a penny across the length of the auditorium floor with my nose, hands behind my back. I did it in record time, but I was sure left with a nasty blister on the end of my nose that took two weeks to heal. Another freshman was blindfolded and sat down at a table with her hands behind her back. She was then told she had to eat the plate of worms they then placed in front of her with no utensils. Of course, the freshman did not know that it was actually spaghetti that they had sprinkled with loose dirt and water so it would taste like "worms." I was so glad I didn't get that one. The penny deal was so much better.

I was 13 when I started freshman year at JMA, the youngest of the class. I did well all through high school, always maintaining a 93% average. There were no

"A" or "B" or "C" grades. It was strictly points. I began taking art lessons from *Mère* Marie Eymard. She was such a gifted artist, especially portrait painting. She painted the portraits of all the Monsignors and Bishops in the Fall River Diocese. I loved art classes with her. I preferred still life or scenery painting. I liked working in oils best of all. Pastels were my next favorite medium.

I joined the drama club and loved that, too. One of the plays I was in during my senior year was a one-act comedy called, "Be a Little Cuckoo," written by Howard Reed. I played the part of Marjorie, a student in a hurry to finish her education. I recall Annette J. sat by my side on stage. She played the part of another student. Diane C. played the part of the teacher. I also remember that Diane was the star of our debate club. It was so funny. Monsignor Bonneau, the pastor of *Nôtre Dame* Parish, who was sitting in the front-row-center-seat-of-high-honor, laughed out loud when Annette Hubert (later Annette Golembewski) slid across the stage to the center front at the end of the play with her line, "Be a little cuckoo." It was surely the performance of a Broadway star.

She was dressed as Lizzie the charwoman, a cleaning lady, in her frumpy apron, disheveled hair and old work boots, holding a galvanized bucket (no plastic buckets back then) and a grey, stringy mop. She ended the comedy with that line, "Be a little cuckoo," while she slid down to center front stage on her knees. It brought down the house. Monsignor laughed so hard, as did all the others, that he actually was crying and wiping his eyes. We had four curtain calls. They just would not stop applauding us. Annette deserved to win a "Tony Award" for the best performance.

My sophomore year was my true "mischief" year. I skipped school (only once) with Claire Roy one warm spring day and we took two buses to the end of Stafford Road where we then walked to her family's summer cottage to go swimming. Of course we got caught because the nuns called each of our mothers to find out why we weren't in school that day.

I got called to the principal's office more times than any other student. One time was for powdering the nun's chair with the blackboard eraser full of white chalk dust before she entered the classroom to begin the teaching session. When she sat down, she had no idea the chalk was there. When she got up to write on the blackboard behind her desk with her back to us, all the girls started laughing at her white bottom. She got annoyed and told us all to stop laughing, threatening to punish us with extra homework if we didn't stop. Some girls could not control their giggles and she finally asked what was so funny. No one answered. Then the "bomb" fell. If we did not tell her what was so funny, she would give us all three hours of homework that night.

So, one of the girls finally told her she had while chalk all over her posterior end. She twisted around to look and was mortified. She brushed herself off, while all the girls continued to giggle. She figured out that someone had powdered her chair. So the *ultimatum* was given. Either the guilty girl came forward and admitted to this prank, or the whole class would be given four hours, no longer just three hours, of homework for a whole week. That was a bit too much I knew. My classmates all knew it was me. They were not asked to tattle, rather the "guilty" one had to come forward. I had no choice. I stood up and admitted to my deed.

So, off I was sent to the principal's office to confess my transgression. I got detention for a week and had to mop and dust the reception room every day for a week. It was very large room with antique tables and chairs (at least 50) that the nuns used to receive their visitors and company. That's why today I hate to dust. I had my fill of dusting that week.

On junior-senior day, when the seniors bequeathed titles on us, other classmates received titles of: Most Intelligent, Most Helpful, Happiest, Most Resourceful, etc. Guess what title they gave me? Yup, it was Most Mischievous. My mother asked me why they had given me that title. I said it probably was because all the others had been assigned to my classmates and that was the only one left when they got to me, which is why I got stuck with it. She had no idea of all the mischief I had gotten into, or of the numerous times I had been sent to the principal's office.

Junior year's highlight was Career Day. I was chosen to be dressed as a Sister of Charity. The nuns really pushed religious vocations. The reason I was chosen was that my mother had been a postulant in the Sisters of Charity Order. These nuns staffed St. Joseph's Orphanage, located next door to JMA. I was sent to the orphanage to be fitted with the official habit of the religious order. On Career Day, I looked very authentic as a young nun, so much so that *Mère* St. Laurent did not recognize me.

I have a photograph of me dressed up in that nun's habit with two of the girls from the orphanage who also attended JMA and one with my mother. One of these girls was Dottie who you will read about later. My mother, of course, would have loved for me or one of my sisters to enter the convent after high school. No way José! That's what I said back then. Now, in retrospect, I wish I had at least tried it. Who knows? Maybe I would have outgrown my "mischief" days and made it as a full-fledged nun. Had I made it as a full-fledged nun, I feel that my life would have been easier than it turned out to be. Besides that, with the changes that came forth with Vatican II, a nun's life was not so bad later on. They got to wear secular clothes, were not so restricted, and they could go play Bingo on Tuesday and Thursday at the parish hall. Not bad, except I really don't care for Bingo.

I recently called my *Tante* Yvette in Canada (*St. Lambert*), *Oncle* Joe's wife, to ask her to ask her sister, who is a nun in a convent in *Québec*, if there was a possibility of getting me in the convent now. I had no luck with that desperate idea. I also went as far as to search the Internet for a religious order that would accept an over-sixty-year-old lady; none will. I'm just too dang old now. Too bad, because I'd be the most obedient, non-mischievous nun they ever had. Their loss!

Other memories of high school are dancing to 45 records in the auditorium before the bell that announced the start of our school day. We had some great dancers in our class; Claudette C., Jackie C., Dot D., Claudette G., and Georgette C. are just a few. Actually, 90% of the girls of our class were terrific dancers.

Many had beautiful voices and sang in the Glee Club. Mary Ann L., Rachelle L., Lorraine St.-G., Annette H. and, of course, Jeanine B. who I remember singing "Summertime and the Living is Easy." I have never heard anyone that could sing that song like she did. Jeanne P. played the huge harp in our school orchestra.

The quiet ones of our class were Lorraine D., Rachel C., Gert L., Jeanne L., Muriel L., Annette P., and the Nadeau sisters. Claire P. and Sylvia M. were boarding students who "obeyed" the "alpha boarder", Maureen. If they didn't, she'd retaliate when they roller skated in the school auditorium on weekends by leading "the whip" and flinging them to the far end of the auditorium floor. The "real quiet ones" were Lorraine B., who we viewed as a "snitch" and Pauline G., who we called "pigeon." They were both older girls and kept to themselves, often intimidated by our youthful exuberance.

Louise (Pewee) was one of the stars of our basketball team. She drove the "Woody" (a beach wagon or station wagon) to school each day from Westport where she lived. After school we would all pile into her "Woody" and go bowling or somewhere. Terry P. and Claudette G. often screamed when one of them found a tick on themselves. Pewee had dogs and lived in a wooded area of Westport, so inevitably, ticks would get into the "Woody."

Jeanne R. and Katie G. were the top class "blushers."

CHAPTER 14

I got my first real job during my junior year of high school. Before that, I had a job cleaning Dr. Shand's house at the Highlands. This was the "rich" section of Fall River, near where the Catholic Memorial Home is now. I would have to take two busses on a Saturday morning to get there. I would clean and scrub for six hours and receive four dollars pay. Out of those four dollars came the cost of the four regular bus fares, two to get there and two to return. These were twenty-five cent fares, so there went one dollar of my wages. I made a *net* three dollars a week for that drudge work.

When I was 14, I got a job as a waitress at Gow's Chinese Restaurant, which was right around the corner from 21 Hamlet Street, where we now lived as we had moved to the other end of Hamlet Street in 1956. My Dad had a disagreement with *Tante* Elmire. She was backing out of her agreement to let my father purchase the house on 266 Hamlet Street after he had converted that third floor to a small apartment for her. He had done all this work free with the understanding that she would sell the house to him after she was installed in her apartment.

Getting back to Gow's, it was on East Main Street and was a family-run business. Elizabeth was the cook, Jimmy was a waiter, and Joe was the owner and keeper of the cash register. He was also Elizabeth's husband.

I worked on Friday afternoons after school from 3:00 to 8:00, on Saturday from 11:00 to 6:00, and on Sunday from noon to 6:00. The pay was eighty-five cents an hour, but the tips were good. I averaged about $35 a week. I was making big money now. So, I quit my drudge job as a house cleaner and became a Chinese restaurant waitress. I kept that job until I graduated from high school. I had to give it up when we moved to Ocean Grove the summer after graduation.

From that time on, I had to basically pay my own way. I had to pay for my school bus passes, which were $1 for ten rides. I got a ride to school in the morning, either from my Dad, Cousin Philippe, or Lorraine St. George's dad. I had to take two busses to get home, costing me two student bus passes each time. First, I had to take the bus on Pleasant Street to downtown then change to the Globe street bus that took me to the corner of East Main and Hamlet Streets.

One student-bus-pass card lasted about one week. To save, I'd walk home from JMA when the weather was good, saving two punches or rides on my pass every time I did this. Imagine that; it was ten cents a ride! By walking home about two miles, the back way via Alden Street and the mills, I could save enough pass punches so that instead of buying a new pass every Monday, I could delay that expense for a few days and stretch that almighty dollar. I guess I got that from my Mom.

With my waitress wages, I also had to buy any clothes I needed or wanted and pay for my own school supplies. Mom taught us early on that we had to learn to take care of ourselves. We were not pampered, believe me. Today, I thank God for the way my parents raised me. I was taught early on to defend myself (remember the boxing lessons?), to pay my own way and to be thrifty. There is no doubt in my mind that, had I been pampered, I would not have survived the life experiences and those tough roller coaster rides that were to come later in my life.

In September of my junior year (1956), my sister Dee Dee and I were invited to a birthday party to celebrate my Cousin Roseanne's sixteenth birthday. The party was held during the day at her house on 16 Nelson Street, and my parents also went. Her parents were *Oncle* Sam (Aimé was his real name), Mom's brother, and Aunt Julie. The adults played cards, mostly a game called Scat, in the kitchen while chaperoning that party. This is where I met Bob, Richie Legault and his brother Kenny, Red Papineau, Smithy, Tommy, Chuckle Bunny, Charlie, Joyce, Mary Lou, Pauline, Diane and all the others in the "gang." My cousin Roseanne and her brother Richard, who everyone called "Fiefe" (pronounced "feefe"), and all their friends attended Durfee High School. My sister Dee Dee and I were the only two Catholic school girls there. We all received permission from the chaperoning parents to pile into the boys' cars for a ride to Newport. We ended up at Newport Creamery® where we all indulged in "Awful Awfuls®."

Bob had quit school just about a year before that party, after completing his ninth grade at Morton Jr. High. That's where he had met my cousin Roseanne and the "gang" that all attended her party. He also had been a soda jerk at DeVillers Pharmacy while he was still a student at the junior high. Even though he no longer attended school, he remained part of the "gang."

I think Bob was dating Mary Lou at the time. I didn't get to start dating him until later on, after they broke up. I don't remember exactly when that happened, but it was a few months before I celebrated my fifteenth birthday. Once I got my "hooks" into him, he never dated another girl.

When my sisters and I began dating, my mother had a few main rules we had to follow. First, we had to be home by 9:00 p.m. When we got a bit older, we graduated to 10:00 p.m., and then 11:00 p.m. Second, she had to approve of what we would be doing, or where we were planning to go. The third and most perplexing rule was this: she told us never to come with a package.

We never questioned my mother's words, but none of us really understood why we couldn't come home with a package, as we all thought she meant a package from the store. The word *naïve* doesn't even come close to describing the three Dube girls. Why did she not want us to do any shopping with boyfriends or dates? We really did not understand her reasoning, but we didn't question her rule. We never dared to ask "why?" when she laid down a rule.

Many years later, after we were all married, we finally figured out what she meant by that perplexing rule. Then it made sense. It was her way of telling us to behave ourselves and not to come home to tell her we were pregnant. We often had some good laughs retelling the story of that "rule," and how we used to hide a small package from the local drugstore to sneak it in the house if we had stopped to buy an item while out on a date.

On dates, Bob and I went bowling at the alleys located at Globe Five Corners. There was also a movie theatre in that area, which was not far from Hamlet Street where I lived. We could walk to the bowling alleys or theatre for our dates. Sometimes, we went to Anne Gagnon's house to play a game of Monopoly® or cards. Anne was Bob Binette's girlfriend and Bob Binette was best friends with my Bob. When Bob was able to borrow his dad's car we went on double dates with Bob Binette and Anne Gagnon, or with Annette Hubert and Stanley. Bob was my date for my senior prom. Before I started dating Bob, we girls were allowed to go to dances on Friday nights either at Club Calumet or The Forresters. After I started dating Bob, I never went dancing alone again.

When Richie had to baby sit his kid sister Nancy on Saturday nights, we would assemble at his mother's tenement for our parties. Everyone would be waiting outside, but far enough not to be seen by his mother when she left Richie in charge. We would all be watching for "the signal" that the coast was clear. Richie would lower one shade in the front room of the second-floor tenement where he lived. Once we received the secret signal we all descended on Richie's place and we would listen to 45s (records) and dance to the great music of that era, or we would play games. One time when we played hide and seek, Kathy, another girl in our gang, climbed up into the attic through a trap door in the ceiling to hide. She was klutzy and didn't watch her step. She came crashing through the ceiling leaving a sizeable hole. Boy those guys scrambled to locate some Plaster of Paris and whatever else they needed to repair that hole before Richie's mom returned around midnight. The girls who had an early curfew like me (by then I think it was 9:30) left, and the boys were on their own. Somehow they managed, and Richie's mom never found out about the big hole in her ceiling, or that we had that signal for the "parties" when she went dancing on Saturday nights.

I have lots of good memories of the gang and of dating Bob. The gang back then simply meant a group of us who all hung around together. Did I forget to mention that gas was 25 cents a gallon back then? I recall four or five of us all pooling our quarters to put a few gallons of gas in Kenny's car to cruise around Fall River and Tiverton, ending our adventure at our favorite hang-out, Bottomley's Ice Cream Parlor on Stafford Road. Kenny was Richie's older brother.

I must not forget to tell you about Richie's 45s collection. He guarded these records with his life. I believe he still has that collection of the 1950s music and, he is <u>still</u> guarding it with his life today, more than fifty years later.

*   *   *

I wanted to go to college after high school but my father would not even consider it. First, he could not afford to send me and, second, he truly believed that I would become a wife and mother and never work a day in my life outside the home, as my mother had done and all the women he ever knew had done. He certainly did not see the winds of change coming. After all, that's how things were back then. He said, "You don't have to go to college to learn how to do housework and change diapers." That was end of that dream. I don't resent him for that. It's just the way things were in the 1950s.

Very few girls went on to college. All of them that did were from financially better-off families. A few received partial or full scholarships. Katie, of course, was one who received a full scholarship. She was the "brain" of our class, graduating with a 99% average. She really achieved a perfect 100% but those nuns just would not give her the 100% perfect grade. I have become close friends with her in the past fifteen years or so, as we collaborated on re-creating our school newspaper for three of our class reunions. She visits me and meets me in New Hampshire when I visit my oldest son. I always tell her she is my "mensa" friend, and I am her "densa" friend.

Much later in life, in fact, when my father attended the momentous occasion of my oldest son Jerry's graduation from Wentworth College in Boston, Dad said to me, "I wish I had helped you to go to college when you asked to go." He realized then that the world had, indeed, changed and education was the key to a good life. He had seen how I had encouraged my kids to go to college and paid those outrageous tuitions. Now, his first grandson, named after him, was an engineer with a solid future ahead of him. He would have a much easier life than either my father or I had. He also realized that, in view of what life had thrown my way, I certainly would have fared better had I obtained a college education to fall back on. Hindsight is 20/20 they say and are they ever so right! If only we could know what the future holds so that we could make the right decisions and choices now. As I said before, I told him I didn't resent his not helping me to get to college all those years ago because I realized that's how things were back then.

I just gave you a few hints, in that last paragraph, of things that were yet to be. It will all become clearer to you as you continue reading my story. It just occurred to me that this is sort of an auto-biography, intertwined with history lessons (e.g., 1938 Hurricane), geography lessons (e.g., Canadian villages in the *Gaspée* area) and now, with that last paragraph, a bit of a mystery too. My dear grandsons, isn't your *Mémère* the clever one? (chuckle)

CHAPTER 15

I graduated from Jesus Marie Academy in 1958 and celebrated my seventeenth birthday six weeks later. By then I had found my first office job at the Ross Matthews Corporation in Fall River which was an elastic and braiding factory. Our family had moved to Ocean Grove Avenue in Ocean Grove that summer. Dad had finally managed to buy his first home, almost twenty years after my parents were married. He was the only bread winner since Mom never really worked outside the home.

I still did not drive and, even if I did, having my own car was not financially possible. So, in the morning, I got a ride with Uncle Walter, Bob's uncle, who lived past the Bluffs, the local skating ring and beach area . . . and what we always referred to as "down the point" in Ocean Grove. He was the all-around handyman for Mr. Gingras who owned an insurance agency and had several rental properties in Fall River. Uncle Walter would drop me off in Fall River at the bus terminal where I would catch the bus to the Flint section. I'd get off at the corner of Eastern Avenue and Pleasant Street and have to walk about six blocks down to the end where the factory was located.

This first job paid me $1 hour. "Wow," you must all be saying. That WAS truly the minimum wage and the starting wage for a recent female high school graduate. I helped with payroll and took shorthand for letters going out to customers. I also prepared sample cards with the products that the company manufactured. One day, there was an incident (actually, it was sexual harassment) that scared me and caused me to come home crying. After I told Mom what happened, she forbade me to return to that job so I had to look for a new job.

After a few weeks of having no luck in the Fall River area, friends of the family who lived in Attleboro, Massachusetts, offered to have me stay with them for a while, so I could submit job applications to all the jewelry companies in that area. After a month, I was hired at SWANK, a men's jewelry manufacturer, in September 1958. I worked there until January 1961, when my first child was born.

I was put in the typing pool for the accounts receivable department. I loved this job. I made friends with Dottie Nevius who was the head typist, and with Zenna, too. During our one-hour lunch break, we hurried to eat our bag lunches and then we played card games like Pitch or Hi-Lo Jack. On Fridays, we would all pile into one of the girl's cars, usually Irene's, and go to the bank about a five-minute drive away, cash our paychecks, then shop at the local department store for bargains. When the busy season came around, the typists were offered a lot of overtime. I would stay overnight with Dottie and wash out my *undies* for the next day. She would let me borrow a fresh blouse for work (which I later returned after I had laundered it). She was very kind to me. We remained friends for the two years I worked there. She came to my wedding and we kept in touch for many years. She is in the photos of my son Jerry's christening, along with my boss Bob and his girlfriend Carol.

After I had secured the job at SWANK, I moved back home to Ocean Grove. I had found a ride to Attleboro from Ocean Grove. Kenny Aguiar, who lived a few streets over from our family and who also worked in Attleboro at Texas Instruments, would pick me up in the morning. He would drop me off at the corner of the street where SWANK was located and, at night, I would walk up to that same corner where he would pick me up for the ride back to Ocean Grove, which took about forty minutes back then. We had to travel Route 118, no super highways to shorten our commute. I had a back-up ride also for the days when Kenny wasn't going in to work. I did what I had to do to get to work, even if I didn't have a car.

Sometime during that first fall and the winter after graduation Bob got his first car. It was a black 1949 Plymouth convertible. I say convertible and laugh. It was old, almost ten years old, in fact. That convertible top had so many tiny pin-prick holes in it that whenever it rained, you felt like you were in the shower instead of a car. I learned to drive in this car.

It was a standard shift and the gears were kind of messed up. When you put it in first gear, it looked like you were in neutral. Finally, after many driving lessons with Bob and hours of studying for the written exam, Bob took me down to Fall River for my driving test. It was a rainy day and that poor inspector kept looking up at the convertible top. The registry was near Ruggles Park; this was the area where road tests were administered. I had to turn the car around in the street using a three-point turn and not using any driveway. When the inspector saw me shifting the gears he had a puzzled look on his face and asked if I was sure I was in right gear. I said yes, knowing the position of the shift gear was deceiving him. Well, I didn't stall the car on the turn in the street and didn't touch the curb with the tires. I passed my road test. I really think the inspector did not take me through the complete test, as he was annoyed with the rainy roof and HE was confused with the gear shift positions, although he never came right out and admitted it.

After obtaining my driver's license, Bob would let me take the car to Attleboro when the overtime season came. This way, I could return home every night. Up until Bob got his first car, if he was not able to use his father's fawn gold Pontiac, he would hitchhike to Ocean Grove to see me, and then his Uncle Walter would drive him home because he didn't want him hitchhiking at night.

Bob had bought me a Lane® hope chest for graduation and soon after my seventeenth birthday, he gave me my engagement diamond. My sister Dee was also engaged. Her wedding was planned for September 1959. Bob and I wanted to get married the following spring, in April 1960. My poor Dad had two daughters getting married seven months apart.

My parents thought I was too young and wanted me to wait another year. I argued my case. I had been with Bob since I was just past 14. I didn't want to wait an extra year. So, two weddings were planned for the Dube sisters. Bob and I had a large "stag and shower," which was customary in those days. This was a couples and singles event held in a large facility (White's at the Narrows) and included a dinner and entertainment. The tickets sold for this event generated a nice cash purse for the engaged couple. Ours was a huge success with more than five hundred in attendance. Flossie Labecki put on a stage show. She was a local amateur comic and also *Mémère* Sevigny's (Bob's mother) hairdresser who always directed the annual fundraiser Minstrel Show at St. Jean's Church.

Dottie Forest (not the same Dottie I worked with at SWANK) and my sister Lou threw me a home bridal shower. Dottie gave me a Betty Crocker® picture cookbook as a shower gift and I remember that Anne Gagnon (later Binette) gave me a large aluminum roaster pan. I still have and use those gifts today, more than fifty years later. My future mother-in-law gave me a beautiful white peignoir set embellished with tiny baby roses. My Mom gave me a blanket and a set of lace-topped sheets and pillow covers.

I had been running the Popular Club catalogue plan since high school. Each week members would put in a set amount of dollars and each week, one member would place her order and receive it. On the tenth and final week, all had received their selections. It was sort of a lay-a-way plan. With my free gifts as club secretary, I got my Bluegrass China, my silver plate, some linens and my copper-bottom pots and pans. I still have some of these plates and most of the pans (the plates that survived the child raising years) to this day, more than forty-five years after I got them.

Dottie Forrest, a bridesmaid for my wedding and my bridal shower co-host, was a girl I had been friends with for years. She graduated with me in 1958. Dottie was living at the orphanage at that time because her grandmother could no longer care for her. She had been placed in a rest home for the aged. Dottie's parents had divorced when she was young, after which her paternal grandmother had raised her up until the time she went to the orphanage at age 14. She was 18 when she graduated and could no longer stay at the orphanage. She had nowhere to go. I asked my mother if Dottie could come live with us after graduation. My Mom said sure.

So, that's how Dottie became a member of our extended family. She called my parents Ma and Pa and truly was like another sister to me. We shared the same room and double bed in Ocean Grove. Dee and Lulu had their own bedrooms. She was a bridesmaid at my wedding, and we remained friends for many years.

On Sundays, my parents would go with Dottie to get her grandmother so she could spend the day with our family. *Mémère* Forrest did this until she was no longer able to get out. My parents were good Christians who lived their faith in actions. "When I was homeless you gave Me a home." They never hesitated or asked WWJD. (What would Jesus do?) They certainly knew and they willingly did. They gave to those who had less than them, like offering Dottie a home when she needed one, and caring for the elderly, like when they brought *Mémère* Forrest to our house on Sundays.

Kids: Do you all now understand how I took in your "stray" friends, Bobby Doyle and Bob Jaekels, when they needed a roof over their heads? Isn't it interesting that they were all named Bob?

Later on, Dottie and her husband Frankie were godparents to my daughter Melissa. They had only one daughter, Lynn. Sadly, Dottie died at age 50 from lung cancer. She was the very first one of our graduating class to pass away.

Bob had been working at a lighting fixture plant up until right before we were married. Then he went to work for Nelson's Dairy as a milkman. He had his early morning route and had to travel to Dartmouth (Massachusetts), load his truck and then drive it to Fall River where his route was. We both saved as much as we could from our wages. Of course, that "stag and shower" helped us a lot.

My parents did pay for my wedding, and Bob's parents contributed to their share of the wedding dinner. As there were more on Bob's side than mine, it cost them plenty. Of the more than 500 guests at our wedding, well over 350 of them were from Bob's side, including family and friends.

I bought my wedding gown at Louise's in Fall River. It was expensive. My sister Dee had got a sample gown for $100. She was so tiny back then, weighing just about one hundred pounds. I wore a size 12, and I had expensive taste. My gown cost more than $300, a lot of money in those days.

We were married on April 30, 1960 at St. Michael's Church in Ocean Grove. The only Canadian relatives that came for my wedding were Dad's cousin Gérard and family from Ontario. Others from *Amqui* had come for Dee's wedding in September and could not afford a second trip just seven months later for my wedding. My maid-of-honor was my younger sister, who everyone now called Lou. My bridesmaids were my surrogate sister Dottie Forest and Charlotte Cabral, yet another surrogate sister from my childhood days on Jenkes Street. The maid-of-honor's dress was the traditional blue of that time. The bridesmaids were of the same style in lemony yellow. The best man was his friend, Bob Binette. Ushers were Pitou (actually his name was Stanley and he was a first cousin to Bob), and Ronnie, Bob's only sibling.

Our professional wedding photographs were taken at Ataman's studio. Our dinner and reception were held at White's at the Narrows in Westport, Massachusetts in the Grand Ballroom which could accommodate those 500-plus guests. It was a beautiful, warm spring day—a perfect day, in fact.

We had already rented our first apartment on June Street in Fall River. It was a three-room tenement. Rent was $16 a week. I could get a ride to Attleboro from some people who also worked at SWANK. There were five in the car pool. I paid $3 a week for my daily ride to and from work. We went to that apartment on June Street to change into our traveling clothes after the wedding and reception. Bob Binette and Anne accompanied us. My travel suit was tan. I also wore a fuchsia hat. Yes, ladies always wore hats back then. Bob's suit was brown, so we complemented each other. (The home movies of our wedding were later converted to CD's by my oldest son, Jerry.)

After returning to White's with our traveling attire we bid everyone good-bye and left in that 1949 convertible headed for Pennsylvania and the Pocono Mountains for our honeymoon. We drove old Route 6 all the way practically. At around 8:00 p.m., we were well into Connecticut and stopped at a motel for the night. We were truly exhausted. It had been a long, tiring day.

Some day when all you grandchildren are much, much older you can ask your parents about Mémère's honeymoon night. I can't tell you now, or even think to ever put it down on paper; but I have told my children about that memorable night when they were old enough to appreciate the story. I'll leave it up to them to tell you the tale if they choose to when you are much older. For other readers of this tale, let me just say that having been raised a proper Catholic girl, I had absolutely no idea whatsoever about what transpired in a marriage bed.

We had a two-week-long, beautiful honeymoon in the Pocono's at a resort named Cove Haven. Forget an antiseptic hotel room. We had our own five-room bungalow with a fireplace. Daily activities were varied. I remember we did take a small plane ride over the beautiful rolling countryside and had a nighttime hayride. There was horseback riding available, but I was too scared to try that. We had live entertainment after dinner each night. I especially remember one of the songs that one of the entertainers sang, "The Bluebird of Happiness." In one of my photo albums, there is a group photograph of the honeymooners. Bob and I are in the center front row. I recall the light bottle-green dress I was wearing was obtained as a free premium from the Popular Club Plan. A good part of my honeymoon wardrobe came from that Popular Club Plan, all free premiums as the club secretary.

On our way back from the Poconos we took a slight detour so we could spend a few days with Terry and Bill Abbott in Lenox, Massachusetts who had married the summer before us. Terry had graduated from JMA with me and we had remained friends. In fact, she too had spent a few years at the orphanage, like Dottie, as her parents had died. She often came to spend weekends with our family while we were in school. The nuns at the orphanage knew my mother well (knowing that she had once been a Postulant in the Sisters of Charity Order) and always gave permission for either Dottie or Terry to spend some weekends with us.

*   *   *

The Bean Story: A Story of My Naiveté

When Bob and I were dating we sometimes were invited to his Auntie Nellie and Uncle Walter's home for a Saturday night dinner. On one occasion Auntie Nellie served us a scrumptious ham with home-made baked beans. I asked her for the recipe and she wrote it all down for me. When she handed me the paper, Uncle Walter asked to look at it. He said he wanted to be sure the "secret" ingredient had been listed.

I gave it to him and continued chatting with Auntie Nellie about other recipes she might be able to pass on to me. When Uncle Walter handed me the recipe back I just placed it in my handbag without looking at it.

After Bob and I were married, I decided to try my hand at Auntie Nellie's recipe one weekend. I bought all the ingredients listed and on Friday night I began with step 1, which was to soak the beans overnight. The following morning I drained the beans as instructed in step 2.

I next skipped down to the last three lines. These were hand-printed lines, with very large letters, underlined, and definitely not the handwriting that was on the first part of the recipe. When I had read the recipe prior to purchasing all the ingredients, I had taken special note of those last three lines.

After following the directions listed on those last three lines, I returned to step 3 to continue with the directions that Auntie Nellie had written down. The beans baked all day and I served them with frankfurters for our supper that night. I was so proud of myself for having succeeded at baking the beans that were just as delicious as the ones Auntie Nellie had made.

The very next time we saw Auntie Nellie I told her I had used her recipe and succeeded in baking those delicious beans but I added that it sure took a long time. She said that yes, they did have to bake slowly all day. I told her that wasn't what I meant. It was the "secret part" about sticking each soaked bean with a sterilized needle to release all the gas that had frustrated me.

She said: "What?" and Uncle Walter began to laugh out loud. Auntie Nellie asked him, "Walter, did you write that on my recipe?" He admitted that he had, all the while continuing to laugh.

Auntie Nellie explained to me there was no secret and Uncle Walter had written that as a joke. He probably figured I would just laugh when I read what he had written and I would realize that it really was not necessary to prick each bean to let the gas out. What Uncle Walter had not realized was that I was so naïve, I believed everything. Besides that, I always did as I was told. That's the way I had been raised.

I was so embarrassed at my naiveté. Believe me when I say that was the one and only time I ever made baked beans in my lifetime. My bean pot was officially retired and hidden away. I gladly passed it on to my daughter many, many years later. I don't have to tell you it was in "pristine" condition having been used only once.

PART II

CHAPTER 16

After we returned from our honeymoon we settled in at our first apartment. This had three rooms and was on June Street off President Avenue in Fall River. I had already arranged for my transportation from that area to SWANK in Attleboro, since we just had that one car. The carpool included four people plus the driver. Bob was working as a milkman for Nelson's Dairy.

It was just a few days after our two-month anniversary that I realized I was pregnant. Yup, I had conceived on my honeymoon. Luckily, I wasn't too sick with morning sickness. I ate dry saltine crackers in the morning to settle my stomach so I could tolerate that forty-five minute ride in the car pool to get to work. I don't think I missed more than a few days of work during my whole pregnancy.

Now we had to prepare for the birth of our first child. I was still running the Popular Club Plan and was able to get the crib and mattress, a small dresser, a baby bottle set, complete with the large sterilizer pot for bottles and nipples, and a car bed as free premiums for being the secretary. My Mom and mother-in-law purchased baby clothes every week or so, and gradually I had a complete *layette* ready. A layette was comprised of all that was needed for the care of a baby, including receiving blankets, sheets, diapers and nightgowns etc. I did not have a baby shower but after Jerry's birth I received many gifts from friends and relatives among which were beautiful hand-knitted sweater sets and baby booties.

We tried to save as much as we could after the bills were paid, as Bob wanted me to stay home after the birth of the baby. He said he would take an extra part-time job so we could make ends meet. We also had to find a larger apartment. We found one on Eastern Avenue on the second floor. It was a small two-bedroom unit but it would meet our needs for then. The rent was only $10 a week. We moved there when I was about seven months pregnant.

Since I became pregnant right away I was only able to work up to the very end of 1960. I was due in February 1961. Bob lost his job at Nelson's dairy right about a month before I had to stop working. Things were looking bleak now. I could not work an extra month because my company did not permit you to work past your seven-and-one-half-month point of pregnancy. In fact, it was the law back then. Bob did odd jobs while searching for a new job. Somehow, we managed to scrape enough money together for the rent, utilities, food and also make the credit union loan payment we had taken out for basic furniture. We dug into our meager savings if we were short. Somehow we managed.

My due date was February 3 but your father Gerard (named for my father, your great-grandfather) was born almost three weeks early on January 16, 1961. It was an easy labor, under two hours in fact, and without complications. The girl who was in the bed across from me in the four-bed maternity room, Carol, listened to my dilemma of Bob having recently lost his job and that our funds were truly low. She asked her husband if he could possibly help Bob get a job at the boat company where he worked. This place was right over the Brightman Street Bridge on the Somerset side of the Taunton River. They painted boats. Her husband did help Bob get a job, but not too long after that they both secured a job at Electric Boat (EB) in Groton, Connecticut. That's how Bob began working as an outside machinist at EB in 1961. That meant a long travel time to and from work for Bob but the pay was good and he had a secure job.

Jerry, as I nicknamed him, gave us such a scare when he was not quite four months old. *Tante* Roseanne, who was *Mémère* Sevigny's aunt, had come over one morning to baby-sit while I went down to the unemployment office to collect my benefit check. I was eligible to collect my unemployment benefits six weeks after Jerry's birth and I was able to collect for six months.

Jerry had been somewhat fussy that morning when *Tante* Roseanne had come over to baby-sit. When I returned from the unemployment office *Tante* Roseanne told me Jerry had been unusually fussy all that time and she was concerned. She had babysat him before many times and knew that he was usually so good. Also, she had raised a large family and her instincts just told her something was not quite right. By the time Bob arrived from work, Jerry was even fussier. We decided to bundle him up and take him to Dr. Witmer's office for a check-up. Dr. Witmer had evening hours up to 8:00 p.m. four nights a week. You didn't need an appointment. You just went and seated yourself in the waiting room and waited your turn. He was sort of the county-type doctor with no receptionist. He was the family doctor, the gynecologist, the surgeon and the pediatrician all wrapped into one.

Some kind people ahead of us in the waiting room could see the baby was very fussy and they let us in to see Dr. Witmer ahead of them. We were the beneficiaries of a kind and charitable act. Dr. Witmer listened to my account of how Jerry had been fussy all day and then he examined him. After he completed a thorough exam,

I dressed the baby and we sat in his little office to hear what he found. He told us we had to bring the baby to St. Anne's Hospital immediately. St. Anne's was right around the corner from his office. Jerry would need emergency surgery for the strangulated hernia the doctor's exam had revealed.

Dr. Witmer said he would call ahead to get things in motion without any delays and that he would close his office to get to the hospital to do the surgery within the hour. This could not wait. It was an emergency. Those other patients who were waiting for their turn were told of the emergency; they would have to return another night to see the doctor.

The surgery went well. Later, Dr. Witmer told me that had we waited to call or see him the next day, instead of going to his office that night, Jerry would have died from that strangulated hernia. The next day would have been too late. He then told me Jerry had another hernia on the other side, but this one was not strangulated. Surgery could wait until he was a bit older. Jerry had been born with the double hernia.

Today, more than forty years later, when I think about all that, I realize that God had a hand in getting Jerry to surgery that night. First there was *Tante* Roseanne who just knew something was not right, then our decision to just go to Dr. Witmer's office that night, and then the kindness of those people in the waiting room who let us take their turn because the baby was so fussy. That strangulated hernia was a killer. God knew this and He intervened.

Because Jerry was born with the hernia, our insurance would not cover the cost of the surgery and the hospital bills. That was the way the insurance worked back then. Bob and I had to apply for an emergency loan of $300 from St. Jean's Credit Union to get Jerry out of the hospital. We could pay off Dr. Witmer a few dollars a month. His surgeon fee was $75. His office visits were $4. Unbelievable, isn't it? The balance on our furniture loan was around $200, so we consolidated this with the new hernia loan. The weekly payment to retire that new loan was higher than we had budgeted for, but I managed by *putting more water in the soup*. The important thing was Jerry had been saved and would be okay. This little emergency had happened when we were married just a little over a year.

So, in a bit more than one year of our marriage, I had become pregnant right away, Bob had lost his job, our first son had been born and had to have emergency surgery at less than four months old, and we had to squeeze our already tight budget for that higher weekly payment to pay for the new consolidated loan. In retrospect, I know this is where I really learned how to put more water in the soup and stretch that almighty dollar. In other words, I learned to never waste anything. This is when I first learned to survive and surmount every little crisis that would throw monkey wrenches at my idyllic, optimistic, naïve, newly-married plans, hopes and dreams. I was 19 years old. I celebrated my 20th birthday a few months later.

I thought things were unpredictable and rough when this happened in the space of a little more than a year, but little did I know that more rough times were waiting in the future. I guess when they say that it's best we don't know ahead of time what's coming they know what they are saying. I do know now that had I known what was in the cards for me, how my life would have many ups and downs and how the bumps in the road would become even bumpier, I probably would have thrown the towel in long ago and not become a survivor.

I had a miscarriage right after that scare with Jerry's hernia. I wasn't even sure I was pregnant, but when I miscarried at home, I figured I had become pregnant before Jerry was even two months old. Had I not miscarried, I would have had a second child ten months after the birth of my first child. It's pretty obvious that my body was not ready to carry another pregnancy so close to the first. The stress and anxiety from Jerry's emergency must have contributed to that miscarriage.

Life went on and the days and months passed. Bob worked overtime on Saturdays whenever it was offered, and he also worked a part-time job at the Firestone® tire store on Pleasant Street. Since I had collected unemployment benefits for only six months, we needed that additional income to make ends meet. My Mom and mother-in-law helped out tremendously, buying new clothes for the baby when he outgrew what I had. That sure helped.

I got pregnant again when Jerry was nine months old. Our second son, Lawrence (named after Bob's father) was born on July 3, 1962. He, too, was born early as my due date was July 23 (my birthday). Jerry was eighteen-months old. Larry, as we nicknamed him, was a healthy baby, but definitely not of the same temperament as Jerry. He required more attention and settling down before he would go to sleep or take a nap. I recall the doctor telling me he was just a bit overactive and that he would outgrow it. Later on as a toddler, he would be the mischief-maker and little instigator.

Somehow we managed with another mouth to feed although we were only able to add a few dollars a week to our savings account for a rainy day. Believe me when I say the budget was strictly followed. In order for Bob to buy a new pair of work boots, we had to squirrel away a dollar here and there for four months, at least. Everything was purchased with cash. There were no credit cards in those days. Bob and I made do with whatever clothes we had before getting married. We received some new things as gifts at Christmas and on our birthdays. We always received practical gifts of clothing. It was never something like a new radio or jewelry.

Nine months after Larry's birth I got pregnant again. It's a wonder they didn't start calling me "fertile Myrtle," or that my mother-in-law didn't give me a chastity belt for Christmas that year. Her reaction to yet another pregnancy was, "Oh no."

A new young couple had just moved in the downstairs apartment just below ours. Terry had also become pregnant right away on her honeymoon but she was not as lucky as I was and suffered from morning sickness and fevers her whole pregnancy. I recall making her tea and toast and bringing it down to her so she could eat as she was so sick. I used to sit Jerry in his bouncer chair in front of the television so he could watch "Captain Kangaroo" and place Larry in the playpen while I brought Terry some tea and toast. Later on in this story, you will see how fate and destiny played a part in Terry and me meeting as we remained friends throughout the years.

My third baby was due on January 16, 1964, which would be Jerry's third birthday. This baby came early too and was born New Year's morning. I recall that morning when Bob returned from the early 6:00 a.m. Mass and I was ready to leave to attend the 7:00 a.m. Mass while he stayed with Jerry and Larry. Bob looked at me and asked how I was feeling. I said I had a stomach ache but it would pass. As we had been at his parents' house the night before for the family New Year's Eve party, where I had feasted on pork pies and *cretons* after midnight, I really thought I had an upset stomach. I remember that it was Rita Canuel who had babysat for us that New Year's Eve. She was my childhood friend who I had played cowboys and Indians with on Arizona Street. We didn't get a babysitter often but whenever we did, it was always Rita. I trusted her with my babies.

Bob told me to call the doctor as he was worried. In reality, Bob was probably scared that I would go into labor and have a quick delivery like my first one.

After speaking with Dr. Witmer and describing how I felt, I was instructed to meet him at the hospital in an hour. There he would check me out and if everything was okay I could leave to proceed with our plans to visit my parents for the traditional New Year's Day family celebration. So we bundled up the two babies and drove to my in-laws so they could baby-sit while I reported to the hospital. I recall having a cup of freshly-brewed coffee there before Bob ushered me out to the car for the drive to St. Anne's Hospital just a short distance from my in-laws' home.

After Dr. Witmer examined me he told me the baby was about to be born and it would be very soon. He then told me he was going to the cafeteria for some coffee as

I had awakened him before 7:00 a.m. on New Year's morning and he had not even taken the time to grab a coffee. He instructed the nurse to stay with me. Not five minutes after he left, taking the elevator that was right across the hall from the labor room I was in, I experienced strong labor contractions causing me to want to push immediately. The nurse threw off the bed covers. Apparently, she saw the baby's head and she told me not to push. She then left me to page the doctor. Her words over the loudspeaker were: "Dr. Witmer, emergency delivery, stat." She returned to me with another nurse and they plopped me onto the gurney for transport to the delivery room.

In actuality, I would describe this transport as "the race of the century." I kept pushing with each contraction that seemed to come every five seconds and they kept telling me not to push. They managed to get me on the delivery table with my legs in the stirrups when Dr. Witmer appeared, took off his suit jacket, rolled up his shirt sleeves and literally caught the baby as he was born. Eleven minutes had transpired from the time Dr. Witmer had examined me and the time Roger was born.

He told me I had another son and my first reaction was, "Oh no, my mother-in-law is going to kill me." When I became pregnant for my third child I hoped for a girl. My mother-in-law also hoped she would finally get a granddaughter. I had already given her two grandsons, so now it had to be a girl. It sure was a shock to us when Roger was born. We were all so sure it was a girl, except Bob that is. He said it was going to be another boy because all he wanted was "suns" and no "moons."

When Bob was finally allowed to see me after I had been moved to the ward from the delivery room, proud as a peacock that he had another son, he asked me what we would name him. I said, "I don't care, you name him." I did care, but I really had no name for a boy as I had been so sure it would be a girl. I had chosen the name Denise Renee for my anticipated daughter and my mother-in-law, equally sure it would be a girl, had shopped at McWhirr's Department Store for a total pink layette and coming-home outfit suitable for her new granddaughter. So, Bob named our new son. He chose Roger after his uncle, his mom's brother, who had been killed at Pearl Harbor. Bob was only about four when that had happened, but he had some fond memories of his favorite Uncle Roger.

Now, with three boys, our little two-bedroom apartment was certainly getting crowded. We definitely had to do something about more room. Either we had to find a bigger apartment or buy a house, *as if that was possible.* Bob was the only one working. I was a stay-at-home mom. There was very little extra money and very little savings. We had a loan from St. *Jean-Baptiste* Credit Union on the used car, on the furniture and for Jerry's emergency hernia operation. We were lucky to save $3 a week. As it turned out it was almost impossible to find a three-bedroom apartment we could afford or that a landlord would rent to us with three young boys.

Before I continue with this part of my story, I must mention that the Labor Day Weekend before Roger's birth, when I was about four months pregnant, we took a weekend trip to the Laconia area of New Hampshire for two days with Bernie and Roger Banville. This was possible only because Roger and Bernie generously paid for our accommodations and all we had to do was pay for our food. This was the only vacation we had taken since our honeymoon more than three years earlier.

On Sunday afternoon of that weekend, we went to a church auction and fundraiser where Bob bid on a carved wooden statue from some island. He won the bid and the statue came home with us. I'll leave you hanging for now, but I will tell you the complete story of that Headhunter Statue, as we called it, later on. It's a good example of fate and destiny. It also was important that I mention this weekend in New Hampshire at this point of my story. You will understand why later.

CHAPTER 17

The inability to find a new affordable tenement/apartment with three boys left us only with the hope of somehow buying an older home. We didn't know how we would do this, but we hoped God would answer our prayers. Believe it or not, He did. The Manchesters who lived on Kennedy Street in the Maplewood section of Fall River were retiring and moving to Florida. They put their cute little four-bedroom cottage up for sale.

This house was on the next street from my in-laws and the backyards were almost lined up, with just one house separating the property lines. When Bob heard that house was up for sale, he dreamed of getting it. He went and talked to the Manchesters, explaining his dilemma of not being able to find a larger apartment. They agreed to lower their asking price to $10,000 because they truly loved Bobby as a son. When he lived on Grattan Street, he was always offering to help them with yard work or shoveling. Never say never. God does answer prayers.

With them lowering their asking price, we needed $1,000 for the down payment. Well, Bob asked his father for a loan for the $1,000. His father kindly agreed, knowing our predicament of being overcrowded in that tiny two-bedroom apartment. That was one money hurdle. Next, we needed to come up with approximately $300 for the closing costs, escrow and moving van costs. Our savings were very meager. No way could we save or come up with that amount in a short six weeks. We were already saddled with those previous loans at the credit union, but God provided. Roger and Bernie came to our rescue. They loaned us the $300 that we needed. God Bless you both, Roger and Bernie.

We happily moved into our little house on Kennedy Street in early May 1964. It was an older home, needing upgrading for sure, but it was in very good condition and had a huge back yard and an adjacent side lot. It had four upstairs bedrooms. *Pépère* Sevigny's backyard on Grattan Street was practically lined up with ours and our little house was the perfect place to raise our three sons.

Bob worked full time at EB in Groton as he had since the time right after Jerry's birth. He also continued working that part-time job at the Firestone Tire Store on Pleasant Street on weekends for the extra money to support his little family and pay off the kind loans from his Dad, from Roger and Bernie and the one consolidated loan from the credit union. Those loans from *Pépère* and Bernie and Roger had made our dream come true of having our own little house. Besides the two jobs, Bob would simonize family and friends' cars in his spare weekend hours. He knew he could shovel driveways and walks for others in the winter months, or pick up a side job painting to help pay off those extra loans.

All of this made it possible for me to continue to be a stay-at-home mom. He always said he didn't want me working and the boys raised by others and he meant it. He would work and provide. He did! There wasn't a lazy bone in his body. I'll add here that his boys all inherited his work ethics. None of them is lazy, either. Jerry, Larry and Roger you ALL are certainly your father's sons.

Not eight weeks had passed since moving into our little house when our lives changed. Bob was home the Fourth of July week on a vacation week. In the middle of that week he began having problems climbing the stairs to the upstairs bedrooms because he suddenly had difficulty breathing. He began to sleep in the big chair in the living room. His parents and I finally convinced him to go to the doctor. Our family doctor was away on vacation so he saw a Dr. Morganstein who diagnosed it as walking pneumonia. He prescribed something and told him to drink plenty of fluids and get plenty of rest.

By July 13 he definitely was not getting better. I called Andy DeVillers, the pharmacist who knew Bob, as Bob had worked for Andy as a soda jerk when he was a teenager. DeVillers Pharmacy is still there today on the corner of Rodman and Brayton Avenues. Andy had a brother who was a physician. He was able to get us an appointment for the next day, July 14. Bob went to that appointment alone. When he returned, he told me he had to check into the hospital that afternoon because the doctor wanted to run some hospital tests. So, he checked into St. Anne's on the afternoon of July 14.

The next morning, around 11:00 I think, his father came over to baby-sit the boys, so I could go to the hospital to see Bob. His father was a firefighter on the Newport Naval Base and worked 24-hour shifts. He was off that day. On top of all that, our white 1957 Chevrolet Bel Air was on the blink and would not start, so I had to drive *Pépère* Sevigny's fawn gold Pontiac, his pride and joy.

When I arrived on the hospital floor that Bob's room was on (it was the room right above the old portico entrance on Middle Street), Dr. DeVillers was waiting for me outside Bob's room, a little distance from the door, so Bob had not seen me. Dr. DeVillers guided me to a tiny little conference room. There, he began with, "We have results of the tests." I said, "Wow, you ran tests already. He just checked in yesterday afternoon." He replied, "Yes." Then, I asked, "Well, what is it?" Dr. DeVillers did not answer. So, I asked if it was his heart, or a lung infection, or something like that. I asked about any known conditions I could think of. Finally, Dr. DeVillers said, "It's cancer."

Talk about shock. I cannot describe what I felt at that moment, but being the optimist that I am, and after a few moments to recover somewhat from what had just been announced to me, I said to him, "Well, you are going to fix him up. He'll be okay." He shook his head indicating no to that comment. I asked, "What are you telling me?" After a few seconds, which seemed like an eternity to me, he said, "The cancer is *acute adrenal insufficiency, embryonic cell carcinoma with metastasis.*" I had no idea what that meant, but I would find out when he next spoke. He explained that the cancer was in his total lymphatic system and was still growing and spreading, doubling in size every six weeks, and that Bob's life expectancy was four to six weeks. I broke down of course, crying uncontrollably, and really couldn't speak for quite a while.

He next said that at this stage of the cancer, there was no established treatment available. This was in 1964. It was just too far advanced. I asked him if he had told Bob all of this. He said no. Bob was under the impression that he had some kind of stomach virus or ailment. Dr. DeVillers had not confirmed it or denied it when he had spoken to Bob earlier. I said I didn't want him to know just yet, as I needed time to absorb this devastating news. He agreed not to say anything unless Bob point blank asked him what was wrong. He could not lie to his patient.

I went to the ladies room, washed my face with cold water and blew my nose. I asked God to give me the strength to walk into Bob's room, act happy and not break down. After fifteen minutes of pulling myself together, I walked into Bob's room. God answered my prayer. I kept the conversation light and did not break down. I did cut that visit short, with the excuse that I had to return his father's car because he had to finish running the errands. I told him that either I or his parents would visit during the next visiting hours. I had to leave because I didn't know how much longer I could hold it together.

To this day I don't know how I drove *Pépère's* car from St. Anne's Hospital to home. It was less than a mile, but as soon as I got into the car the flood of tears descended on me. When I finally parked the car in front of our little house on Kennedy Street I was consumed with my grief of what the doctor had burdened me with. I slumped over the steering wheel with the horn blaring and sobbed uncontrollably.

Hearing that horn blaring and seeing me slumped over the wheel when he looked out the front window *Pépère* came out of the house after placing Roger in the playpen. He literally had to get me out of the car and into to the house. Of course, he began asking what had happened. Why was I sobbing? Had I seen Bobby? Did I have a car fender bender? I could not speak. I was still sobbing out of control.

Then he asked if I had seen the doctor. I shook my head yes. So, he began asking, "What is it? Is it his heart? Is it his lungs? Is it an infection?" Funny, he never mentioned the word cancer either, just like when I was asking the doctor about possible conditions. Again, I could not speak. Finally, he got angry and told me to tell him. He was such a kind and gentle man. When he raised his voice and said, "Tell me," I knew he had reached his limit. I had never heard him raise his voice to anyone. I had to speak, but I didn't want to tell this man his son was going to die and soon. All I could say was, "It's cancer."

This was like dropping an atomic bomb right over him. He began to cry. We cried together. Then after a while, optimistic too, he said, "Well, they're going to fix him up. Don't worry, Lorraine. Everything will be all right." I shook my head like I agreed and I understood. I withheld the part that I was told Bob's life expectancy was four-to-six weeks. I could not share that horrible part with him. This was his oldest boy, just 26 years old.

That day was July 15, 1964. That was the day that my life began its first, but not last, scary roller coaster ride. That's the day I truly became an adult. I was one week shy of my 23rd birthday.

Chapter 18

I don't know what *Pépère* Sevigny ever told my mother-in-law. She was very optimistic, never crying, always keeping her chin up, always encouraging me by saying, "Bobby's going to be okay." I recall that the word *cancer* was never verbalized in my conversations with her. Whereas, when I talked to my parents, family and close friends, the big "C" word was not avoided.

The next day, when I went to the hospital to visit with Bob, I saw Dr. DeVillers again. He said he would get Bob transferred to Pondville State Hospital in Norwood, Massachusetts. He said there were new experimental treatments that could be tried on Bob. Nothing could be done for him locally. Because of his age, 26, I guess he thought that anything was worth trying. There was nothing to lose.

Within one or two days Dr. DeVillers got a bed for Bob at Pondville. He was released from St. Anne's and his father, Roger Banville and I drove him directly to Pondville. He didn't even come home for an hour to see his boys, his "suns."

When we left St. Anne's Hospital, I was handed a large manila envelope with copies of all the results of the medical tests they had run. When we arrived at Pondville, about a one-and-one-half hour drive away, we had to go to the examination area first where they reviewed the information in that manila envelope, examined Bobby, formally admitted him and finally assigned him a bed. There were four beds in his room. Bob's was the first on the right as you walked through the door.

Over the next two-and-a-half weeks they ran more tests but no specific protocol was implemented. I made that trip to Pondville every single day, catching a ride with whoever could go to accompany me. It was either with my in-laws, always with Roger Banville driving, my parents, or friends like Bob Binette, who had been the best man at our wedding. Sometimes it was one of Bob's uncles, or a cousin or a friend of the family.

Never did I go alone or drive. I could not drive because I was on tranquilizers. I had seen Dr. Witmer within the first few days of hearing the shocking words from Dr. DeVillers on July 15, 1964. The medication helped me to stay calm, not to cry in front of Bob and to "keep it together" for the boys. The three boys were three-and-a-half, two and seven-months old.

I had so much help from family and friends who would come over to take turns to baby-sit the boys so I could make that daily trip to Pondville. They cooked and bathed the boys, did laundry and daily household chores, lightening my load as much as they could. God bless them all!

That daily trip took up to five hours of each day. The driving time alone to and from the hospital took up to three hours, and then when traffic was heavier, or there had been an accident, it took even longer. We had to get off state highway 195 at the Seekonk exit and go up Route 114, then on to Route 1 to Norwood. The Braga Bridge over the Taunton River between Fall River and Somerset had only been completed a few years prior to this.

Blanche, Bob's mom, worked in the curtain factory on the sewing machines. She continued to work every day, going up to see Bobby on the weekends. I refer to him as Bob, but to his mom, he was always Bobby. Larry, Bob's father who worked those 24-hour shifts as a fireman on the Navy Base in Newport, came with me on his off-duty days, always with Roger Banville doing the driving. It was an exhausting schedule for me. I thank God for the many friends and family that helped me in that time period. This daily routine continued with only one exception.

During the next week they ran even more tests and he had to have a surgery. One of his testicles was totally cancerous. They removed it as it was growing in size every day. After the pathology report was available one of the staff doctors called me in for a meeting. He too told me that the cancer was far advanced and that radiation treatments, which were experimental back in 1964, could not be tried as Bob's body was full of radiation. He was at a loss to explain the reason for that high level of radiation which they discovered while administering all the tests.

He told me they were looking into a chemotherapy plan, totally experimental of course, that could possibly be tried. He emphasized that they could not cure him but maybe they could give him a few more months. When I left that consultation room I did not go to Bob's room. His two cousins, with whom I had hopped a ride, were with Bob. I cried so hard, even with tranquilizers. The doctor's words were "*maybe a few more months.*" He did not say "*a few more years.*" This was the second doctor who gave me devastating news. I was always alone when that happened.

The next day, on my daily visit to see him, Bob asked why I had not come to his room the previous day. He knew I had hitched a ride with his cousins. I lied and said I got tied up with insurance paperwork in the front office and that by the time I finished with all the dang forms, etc., the visiting hours were over. He accepted that explanation.

On Saturday, August 8, 1964, Bob called me at home around 9:00 a.m. and said, "Come and get me. I'm coming home." I said, "What?" He told me he had received permission to come home for one night. He had to return to the hospital Sunday night. I immediately called Roger Banville and Bob's dad and we all went up to get Bob. This was a Saturday, so Blanche, Bob's mom, babysat the boys.

That Saturday, after we arrived home from Pondville, Bob drove his father's car (ours was still sitting the driveway on the blink) and took Jerry, the oldest who was three-and-a-half, to Westport to give him some go-cart rides. He wanted to mow the lawn and trim the hedges but his father stopped him from doing that. He played in the big backyard with the two older boys. Later he took a ride over to see his old boss, Andy DeVillers, at the pharmacy.

On Sunday, he asked me if I knew where all the insurance papers were and if I had enough money to make ends meet. He did receive a portion of his paycheck being on "sick leave" from EB, but there was no extra income from the part-time job or the occasional odd jobs he normally picked up to supplement our income. I told him not to worry. I was fine. We never talked about his condition. I still thought he did not know of that devastating prognosis Dr. DeVillers had given me back on July 15th. In retrospect, I now know he knew, because he was asking so many questions about life insurance and the financial situation.

A few of our close friends had stopped in for short visits to see Bob that Saturday night. I remember that Richie and Carol, and also Austin Belanger, an old friend from Westport, made short visits so as to not tire him too much. Later, when we went to bed, he talked about how I was doing and how I was managing with his "suns." He never talked about what he was feeling or of what he knew about his condition. We eventually made love. Before we did, I suggested we use protection as I didn't want to chance getting pregnant. He agreed.

I had gone to confession the week before at St. Anne's Shrine and had discussed my situation with my confessor. Anticipating that he would somehow be able to come home and that we would make love, I was very concerned about getting pregnant, recalling what Dr. DeVillers had told me about life expectancy. My confessor had listened to my story and simply told me that I had to do what I thought was best for my little family. I interpreted his counsel as nothing was a sin if you didn't believe it was a sin. I had been so worried that I would cause Bob to be sent to hell if I insisted on using contraceptives as it went against the teaching of the Catholic faith. We had begun to use birth control after Roger's birth as by then I realized I was indeed "fertile Myrtle" and another new baby every eighteen months just had to be avoided. First, all those pregnancies were taking a toll on my body and second, the family finances were already strapped to the limit.

Before we left to return to the hospital the next day, he took the boys downstairs to the basement area. He was carrying Roger in his arms. He took them to the "cage area" where he kept all his tools locked up. He told the boys to always take care of daddy's tools. Before going out the back door to get in the car for the ride back to Pondville he turned one last time and said to his mother, "Ma, take care of my boys and Lorraine, okay?" That Sunday was August 9th. The following Monday at the hospital they began the experimental chemotherapy course. He received an eight-hour intravenous dosage of the chemicals in the hopes of at least temporarily arresting the progression of the big "C."

Later on I found out that he had made a deal with Dr. Cox at Pondville. When they told him about the chemo plan they had to tell him the full truth of his condition and get his signed permission to try this experimental protocol. He told Dr. Cox he would sign the consent form only on the condition that he would be allowed to go home for the weekend to see his wife and his boys. Dr. Cox agreed and so I received Bob's call that Saturday morning to come and get him.

I was still making the trek to the hospital every day. I was exhausted. On Friday, August 14th, it was my parents and *Tante* Marie (Mom's oldest sister), along with me, scheduled visit to Bob. There was a lot of phone checking and coordinating with everyone to come up with a schedule that worked for everyone and that allowed me that daily "hitch-a-ride." As far away as the hospital was, Bob still had visitors every day. When my parents called to tell me what time they would pick me up I told them I would not accompany them that day. I was so exhausted and I truly needed one respite day. I asked that they tell Bob I was taking one day off to get some needed chores done and that I would see him the next day, on Saturday.

When my parents returned from the hospital they called me to let me know how he was doing. My mother told me Bob had shook hands with my Dad and thanked him for all the help over the years and now. He had said to my dad, "I know you'll take care of Lorraine and the boys." Bob, of course, knew by then that his chances of surviving were very slim. Dr. Cox had to tell him the complete truth the week before when the experimental chemo was planned.

The very next morning at 3:00 a.m., August 15, 1964, I received that devastating phone call from Dr. Cox. His exact words were, "I'm sorry to have to inform you like this, but your husband passed away very quickly just about an hour ago." I know I couldn't catch my breath because I was crying so hard. I mentally asked myself why I had not visited him that previous day. I felt so guilty that I had taken a respite day.

Dr. Cox then asked me if I was alone. I said that I was alone with my three babies while sobbing uncontrollably. He waited patiently and when I was able to speak, I asked him why I was not called earlier so we could be with him in his final minutes here on earth. Dr. Cox explained that they did not know he was dying. He further said that at the last bed check, approximately one hour before he died, there were no apparent signs that death was imminent. He thought that possibly the experimental chemo therapy caused a heart attack but said he could not be certain.

He then explained what I needed to do next. First, I had to go to the funeral director and make arrangements for "the body" (it was no longer "your husband") to be picked up. I had to drive to the hospital to sign the necessary paperwork for release of the body to the funeral director (no fax machines in those days), and I had to retrieve his personal effects, like his watch and wedding ring, radio, etc., after the paperwork was signed. I told him I understood and would be there before lunch time.

Again, I was all alone when I received terrible news. The children were all sleeping. It was 3:00 a.m. That day, Saturday August 15th, was a Holy Day, and the plan was for his mom to come over at quarter-to-six so I could go to Mass at St. Jean's, which was one block away. Then she would go to a later Mass. Later, we would all go up to see Bob.

I began to think. My God, she is going to show up here promptly at quarter-to-six. I can't tell her Bob died and about that call I received at 3:00 a.m. when the two of us will be alone with just the three kids. What am I going to do? I silently asked myself.

I immediately called my parents and told them the horrible news and my dilemma about how I was going to tell my mother-in-law her son was dead. Mom said that Dad would be at my house before 5:30 a.m. and he could stay with the boys. She would come later with either Eddie or *Oncle* Paul St. Amand giving her the ride. She needed a few hours to pack a bag and do a few things as she planned to stay with me for some time.

My Dad arrived at my house before 5:30 a.m. and we hugged and cried together. I made sure Roger's diaper was changed and told my father to give Jerry and Larry breakfast of cold cereal and toast. He could give Roger just his bottle and my Mom could feed him a bit later when she arrived. I then walked over to my in-laws and knocked on the door. It was not more than five minutes after 5:30 a.m. Blanche asked what I was doing there so early, saying she was just about to walk over so I could go to Mass while she babysat like we had planned.

My eyes were all red and puffy from crying. She asked what the matter was. She really had no clue. After a few minutes I told her about the call from Dr. Cox and the few details he told me about Bob's passing. Here again, it was as if I dropped an atomic bomb on her. She said, "Oh no," and she too sobbed uncontrollably. Ronnie, Bob's only sibling who at the time was only 19, came out of his bedroom having heard his mother's loud sobs. I then had to tell him about the call and there was more sobbing and hugging by all three of us.

Bob's father was on his way home from his shift at the Newport Navy base, due to arrive at around 8:00 a.m. He had to be told when he arrived home. I called Roger Banville, who lived across the street from my in-laws, told him about Bob's passing and asked if he could come over to my in-laws to be there when Larry arrived home from Newport. I wanted someone else there with me because I was truly afraid of how he would take this heartbreaking news.

My father-in-law arrived at about 8:00 a.m. When he walked in the house into the kitchen, he saw his wife, young Ronnie, Roger Banville and me. I didn't have to say anything. He cried out, "Oh no. Oh my God, no. Bobby's dead." He sobbed uncontrollably with Roger Banville at his side telling him to let it all out and trying to comfort him.

The next hour is a blur but at some point I told them about having to see the funeral director, then driving up to Pondville to retrieve Bob's personal possessions and signing the necessary paperwork for Bob to be released to the funeral director. Roger Banville, of course, was right there offering to do all the driving. My mother-in-law asked who was with the kids. I told her my Dad was and that my Mom would be down later in the morning and would stay with me and the boys at least for a while.

So by 9:00 a.m. we were on our way to Boulé's Funeral Home. I had called my little house just before we left and asked if my Dad was holding up okay with his three grandsons. He said, "Worry *pas*," his typical half French/half English dialect which meant "not to worry."

We were greeted at Boulé's in the first big room as you walk in. There were a few stuffed chairs and the secretary desk where the information for the wake and funeral would be gathered. I remember Mr. Boulé telling me he was so sorry about the loss of my mother. He assumed because I was with an older man and Roger that I had just lost my mother. I told him it wasn't my Mom; my husband had just died.

That startled him. He asked if it was a car accident. I told him what happened. It was a total shock to him and to so many others as they all heard the unbelievable news, because Bob was only 26 years old.

After the necessary paperwork was completed for the funeral and for picking up the body at Pondville, I had to go into the casket room downstairs and select the coffin for my young husband. Roger and my father-in-law came with me, of course, but I chose the first nice one and had to leave that room immediately. It was like I was living a nightmare.

We drove to Pondville. We met with Dr. Cox who expressed his condolences to all of us. I was handed a large manila envelope with his small personal effects. I was given his wedding band, portable radio and anything personal he had with him at the hospital. The paperwork was signed.

Then Dr. Cox asked if I would give permission for an autopsy. Immediately my father-in-law said, "No, you're not going to cut him up. He's dead, let him be." I could not go against his wishes so I did not agree to an autopsy. Dr. Cox tried to explain they were guessing it was heart failure that took him and that they would really like to determine if it was, in fact, a heart attack. He did not verbalize what I think he was thinking at the time although this thought did not come to me until much later. He wanted to determine the cause and extent of Bob's body being so full of radiation that they couldn't give him one radiation treatment. I wish he had gone into detail about that with Bob's father and me right then and there. Maybe he would have received that permission for an autopsy.

Many years later when we could talk about what happened to Bob, and after we found out that all the guys who worked as outside machinists in the "Pill", the reactor compartment in the submarines, had died, we began to wonder if EB was where they all got sick. Much later on after Red Scanlon's son (Red was one of Bob's co-workers) had done some research, with Ralph Nader helping him, they had figured out that it was possibly the radiation gauges worn while working in "the pill," the reactor room, that were the culprit.

Those gauges had to be defective and not properly registering the amount of radiation each man was exposed to. They all died of cancer, Bobby being the first and eventually Red Scanlon himself. Red Scanlon's son tried to pursue this further with legal action after his dad passed away but was unsuccessful as they couldn't prove it without records. What was needed, especially, were the records of their exposure to the reactor room while wearing those gauges. At that time, because EB was doing government work, all those records were "classified" and not available to the public. EB was off the hook.

CHAPTER 19

Roger Banville, Bob's dad and I made that last return trip from Pondville. Later on in the afternoon his mom and I went downtown to McWhirr's Department store. The boys were being cared for by my Mom. I recall bumping into Ruthie, my old friend, and telling her the terrible news.

Blanche bought me two black, two-piece dresses, a black slip, black shoes and a black handbag, garments appropriate for Bobby's widow. She purchased two outfits for herself, also appropriate for the mother of a deceased son. I know she must have been devastated by the death of her son, which was announced to her just that very morning, but Blanche was a trooper and had her sense of etiquette and propriety, so she did what she had to do. She made sure I would have the proper clothes to wear to the wake and funeral. She paid for all of this knowing I could not afford to buy anything. She had always been generous to me. She was ever-so-generous then, and she continued to be generous to me for her whole life, up until the day she died at age 89. I loved her dearly.

Her heart must have been broken in a thousand pieces but she held it together for her husband, for herself and for me, too. She was the force that anchored everyone else.

In the late afternoon and early evening hours of that terrible day, August 15th, my in-laws made telephone calls to friends and family living locally and those living in Springfield, North Carolina and in Maryland. I made calls to family and friends, both locally and out-of-town. My Mom, who planned to stay with me at least until after the funeral had made her calls to family and friends in Canada and the U.S. We all were the bearers of that sad news, and each time we had to say those horrific words to whomever it was that received our call, we relived the initial shock of that first moment in time, over and over again, when each of us had learned Bob had died (I, myself, at 3:00 a.m. that morning).

How I ever got through that day I don't know. I guess God did send me the strength and courage. It was one of the longest days of my life. In actuality, there would be more "longest days of my life" to come. I did not know that then, though.

The wake period before the funeral was long in those years. The first viewing and wake period was the following night, Sunday. There were two more days of waking before the funeral on Wednesday. I, my in-laws and Bob's brother Ronnie, arrived together a little earlier than the scheduled calling hours of the wake Sunday evening. We did not drive. Boulé's Funeral Home sent the limo to pick us all up.

Describing the instant we approached Bob's coffin and viewed his body is difficult. I can only try to describe my feelings. He was laid out in the clothes I had chosen and which had been delivered to Mr. Boulé by Roger Banville. It was the suit he had worn on our wedding day, just four years earlier, when we left the reception for our honeymoon in the Poconos.

"How could this be happening?" was one of the thoughts running through my head. He was 26 years old and looked like he was just sleeping very peacefully with not a wrinkle or crease on his face. It was unreal. I can only imagine the emotional turmoil and the feelings his parents had. That was their first-born son in that coffin. Ronnie's thoughts must have been similar.

A short time after that initial shock of seeing my young husband in his casket and then taking my place in the first chair of the family line, the visitors started arriving. They each, in turn, would kneel before the casket and say a short prayer for the repose of his soul. Then, starting with me seated first along the right side of the wall near the casket and then his parents and brother, they would kiss and hug me, or just shake my hand, offering up their sincere condolences for my loss, for their loss (to his parents) and for his loss (to his only brother).

CHAPTER 20

So many friends and family members recounted to me a special memory they had of Bob, of his generosity, his thoughtfulness and of his love of life.

I will digress some here to relate a few of my own precious memories of Bob's generous spirit for the benefit of his grandsons who never knew him. His generosity was but one of the character traits that endeared him to everyone he met and why the visiting line for his wake was so long.

First, the one and only time I gave Thanksgiving dinner in the three years we lived in that tiny Eastern Avenue apartment was the one when Jerry was not yet two years old and Larry was about five months old, so I can calculate it was in November 1962. Our usual routine was spending the major holidays with either his parents or with my parents, alternating, to be fair to both sets of grandparents. That routine was not followed that particular year.

About two weeks before that Thanksgiving, when Bob returned home on Saturday afternoon from his part-time, weekend, extra job at Firestone, he told me he had invited a co-worker and his wife who he worked with at Firestone to Thanksgiving dinner at our apartment. They were a young couple like us but with no children yet. "What," I said. "Where are we going to put them?" I didn't even know these people.

The tiny kitchen was no more than eight feet long by eight feet wide in size. As you walked into that room, along the right wall were the long white porcelain kitchen sink and the short lower cabinets. Above the sink on half of the wall space were the upper cabinets. Now, remembering that I said this was an 8' x 8' size room, imagine that wall's length taken up by the doorway, by the only short counter to the right of the sink and by the only tiny wall cabinets in that room. The facing wall had one window way over to the left and the remaining wall-only space. The right side wall, starting at the far end of the room held the apartment-size refrigerator (our wedding gift from his parents), the washing machine and the apartment-size stove, a 20-inch Glenwood. At the end of this stove there was just enough room, not quite three feet, to stand at the kitchen sink on the other wall area.

The left side of that tiny kitchen was where the dinette set was backed up against the wall with one chair at either end and two chairs on the outer side. We could not pull the dinette table away from the wall to place the chairs all around for seating; there just wasn't enough room. With the back of the chairs in the front of the washer and cooking stove, there was just enough room to pull out the chairs and sit. We were barely able to squeeze by to retrieve something from the refrigerator. The high chair was on the back wall just to the side of that one window.

After my reaction, Bob told me that this co-worker had no family in the area. Both he and his wife had moved to Fall River recently from another city. He, too, was working an extra job to make ends meet. They were struggling, just as we were. He said he felt sorry for him and didn't want him and his wife to spend the holiday alone, so he invited them to share Thanksgiving with us. I pointed out to him that we would be packed like sardines in that tiny kitchen. In all, we would be four adults, one toddler (Jerry), and one infant in the infant chair on the floor (Larry). I also worried about setting a proper table. The table HAD to stay against the wall and two had to be seated on the chairs whose backs literally backed up to the cooking stove. He calmly replied, "We'll manage."

Somehow we managed. The turkey and fixings were purchased. The table was set with my best linen and Bluegrass china and silver retrieved from the large all-purpose storage closet that ran along the wall in the hall area leading to the even tinier bathroom. I'll never forget that dinner. We truly were "packed like sardines" and that's putting it mildly. Nevertheless, we did set a good table and shared our Thanksgiving with two people who needed the kind invitation Bob had extended to them. I can't even remember their names as that was the one and only time I saw them. I think they moved on to greener pastures by the time the next Thanksgiving rolled around. In any case, Bob did not extend a second invitation to them, as I'm sure he would have if they were still in the city with no family for the holidays.

Now I'll tell you the story about Jeanine and Conrad. Jeanine was a third cousin of mine. I was a bridesmaid at her wedding. They lived in the Flint section of Fall River, within a short walking distance to our apartment. Neither of them drove a car, so they walked everywhere. They had one little girl, Irene, about a year older than Jerry. They had even less than we did, as they both worked in one of the commercial laundries in Fall River, earning just the minimum wage of the time. On one of their visits to us, which I recall was in late fall because it was starting to get cold outside, Bob had apparently noticed that Conrad was shivering when they first came in. His light jacket was appropriate for spring and even very early fall, but this late in the season, that jacket was not keeping him warm. I guess Bob figured out that Conrad had nothing warmer to wear for this pre-winter season.

I'm guessing here as to what Bob was thinking because he never voiced his thoughts. He just instinctively acted. Bob did not have a spare, warmer jacket suitable for that time of the year, but he did have something that would be warmer than the light jacket Conrad was wearing. He opened his closet, located to the left of the gas space heater in the living room. Our bedroom closet was so tiny that only his very best suits (he had two) were kept there along with my clothing. His work clothes and his casual clothes were kept in that other closet. He retrieved what he had thought of and handed it to Conrad saying that he was sick of it and it was getting too tight for him. This was not true as Bob's weight stayed the same from the time I met him until the time he got sick. He then said Conrad should try it on and if it fit he was welcome to it.

That was very tactful of him. He knew there was no need to embarrass Conrad by mentioning he had noticed him shivering. Conrad was slim like Bob and just an inch or so taller. Bob knew it would fit him. Conrad's face lit up like a child who had been given a pleasant surprise and he said: "Are you sure?" "Of course," Bob said. It was a heavyweight, bottle green, wide-wale corduroy sports coat. Bob usually wore this with casual slacks on Sundays when we visited with his parents or mine. It was not really out-of-style. Bob could have worn it for many more years. But, when he had noticed Conrad's shivering and his inadequate jacket, he instinctively realized Conrad couldn't afford to buy something warmer, and he generously and tactfully gave from his heart to someone in need.

Beginning at the time of Jerry's birth and continuing after the births of sons #2 and #3, we began attending Sunday Mass separately. In those days, no one brought an infant to church to distract the other worshippers. It would have been nice if we had had Saturday evening Masses back then. One of us could have gone on Saturday night and the other early on Sunday morning.

Instead, our routine was that Bob would get up early enough to make the first one at *Nôtre Dame* Church at 6:00 a.m. When he returned, I would have enough time to drive to church just a short distance up the top of Eastern Avenue to attend the one at 7:00 a.m. When I returned a little before 8:00 a.m., he would have my Sunday breakfast ready for me. He pampered me with those Sunday morning breakfasts. Besides preparing that thoughtful breakfast for me he would have the boys all washed, dressed and fed. He did this all in the space of the one hour I had been gone. After the kitchen was cleaned up and I had changed my clothes and packed up the diaper bag and what we needed to take with us, we left by 11:00 to go to either of the grandparents' houses. We alternated going one week to *Mémère* and *Pépère* Dube's and the next to *Mémère* and *Pépère* Sevigny's to spend the day, usually returning home to our little apartment by 7:00 p.m.

I had never asked that he cook my Sunday breakfast and have it waiting for me when I returned from church. I had never asked him to help me out by getting the boys washed and dressed and fed while I went to church. He was just a kind, loving and thoughtful man. His kindness was part of the fabric of his character. He definitely wasn't a chauvinist.

He never forgot my birthday, our anniversary or Mother's Day. I imagine he saved some money from the odd jobs he did to pay for my gifts. He never once asked me for extra dollars. He always turned in his paychecks from Electric Boat and Firestone as I was the one who handled the family budget and finances. It must have been when he did some of those odd jobs like shoveling snow, washing and simonizing someone's car, washing windows on the outside for aunts or cousins, or helping someone to paint their house that he squirreled always a few dollars for my birthday and our anniversary.

Those are just some of the odd jobs he picked up. He was versatile, a kind of jack-of-all trades type. Because he was so dependable and did everything so well, he never had trouble lining up a few jobs for the next weekend or weeknight. He didn't do this to keep some of his hard-earned money to splurge on something he wanted. He did it so he'd have money on hand when my birthday, Mother's Day or our anniversary came up and of course to supplement our income. There wasn't a selfish bone in his body.

I have to relate at least this one more story about Bob's clowning around. This wasn't part of his character; he was a character, truly the life of the party and a good sport. This incident happened one Halloween when I was about seventeen. My family was then living on Ocean Grove Avenue in Swansea.

After hearing someone knock on the front door, my Mom went to answer the door. When she opened the door there was this nicely dressed lady in her thirties wearing the brightest red lipstick my Mom had ever seen. The lady had on a matching outfit. I remember the winter coat she was wearing was a deep grass green. She also had a beautiful hat and bag and stylish shoes. The lady asked my Mom something in French (I forget what it was) but as soon as my Mom heard the voice she burst out laughing. She recognized that voice. It was Bob dressed up as a "lady" for Halloween wearing his mother's clothes. We took a photo of him in that get-up. I hope I find it when I look through my photo albums.

If all my sons are "clowns" from time to time, I hope that they remember that they got that from their Dad and not their mother. Besides that character trait, they also are all like him in acts of kindness and in being dependable. When I see Jerry helping Sheree with the boys my mind goes back to Eastern Avenue and I recall those Sunday mornings when Bob gave me a hand with my little munchkins. All three of my boys are thoughtful, always ready to help someone out and versatile, too. They will all take on extra side jobs for extra money. When they do, they are conscientious and do a good job. They are truly their father's sons. If he can see them all now from his heavenly home he certainly is beaming with pride.

CHAPTER 21

Now I'll return to the wake period. There was never a single lull or break in that continuous line to view the young man who had died so young. The Lafleur family (Blanche's side) was large. The Sevigny family was smaller but there were numerous members nonetheless. My mother's side of the family was large. My Dad's family was all in Canada. Friends and acquaintances of all of us, including myself, my in-laws and Ronnie were numerous. All those who paid their respects signed the book. Those pages were filled almost to the very last line on the very last page.

I remember when Andy DeVillers paid his respects. He told me that he had seen Bob the Saturday he had come home for that overnight stay. He told me Bob knew he was going to die, but he told Andy he wasn't worried. He knew that his parents and my parents would take good care of me and his sons. Can you imagine? He was thinking about me and the boys even when he knew he had only a short time left to live. Always thoughtful and totally unselfish, that was my Bob.

By Monday night Mr. Boulé had to ask the visitors not to kneel before the coffin but just to take a brief view, say a short prayer and to move through the bereaving family line as quickly as possible. He could see the people lined up outside in a long queue waiting to get into the funeral home to pay their respects. After visiting hours on that Monday, he asked me if Bob had been a politician. He commented that he never saw so many people lined up for just an ordinary man. He had to be in politics or famous for something. What was it? I said, no, he wasn't, but he was known to many and loved by all who knew him.

His teen-year buddies, Smithy, Chuckle Bunny, whose real name was Andrew, Richie, Kenny, Tommy, Red, Austin Belanger and too many others to name from "our gang" all came. On Tuesday evening, the last night of the wake, Richie (Legault) came over to me and handed me an envelope. They had taken up a collection, all those buddies of Bob, and gave me $300 to help me out a little with the finances, guessing that I didn't have much to fall back on right then. God bless each and every one of them.

The funeral was held on Wednesday, August 19th. Before departing for the church service, after all the cars had been aligned for the funeral procession, I, along with his parents and brother, were the last ones left sitting at the side of the coffin. We all delayed getting up from our chairs and viewing Bob for the last time. Finally, I got up and knelt on the *prie-dieu* before the casket and said a short prayer. I then went to the head of the casket, bent down and kissed Bob on the cheek, all the while sobbing uncontrollably. Mr. Boulé came to my aid, took me by the arm and led me out to the family limo waiting at the front of the funeral home. A few minutes later, his parents and Ronnie joined me in the limo. No one spoke, as we were all sobbing.

The pall bearers were his friends and cousins. They were: Pitou Indyck, Bobby Gagnon (both his cousins), Richie Legault, Austin Belanger, Roger Banville and I can't remember the last one. It could have been Stanley Lafleur, another cousin, who was Uncle Romeo's son. The church was filled to capacity with all those who participated directly in the funeral home procession and so many others from our parish, and other parishes, who had a connection to Bob, even if they only really knew him by association. I will be bold enough to say that he had a funeral comparable to that of a well-known politician or celebrity. That bold statement is not really far from the truth or an exaggeration. Bob, in his own way you could say, was a politician and a celebrity.

Next was the short trip to *Nôtre Dame* Cemetery. It was a gravesite service, not a cemetery chapel service like we have today. After the gravesite prayers and short service came the lowering of the casket into the grave. This is where I had to leave, and so did his parents and Ronnie. *We could not bear to watch Bob being lowered into that deep, dark hole.* That was just too much.

I almost forgot to mention the flower arrangements and the Mass and sympathy cards. There were so many flowers they spilled over into areas where usually there would be no flowers. The Mass cards, both enrollments and cash offerings, were overwhelming. There was enough money to have a Mass said every week for one full year.

Today, some forty-plus years later, I have reached the conclusion that he didn't need prayers said for the repose of his soul. Bob was admitted to heaven after only the very shortest stay in purgatory. He was such a good, unselfish, kind and gentle man, a true "gentleman," always doing for others and striving to never offend anyone. At 26, his transgressions or little sins were not many, and nowhere near as many as my own long list of sins and failures. His time in purgatory in expiation of those minor transgressions had to be a *Reader's Digest*-type, meaning it was surely a short, condensed stay. He was welcomed through the gates of heaven very soon after his untimely death. I'm certain of it. I am not certain of many things, but that I am certain of.

CHAPTER 22

On Wednesday evening, after all the family and friends that had joined us at my in-laws for the post-funeral gathering left, I had to return to my little house. My Mom offered to stay with me for a week or however long it would take for me to feel I could stay alone with my three sons, two toddlers and an infant. I thanked her but said I would be okay alone with the boys. If I needed anything my in-laws lived close by, as did Bernie and Roger.

I had been alone with the boys since that first hospital admission on July 14th. I had slept alone every night except for that Saturday night Bob was home from the hospital, when he had cut the deal with Dr. Cox that allowed that home visit for the weekend before they started the chemo trial. This first night alone after the funeral was different. I felt truly alone. So many thoughts, fears and apprehensions bombarded me. I had difficulty falling asleep, but I knew that I had to sleep, as there were those three babies to think about. The two oldest would be up early wanting their breakfast and to go outside to play in their still-fairly-new backyard. The baby, Roger, needed even more motherly care as he was not yet eight months old.

Somehow, I did manage to get some sleep that night and on the following nights. The days passed. Little by little, it became easier to fall asleep and to cope with the daily demands of being a young widow with three little sons all under the age of four. There were so many things to take care of besides being a mom.

After obtaining copies of the death certificate, I had to submit the life insurance claims and apply for Social Security survivors' benefits. When I received the life insurance proceeds, I paid for the funeral and paid off the loan that Bernie and Roger had given us. I had to contact EB, Bob's employer, to find out what benefits I had coming from them and to make arrangements for Red Scanlon to deliver the tools that Bob had left on the job. I had to see the bank official where we had just recently obtained our mortgage.

We had made just three mortgage payments when Bob died. We had not taken the life insurance option *knowing* that we were both young and the house would

116

be paid for long before either of us died. Of course, it was an economic decision, too. The household budget could cover just so much and not one unnecessary dollar more. Mortgage insurance fell into the "unnecessary" slot. The names on the mortgage had to be changed. I would be the only one responsible for paying off that mortgage.

It was during that bank visit that the bank official advised me to put the house up for sale. He said I would not be able to afford the mortgage with my very limited income. Before losing what little equity I had in it, I should sell. I replied that I would not sell the house that Bob bought for me and the kids and that I would never be late with one mortgage payment. I never was late. Later, I sold that house at a profit. In retrospect, the lesson learned here was once again: Where there is a will there is a way.

Between the Social Security survivors' benefits and what was left from the insurance proceeds, I could manage to meet the necessary expenses. I did not have to return to work. I did stay home to raise Bob's sons, as he always wanted me to.

I looked after Mrs. Gagnon's three children, Susie, Brenda and big Jerry. They were all in school, but would come to my house for their lunch and then after school until their parents returned home from work. This gave me some extra income. All my friends who worked and who could afford it would drop off a basket full of ironing. At night, after the kids were put to bed, I would set up the ironing board in the living room in front of the television and I'd iron away, earning $5 a basket. Some friends were savvy and they neatly folded the items that went into the ironing basket. They got more in those baskets than those that just threw them in. Those baskets were not as full and did not take me as long to iron, but they compensated for one another, so the $5-a-basket-deal worked for me. I think, today, that is why I hate to iron. The lesson learned here: You do what you have to do to survive.

The extra income from the Gagnon children care and the baskets of ironing made up the difference I needed to run my household budget with some left over to do a few house improvements and repairs. The major ones were having the heating system installed for the upstairs bedrooms. Before it was installed, heat from the first floor had to travel up the stairway and through the little grate opening in the ceiling just above the kitchen doorway. The second floor bathroom project was started. This involved converting one of the bedrooms into a second-floor full bathroom. Plans to remove the tub in the first-floor bathroom were made. I would have my washer and dryer installed in that tub area, so I would not have to go down to the basement to do the laundry.

There were numerous other little repairs accomplished, always with no labor costs. Either my Dad, the union carpenter, or Bob's Dad and Uncle Walter, both seasoned handymen, would supply the free labor. In the case of the upstairs bathroom, the plumbing work was done by a buddy of my father-in-law, one who truly felt sorry for me having lost my husband at such a young age. He charged me so very little for his expertise that it was in the next-to-nothing labor-cost category.

Every Friday night, my in-laws, along with Uncle Walter and Auntie Nellie would come over with the beer and snacks. They would keep me company and eased my loneliness. They all were so kind and thoughtful and generous.

It took me more than six months before I could gather all of Bob's clothing from the closet and bureau drawers to donate to the St. Vincent de Paul Society. Somehow, I felt that if I gathered all his things, it would really be final and not a dream that I would awaken from. I wanted it all to be a bad dream. I did keep some of his jewelry to pass on to the boys when they were older. I had stalled gathering all his things to be donated because I knew that task would also cause me to relive the memory of having to select the clothes he was buried in six months earlier.

Anyone who has lost a loved one and who has that heartbreaking job of gathering a loved one's belongings to be donated to charity will fully understand how painful that dreaded task truly was for me.

CHAPTER 23

I received help from so many after Bob's passing. I'm not talking about monetary help. Rather, it was all kinds of the "helping-hand" type and always so generously given.

My father-in-law or Roger Banville mowed the lawn and trimmed the hedges. My cousin Claire would walk over with her three kids, all older than mine, and they all helped to rake and bag the thousands of autumn leaves from the four big trees in the yard. One tree was in the back yard. The three others were along the left side of the house where my property line ended.

I have a picture of Bob sitting on an old wooden chair from the cellar and leaning against that one tree in the backyard. This was taken the weekend he came home those two days from Pondville to see me and his "suns." He doesn't look sick one bit. That's why it was so hard to believe he was going to die. He simply DID NOT look sick in the least.

My Dad, of course, was always available to repair something or other. He would have to repair the diagonal slats that enclosed the bottom section of the rear porch at least once a month. There was a little access door in the rear of that porch area. The boys used to go in there and play games like, "it's our fort." From time to time they got carried away and one or two slats would be split, broken or just plain come loose.

Anne Gagnon's mom, who now lived down the street from me, came over to baby-sit if I had errands to run or a doctor's appointment for myself. Friends called often and stopped by for short visits whenever they could. So many friends and family members helped me in so many ways; it would take too long to put everything all down here. I could easily fill another twenty pages of their good deeds. Everyone was so very kind to the little widow and the three little munchkins. God bless them all.

The first few years of my life after Bob's death were my first true survivor years. As a young 23-year-old widow with three boys, ages 3 1/2, two and almost

8 months, and with a very limited income, life was not easy, but I did survive. This was made possible by the many graces the Lord sent to me and through the actions and kindnesses of others who were in my life then and those that later entered my life. I know this now, but I don't believe I fully realized it back then when everything transpired.

I recall Monsignor Hamel taking his daily walks in the Maplewood section of St. Jean's Parish. At least once a month, my little cottage on Kennedy Street was his coffee-break stop. He would take a coffee-break stop at one of his parishioner's homes on each of his daily walks making a parish visit at the same time. I was special, receiving at least one a month, while the others in his flock would receive one only once a year. These were the parish visits that were part of the Catholic ministry back then, referred to as *les visites de paroise*. Today, if you desire your pastor or a priest to come to your home for a parish visit, you literally have to call and make an appointment and get fitted into their schedule.

With the cash donations from the sympathy cards to be used for Masses for Bob, there was at least one said for him every week. Extra Masses were said on significant days like our anniversary or his birthday (or as close to that day as we could schedule it). He was born on December 21, 1937. He was four months shy of his 27th birthday at the time of his passing.

Monsignor would remind me of the schedule for the next four to be offered for Bob and would always ask if I needed anything. The St. Vincent de Paul Society chapter that was very active in our parish would help parishioners in need with clothing, food baskets and even money, perhaps a twenty-dollar bill to help meet a mortgage payment. My mortgage payment was $100 per month, including the escrow account for the house taxes and fire insurance. That was a considerable amount of money for a mortgage back then.

I always said I was okay. I didn't need any help. I had my pride. I was raised that you make do with what you have. Still, many times he would secretly leave a white envelope containing a twenty-dollar bill under the doily on the middle of the kitchen table or under whatever was the centerpiece *du jour*, maybe a fruit bowl or an arrangement of artificial flowers. He instinctively knew I had my pride and, as desperately as I might have needed an extra $20, I would never have asked for it.

I recall one specific visit from him. The two older boys were playing in the back yard with their Tonka® trucks. The backyard was totally enclosed by fencing on the back side and hedges on the other two sides and front. The only access to the sidewalk, or I should say escape route out of the yard, would have been up to the front of the house along the driveway route. They obeyed and stayed in the back where I could keep an eye on them by peering through the one little window facing the back yard. It was just at the place where the stairway turned to lead to the second floor, about three steps into the stairway, if I recall correctly. I should say that Jerry always obeyed, but Larry was the little disobedient one. He often tried to make a break for it from time to time, for which he was, of course, caught and punished.

This is when the "kneel down in the corner" phase of their punishments for disobedience began. Larry was told to go kneel in the corner in the dining room, in the right-hand corner, to the side of the bathroom door and near the cellar door. There, depending on the transgression, he would have to kneel at least five minutes for his punishment. He would always promise to never disobey again as his poor little knees smarted from kneeling on a hard floor with his nose in the corner. Being the instigator of the three, Larry spent many-a-time on his knees for his "penance" and for disobeying. It didn't matter that Monsignor was visiting. Larry's "punishment" (disciplining) would not be postponed.

About that one particular visit from Monsignor I mentioned earlier, I recall changing Roger's diaper on the changing table located in the "all-purpose area" on the inside wall between the door to the kitchen and the door to the bathroom, while Monsignor was seated at the kitchen table with his tea and cookies, or coffee and cake, or whatever it was I had to serve him for his coffee-break snack that day.

The all-purpose area was a baby-changing area, with the bathinette top serving as the changing table, and also the dining room, which did not have a beautiful dining room set but a simple dinette set with chrome legs and padded chairs. Along the wall facing you as you entered this room from the rear egress door was a built-in china cabinet with three large drawers at the bottom. This was an all-purpose china cabinet. The drawers were used for table linens and also served as part of my linen closet for storing the bathroom and kitchen towels. The linens, sheets and pillow cases were stored upstairs in a bureau drawer or in the cedar chest, as there was no linen closet upstairs either. In that all-purpose room, the only other piece was the rocking horse that the older boys took turns on when play was indoors because of rainy weather.

Anyway, while changing Roger, and as I moved around checking on the other two outside, or just sitting for a few minutes to chat with him, Monsignor spoke to me about God and my faith, of accepting the will of God and about praying more fervently for the strength and courage I would continue to need in the coming years to raise my three fatherless sons as a young widow. I recall vividly saying to him I had no time for "fervent" prayer. I had too much to do and take care of. God would be lucky if I said even the barest minimum of daily prayers. I also told him I was angry with God. In other words, I did not want to accept His will. Why had God taken Bob at such a young age? He was a good husband, father and son, a good provider, a thoughtful, true friend to so many and a generous soul who literally would give the shirt off his back to anyone in need. Why had God not taken one of the "bums" that existed who contributed nothing whatsoever and who certainly were not the "good man" that Bob was?

Monsignor did not get angry with me for refusal to accept the will of God and for stating that I was angry with God. He gently spoke to me about graces and the extra graces available to me through a fervent prayer life. God would, without a doubt, give me the courage and the stamina I needed. He would sustain me in my grief and in my needs as a single parent. But, I had to ask God for help. "Ask and you shall receive. Seek and you shall find." God knew what I needed and He would meet those needs, but I had to ask. He also told me that when we ask for something in our prayers that God does not grant us, we say, "God didn't answer our prayers," but, we are wrong. God always answers prayers. He just doesn't always answer in the way we want. If we don't get what we asked for in our prayer petitions, it's because He knows what is best for us.

Monsignor Hamel never gave up on me. I was bold, defiant and angry at God, period. Over the course of time, during his monthly visits to me, he would subtly guide my hurting soul and broken heart to become closer to God through prayer. He would relate stories of others (never using names) that had experienced their life catastrophe and how they eventually learned to accept the will of God and to pray more fervently for their needs.

Now I know that he was telling me that I was not the only one who had suffered a great loss. He gently and in a beating-around-the bush style eventually succeeded in his mission to make me realize the riches that could be gleaned from fervent prayer and acceptance of God's will. He never preached to me about having to accept God's will, never admonished me for doubting God's love for me when I said I didn't know why God had done this to me. Another priest probably would have scolded me and told me to confess my sin of doubting God and given me a hefty penance to expiate my transgression, but he never did that. He knew I really didn't mean to question God. It was not a deliberate, conscious decision. Rather he knew, even if I didn't realize it until much later on in my life, that this feeling toward God was part of my mourning and grieving phase. Oh, how wise he was. No wonder he was made a Monsignor.

His visits continued on for several years. Looking back on them now, I realize these were my therapy sessions. He was my free therapist who let me talk, scream, revolt, question and get it all out. His goal was my finally accepting God's will and practicing the habit of fervent prayer. That would be his "pay" for those therapy sessions. I hope he has a special place in heaven now. He certainly deserves one in my eyes. He was the one who first gave me the Serenity Prayer card. *"God grant me the serenity to accept the things I cannot change, the courage to change the things I can and the wisdom to know the difference."* I still have that card to this day.

I wore black and white every day for one full year, as did Bob's mother. We truly mourned our respective losses the old-fashioned way. I was easily recognized as the little widow wearing that black. I attended all the Masses said for Bob that first year, walking to church one block away in the cold winter months that followed, wearing that expensive coat purchased for me by Bob's mother from McWhirr's. I still have that simple black cashmere coat. It was in the very basic classic style and never went out-of-style.

One day in early fall while I was outside in the front area with the kids, a young woman walked by holding her young son's hand. She stopped and introduced herself. She was a neighbor who lived in the corner house at the end of the street where it crossed Rodman Street, about seven houses down from me. Her name was Lorraine Francoeur and her tiny son's name was Roger. My name was Lorraine and my youngest son was also named Roger. Her brother was married to Cousin Lucille Lapointe, *Tante* Roseanne's daughter. She told me not to hesitate to ask if ever I needed something that she could help me with. We became friends from that day on. She had seven children in all. Their names were in birth order: Michael, David, Denise, Diane, Jeanine, Paul and Roger, the baby. Her husband was a self-employed painter. She, too, was a stay-at-home mom. She did not drive. So, we began chumming together, going to the supermarket, to the park, to the doctors and visiting with each other in our respective homes for afternoon coffee and chats.

Her older daughters, Denise and Diane, were my babysitters when I eventually could leave the boys with someone other than my mother-in-law. Lorraine encouraged me. She was with me the day I had to change my first flat tire, which was discovered when we were about to all hop into my car to go somewhere. My father had taught me how to change a tire after Bob died. He said I may need to do it sometime and I should be prepared, just like when I was a small girl and he had taught me how to box so I could defend myself.

Thank you, Dad, for everything you taught me. I made use of those lessons all through my life. Truly, you were my only "college professor" who taught me the necessary life's lessons. I should have awarded you one of those Honorary College diplomas. You earned that diploma. You only had three years of formal education in Canada yet in my eyes you were more of a success than most college graduates of today.

Lorraine and I were partners for the Ladies Guild projects and events, we were mom's who exchanged tips on raising the kids, and we could unburden ourselves to each other during our afternoon coffee "Klatch" breaks. I realize now that God put Lorraine in my life at the right time, the time when I especially needed companionship. It was through her that I changed family doctors. Doctor Witmer was getting advanced in age. Her doctor was closer and we could schedule the necessary office visits together. She could help watch my kids in the waiting room, and I could watch hers, and she had transportation to those visits, since she didn't drive. She was and still is such a good soul. She was even-tempered and jolly, with never a complaining word uttered from her mouth. With seven children and her calm, soothing character, she was truly a model for any mother to follow. I wish I were even just half as even-tempered as she was. God bless you, Lorraine.

I should relate the how and when of purchasing my own first used car as a young widow. Remember that white Chevrolet Bel Air that was sitting in the driveway since the day Bob entered St. Anne's hospital? The last time it started was that day when I checked him into the hospital on July 14, 1964. I remember at the time I asked, "What else can go wrong?" Bob getting ill and having to be hospitalized, then the car on the blink at a time when I needed it most for daily visits to the hospital, were all happening at the same time. Well, it needed a major valve or piston job, not worth spending the money on. I had to find another used car.

My Dad had a mechanic friend, Mr. Freddy Beaulieu, who, incidentally, was a second or third cousin to Bob's mother. He had a cousin in Westport who bought cars at auctions that had been declared totaled by the insurance companies. Being the good mechanic and body work man that he was, he knew he could purchase some of those cars real cheap, fix them up like new and sell them at a profit. So, the word went out to him through my Dad and Mr. Beaulieu that I needed a good, dependable used car. That's how I bought my first Chevy Nova. It was fawn beige and had four doors, but I don't recall what year it was. It certainly was in the used car category.

The car had been totaled by the insurance company because a large tree limb had fallen onto the roof and compressed it down to the seats. It had broken the side roof struts. Mr. Beaulieu's cousin knew that the motor was undamaged. The damage was cosmetic. He knew he could find another top roof section that was undamaged from the car scrap yard he frequented for parts. So, having been told about the little widow's need for a good reliable used car, he bid on it at auction, loaded it onto his truck and brought it to his shop in Westport.

I went to see it with my Dad while it still had that crushed roof. I asked, "Are you sure you can fix this up?" It was certainly a "total loss" in my eyes. He assured me he could make it look as good as new. We discussed the price and with a nod from my father that it was a fair price, I agreed to purchase it and would pick it up when he had it ready. That took a few weeks. He had to find that replacement roof and do the work. I needed the time to go see Mr. Moreau at the credit union to obtain a used car loan, the first loan I made alone without a co-signer.

Remember I was not working and my income was 90% from the social security benefits. Would they give me a loan? I had a little left in the savings account from the life insurance proceeds, but those funds were for "rainy days" or emergencies, or for the materials for the repairs in my little house. Although those repairs were labor free, the materials had to be paid for. It must have been at this time in my life that I began to use the "ace-in-the-hole" phrase. That meager savings account was my ace in the hole and had to be protected and not used frivolously.

Well Mr. Moreau at the credit union did submit my loan application and it was granted. It was a loan for $1,000. Somehow, I managed to squeeze that loan payment into my already tight budget. This is where I practiced "putting more water in the soup" more frequently.

Life went on, as it does for everyone else who experiences a loss such as I did at a young age. Gradually, things got easier. I gained more confidence in myself and the lonely nights after the boys were in bed were more tolerable. I continued to visit my parents on Sundays and my in-laws, who lived so very near to me, helped me with free babysitting, with handyman work and yard chores. They supplied the free beer and snacks on Friday nights when they would visit with Auntie Nellie and Uncle Walter.

My mother-in-law took her twice-monthly bus shopping trip to McWhirrs. She bought and paid for 80% of the clothing needs of my growing sons, her three grandsons. She bought me new underwear and bras and hosiery (not pantyhose, those were non-existent at the time) and at least one new girdle every year. (Yup, back then ladies always wore girdles.) She bought me a new Easter hat (hats were worn to church back then). She bought me new curtains for the living room and the dining/all-purpose room. Without her generous help, it would have been more difficult to make ends meet. She'd buy a new tube of lipstick for herself, then give it to me saying she really didn't like that "shade" after all and maybe I would like it. If I offered to pay her for the clothes or the lipstick, she said no. She was generous beyond explanation. She continued to be ever-so-generous to her grandsons and, yes, to me, until she died. She was the mother-in-law all girls dream of having.

Now, back to the time when the white Chevy sat in the driveway on the blink since the day Bob was first hospitalized. At the time I said, "What's next? What else can go wrong?" Well, now I know why that car went on the blink just at that time. It was God's doing. Knowing what His plan was and what would transpire in the course of the next month, He "blinked" our car out of commission. Even though Dr. DeVillers had spoken those horrible words to me, "life expectancy was four to six weeks," I never really believed or absorbed that as a carved-in-stone truth. I always believed that all of the Prayers of Petition being said for Bob's health would be answered and, somehow, a little miracle would happen and he would not die.

God knew that would not happen. He had His Plan and there would be no deviation from that master plan for my benefit. To this day I really don't know why that horrific thing had to happen to our little family but I long ago accepted the will of God and no longer question that part of His plan. I do, though, still have many unanswered questions. Surely they will all be answered when I die.

I now know that the car being on the blink was God's way of protecting me. Had that car been operational, I probably would have driven myself to Pondville and to run my own errands. I was taking tranquilizers and was told not to drive. Knowing myself as I do, and especially being too proud to ask for a ride, I would have driven that car, putting aside the admonition of not driving. God made sure I wouldn't do that by disabling my car. The matter was settled. I had to put my pride aside and accept those daily rides.

He knew that I would soon be a young widow with three young sons and that those sons needed me intact. There would be no unfortunate car accident that would jeopardize the mother of three fatherless boys. That was part of His plan. He protected me and the boys. He also knew that I probably would not take those tranquilizers so that I would be able to drive. He knew also that I needed that medication to help me hold it all together for the next month. How wise and all-knowing our God is. I did not know all this back then when it happened, but after much reflection over the years, I am sure of it today. Also, time and experience, contemplation and prayers have given me that answer. Remember the "four-to-six weeks" diagnosis? Well, from July 15, 1964, the day Dr. DeVillers announced that to me, until August 15, 1964, the day Bob died, was four weeks to the day. God knew all that, too, so, as I said before, he "blinked" my car, or put it on the "fritz," as I used to say.

My relationship and closeness to the Sevigny family never really changed after Bob's death. They continued to help me in any way they could. *Pépère* and *Mémère* (as I called them now) were always so generous with their time, money and encouragement. I was always their daughter-in-law and was introduced as a daughter-in-law up until she passed away. I remained close to Bob's only sibling, his brother Ronnie, who is four years younger than me. My boys grew up knowing their paternal grandparents and Uncle Ronnie, his wife Cindy and their three sons, Ron Jr., Scottie and Bobby, as well as the whole clan, especially Uncle Pete (Cousin Pitou Indyck) and his wife, Auntie Carol. We still try get together at least twice a year and sometimes more often because of special celebrations.

I almost forgot about my birthday gift of a new Timex watch. I celebrated my 23rd birthday just three weeks before Bob died. Bob gave me a Timex watch. He had asked my sister Dee to purchase it for him as he was hospitalized. How he paid her, I don't know. I can only guess he asked his father for the money, as he certainly couldn't ask me for it. See how he was so thoughtful and how good he was to me. Even as sick as he was, hospitalized, I was not forgotten on my special day, my birthday. That is but one of the countless, precious memories I have of dear Bob.

In the months that followed his death, I would often look at the snapshot of him sitting on that old wooden chair that was tilted and leaning against the large tree in the middle of the back yard. It was painted celery green and was from the cellar, a leftover from the Manchesters. That photo was taken on that Saturday he came home for the weekend before the chemo protocol was started. I could not believe he was truly gone. He looked so healthy in that photo. Truly, everyone who visited him at the hospital all said, "But he doesn't look sick." He didn't and, as I said before, he looked like he was just sleeping when they laid him out in his casket. Many funeral home visitors made that same comment, "He looks like he's just sleeping."

From the time of Bob's hospitalization through his death and the first few years that followed, I began to hone my survival skills—skills like putting more water in the soup and of always having an ace in the hole. I gradually accepted the reality that life was not always the happy idyllic life of my childhood. There were "pits" and more than a few of them too. The phrase, "Life is just a bowl of cherries, pits and all" finally had meaning to me. I had experienced the first real big "pit" on the day Bob died.

I improved on more skills, like cooking "*les jiblottes,*" a concoction made from leftovers, which I would mix together and create a casserole (I wasted nothing), of making do with whatever I had, of serious budget-following and controlling unnecessary spending. "Where there is a will, there is a way." Literally, I began to grow up with my sons after Bob died. As a single parent, a homeowner and as a woman on her own, I began to strengthen my "juggling act" skills.

All of these skills would be needed in the course of my lifetime; being widowed at age 23 was just the beginning. I did not know it then, but I do now. I think I said it before, but it's a good thing we don't know what lies ahead of us. Better to deal with it when it happens and enjoy the good days that you can in between all the roller coaster rides of life. The first adult roller coaster ride in my life was the unexpected death of my young husband. The roller coaster rides that followed were all adult roller coaster rides. The mother-of-all roller coaster ride came much later in my life.

Besides the generosity of my in-laws and their help, my parents helped tremendously also. Dad was my built-in carpenter, keeping things around the house in good repair. From time to time, Mom would buy one of the many pairs of shoes for the growing boys. It seemed not a month passed before one of them needed bigger shoes. They never wore cheap shoes or hand-me-down shoes. They all needed "cookie" inserts in the shoes to support their arches because all three were flat—footed like their father. They wore Thomas Heel shoes. Mom would knit winter mittens and scarves to keep them warm. No store-bought items like these were good enough for her three grandsons. *Memére* Sevigny knitted sweaters. I especially remember the light blue one with the yellow ducks at the waistline that Jerry wore when he was about three and that the others later wore as a hand-me-down. There were many hand-knitted sweaters from *Mémère* Sevigny in those first growing-spurt years after Bob died.

Mom would often buy extra groceries, mostly cereal and canned goods, and give them to me to help feed my growing boys. They never gave me money, but would have if I needed some and asked for it. I never asked, because I had to manage on my own, had to make do, had to pull myself up from the bootstraps and survive on my own, really. Their generosities to me and the boys in countless other ways were appreciated and very much sufficed. My kid sister, Lou, who gave birth to her first son shortly after Bob died, helped me, too, that first year. She took over the monthly encyclopedia payments for the year. I had purchased these precious books on the installment plan just before we moved to Kennedy Street. These encyclopedias were the cornerstone for my master plan for the boys' future.

One of the reasons I got married so young was that the dream of a college education was crushed, and I thought then that dream was "impossible." I now know after many years of life's experiences that "impossible" should not have been in my dictionary back then. "Where there is a will, there is a way" should have been my mantra way back then.

I often related that conviction to my kids as they were growing up. There is no such word as *impossible* in my dictionary. "Where there is a will there is a way." Never say "never," or "I can't." Say, "I'll try," and keep trying, no matter how many times you fail, until you do succeed. Remember these words because later on in this tale, you will hear how those words to them came back to haunt me.

So the encyclopedia set was for the boys to help them get to college. Because of that squelched desire for my own college education, I vowed that if I ever had kids and they wanted to go to college and were willing to work at it, I'd work day and night to help them get their college educations. I still have that now obsolete encyclopedia set stored in boxes up in the attic. It is, in fact, obsolete because so much *new history* has transpired since the early 1960s when it was published. Besides that, no one needs an encyclopedia set in today's world, thanks to computers and the Internet. All information for learning and research is readily available with the click of a mouse. God bless you Lou (little Lulu) for making those installment payments for one full year and for helping me out when I needed it.

My older sister Dee Dee helped out, too. She loved to iron, so I'd save my family's ironing for her. I was, as you may recall, ironing basketfuls of neighbors' items for $5 for extra money. Dee Dee came over to do my ironing. All I had to do was set up the board where she could watch television, fix her some tea and toast and all my personal ironing got done. I clearly recall blowing fuses over and over again. When I made her tea and toast, the iron was on, as well as the television set, and this all triggered an overload and yet another fuse was blown.

She also sewed on the knee patches of the kids' play clothes. They were typical, rough and tumbling boys. They supplied my sister with many tears and holes that had to be repaired. I did not have a sewing machine at that time. No item of boys' clothing was ever thrown out or discarded until it was absolutely necessary, or until it had outworn its usefulness. "Waste not, want not." "Make do with what you have."

Then there was Mrs. Gagnon, Anne's mother, who did free babysitting when she was needed and who made French toast for the boys' lunch. Bernie and Roger paid for my milkman bill for a whole year and Roger, being a barber, gave the boys all their haircuts for free. There were many others who helped me in small ways during those first few years after Bob's death. Thank you all and God bless!

Dealing with Jerry when he asked when Daddy was coming home was hard. Finally, I got up the courage to tell him about his father's death, improvising a bit to make it more understandable to a toddler who had not yet reached four years of age. He was three-and-a-half when Bob died. The other two were not as affected as him, being as they were too young.

One day, when the other two were napping, I sat with him in the big overstuffed chair by the front bay windows in the living room. I began to tell him the story of his father's absence. I asked if he remembered when I had to go every day to the hospital to see Daddy. I had told him at the time that Daddy had a *boo-boo* that had to be fixed. I told him about God and how we were all children of God. Then I told him that God had come for Daddy because he needed him up in heaven. Daddy knew how to use many tools and was good at fixing things. God had need for his talents in heaven to "fix some things that were in tough shape."

Daddy couldn't refuse because we all had to obey God. That's what grownups meant when Jerry heard them say in the "Our Father" prayer, "Thy will be done." God's wishes came first, not ours. Even though Daddy did not want to leave me and his three sons, he knew he had to say "yes" to God's request. So Daddy was up in heaven with Jesus doing all that repair work he was called there to do. Then I asked him if he remembered the last time he saw Daddy, when Bob had taken the boys down to the cage area in the cellar. I reminded him that Daddy had said to always take care of Daddy's tools. Daddy knew he had to go to heaven and that God had all the tools he would need to do his jobs there. He was leaving his three boys his tools, reminding them to always take care of them.

I told him that one day we would all be together again in heaven. I also told him that his Daddy was watching and protecting him from his heavenly home. If he ever needed help, all he had to do was ask his Daddy and help would come without a doubt. He accepted my story and, after that, he was not as fearful when I had a sitter for them and left the house for my own doctor visits or to go shopping.

My social life consisted of the Women's Guild and going out for pizza once a month with some friends from my high school days: Ruthie Quinn, Claire Roy, Florence and others. My life revolved around my three little boys, visits to their grandparents on both sides and keeping in touch with old friends through occasional phone calls, while writing to those that were out of town. To this day, I still keep in touch with Jackie Thibault (Davis) who is out in Missouri. I have known her since the first grade. She ran away from home at age 15 with the first boy she met and went to Missouri, lied about her age, and got married. She had a tough life growing up. Running away from home was the best solution for her, believe me.

A daily routine evolved: Get the everyday chores done, laundry, floor washing or some other once-a-week household job. Then there were a few afternoons going to the park with all the kids with Lorraine Francoeur accompanying me. Various other afternoon outings were to the market to take advantage of a special sale, or to the shopping center on Milliken Boulevard at the end of Tucker Street. We would stop for hamburgers and French fries at the McDonald's on the corner before returning home. That McDonald's is still on that same corner to this day. We would go to the Flint section to see Lorraine's parents who lived in *Nôtre Dame* Parish. We would keep each other company. There were no spectacular outings like going to the circus or the movies, just simple ones that we "made do" with, as neither of us had the means to splurge—her with seven children and me as a single parent raising my boys on Social Security survivors' benefits.

CHAPTER 24

Most Sundays, I would pack up the car for the weekly trip to my parents in Ocean Grove. Roger was in the car bed behind the driver's seat. Larry was in the car seat on the other side of the back seat and Jerry, the oldest at 3 1/2, sat in the front passenger seat. There were no rules back them like there are today that all children under the age of eight had to be in a special car seat or harness, or ride in the back seat away from airbags. There were no airbags in those days.

In fact, we didn't even have safety belts. Thank the Lord Jerry was so good. He always behaved and listened and sat quietly while I drove. It's a good thing Larry was in the car seat because he was the mischievous one. Eventually Roger graduated to the car seat and the two oldest had to sit on the front seat with me (child seat laws were different back then). I could never chance leaving Larry sitting on the back seat next to his baby brother in the car seat. Lord knows what that little mischief maker would have done. It was best he be right by my side so he couldn't distract me and where my firm arm could restrain him if he tried something. God surely protected my little family as we never had an accident, not even a close call.

Occasionally, *Mémère* Sevigny and I would take the boys for a visit to Newport on a Sunday when *Pépère* was working. The boys loved those visits to the Fire Station. They were treated like royalty and allowed to sit on the ladder truck. They tried on the boots and firemen's hats. It was a great day for them. They always asked when they could go back.

They say that time heals all wounds. In a way it does. Life does go on. I was all the boys had so in retrospect they helped me keep it together and find the courage to go on. I often wonder if I would have "lost it" had I not had my three young sons so dependent on me. Though the wounds healed from that horrible loss at so young an age, they also left many scars. From time to time, even to this day more than forty years later, something will happen or be said that will make me go back in time and recall it all.

Life went on, though, and it got easier as time passed. I became more confident of myself as a single parent and as I had always handled the money and budget when Bob was alive that part was nothing new to me. I was careful. I managed quite well on the little I had. As I said before, I did receive lots of help, not monetary, but help in many ways from my parents, my in-laws, family and friends.

In the spring of 1966 I was introduced to another young widow, Celine, through Bernie. She lived in Tiverton, Rhode Island and had three girls. Her daughters were ages 10, 8 and 3. Her husband Bernard, an insurance agent, had recently died of a heart attack in her arms on the kitchen floor. He was in his early thirties. We started visiting each other. We could talk about our mutual losses knowing that each of us understood. No one else really could feel what we felt. Only those who actually belonged to the "young widows club" could understand. We were both so very young and yes, lonely.

Sometime in June 1966, we decided we were going to go dancing. We thought about it for a long time before we actually went. We decided that when asked about ourselves, we would say we were single, not widows. We didn't want anyone taking advantage of us. So, one Saturday night, Celine drove and we went to the Alhambra Ballroom at Crescent Park in Riverside, Rhode Island for ballroom dancing. I remember the dress I wore. It was a yellow linen, sleeveless, sheath dress with green appliquéd designs on the front. We were as nervous as two teenagers. We stood at the edge of the dance floor waiting to be asked to dance. We reminded ourselves to stick with our "stories." Not too long passed when a tall gentleman asked me to dance. He was at least six feet tall and good looking. Celine got asked to dance too.

At first, we just danced a slow fox trot. They always played three songs to a set. While we were waiting for the music to begin for the second song of the set, my dance partner asked me where I was from. I said, "Fall River." He then said, "How come a pretty thing like you isn't married or engaged?"

All my intentions of not saying I was a widow went out the window. I told him I was a widow and had lost my husband to cancer two years earlier. He said he was sorry for my loss. After a few minutes of silence he asked if I had any kids. I told him about my three sons. That didn't scare him away as he asked me to dance all night. I never danced with anyone else. Celine danced with several others and, before we knew it, it was the last dance for the evening.

My dance partner's name was Russell. He was divorced and had two daughters, Doreen and Holly. Doreen was a bit older than my Jerry. Holly was two years younger than her sister. Russell asked if he could have my phone number. I said no, as I really didn't know him. Besides, he was divorced, and being a devout Catholic, that sent up a warning signal to me. He took a yellow velvet bow I had in the side of my hair. He asked if I'd be back the following week. I said I didn't know when I'd be back. He said he'd be there every week watching for me and if I wanted my yellow bow back I'd have to come back for another dance.

Celine and I got in her car and she drove me home. We laughed and giggled all the way home sharing the highlights of our experience at the Alhambra. She asked if I wanted to go again the following week. I said no. The next three weeks were horrid. I lost twelve pounds, had trouble sleeping, my emotions all in turmoil and my Catholic conscience nagging at me. He was a divorced man!

Celine kept telling me he probably found another girl by now and wouldn't be waiting for me as he said he would. So, after three weeks, I gave in and we returned to the Alhambra on the fourth week. He was there waiting at the entrance inside with the yellow bow in his hands. He said hi and that he was glad I finally returned. Then he led me to the dance floor. We danced and talked all night. I brought him over to introduce him to Celine. He asked me again for my phone number. This time I gave it to him. He said he would call me.

During our conversation that night I found out he also worked at EB in Groton, Connecticut. He worked in the department where they ordered all the materials for constructing those submarines. He lived with his parents in Riverside and was attending Bryant College in Providence at night.

He did call several nights during the week after returning from his classes. He asked me out for the following weekend, and I said yes. I gave him directions to my house in Fall River. We went out to dinner and then returned to my home where we talked some more. Over the summer, we went on picnics with the boys, to Lincoln Park for them to ride the kiddy rides and to visit my parents. I also introduced him to some of my friends. After three or four months, I felt I had to back off, as things were moving too quickly. I said I just wanted to go out dancing with Celine. It was too soon to get serious. He didn't like that, but he accepted it.

The following week Celine and I again went to the Alhambra. Russell was there and I did dance the first set with him, but then I said thank you and returned to the spot where Celine and I always agreed to meet. Not a minute passed before another gentleman asked me to dance. He was about 5'8" with dark hair and a great smile. He could sing all the lyrics to whatever song was playing and was a super dancer too. He was from New Bedford and had never been married. Again with him I did not tell my "made up story." I told the truth. I was a widow with three young sons.

He did not monopolize me as Russell had done that first night. After the first set with him I returned to join Celine. Russell asked for the next set and I danced with him again. So, that night it was back and forth, from Russell from Riverside to John from New Bedford. John was a gentleman, too. He asked for my phone number, and I gave it to him. He said he'd call during the week.

He did call and asked me out for the following Friday night. I said yes. In the meantime, Russell had called. I wouldn't commit to another date. The third time he called that week I told him I had plans for Friday night. He asked if I was going out with that "Port-o-gee" from the Alhambra. I said, yes, I was. He was miffed.

After that, John would sometimes just come over on a Saturday night and bring ice cream for the boys. He was good with the boys. We would sit at the kitchen table and play cards. I couldn't always afford to pay a sitter and spending an evening at home was acceptable to John.

After a few more weeks of keeping Russell at arm's length and continuing to see John, Russell gave me an ultimatum. Either I dropped John and resumed the relationship with him, or he would not call again. It would be over. I told him to call me the following night as I had some thinking to do.

Well, I gave in and dropped John. By the end of fall we became serious. Russell surprised me with a diamond in November. I said yes. Then we began discussing things for the wedding and where we would live. I also explained to him that I had made a promise that the boys would always carry their father's name. If that was going to be a problem for him he should back out now. He said he understood. Since he was working in Connecticut and going to school nights in Providence, and because he didn't want to live in another man's house, we agreed I would sell the house and we would find a house closer to Providence. East Providence was only a twenty-five minute ride from my parents home in Ocean Grove, so I said, "That's as far as I'll go. It's no further for you as you are traveling from your parents' home in Riverside now." He agreed.

We went to see Monsignor Hamel as I did want to be married in the Catholic Church. After Monsignor questioned Russell about his first marriage it was revealed his first wife was a Catholic divorcée who had been previously married to a Catholic. Thus, the Catholic Church did not recognize Russell's marriage to her as valid. It was like he was never married. I could have a nuptial mass in the Catholic Church.

The wedding date was set for January 21, 1967. My house was put up for sale. My Dad insisted on paying for the reception and dinner a second time. God bless him. Dee and her husband Eddie were our matron of honor and best man. We had a small wedding, about fifty people. We went to New York City by train for a long weekend for our very brief honeymoon. Mom and Dad stayed at the house with the boys.

The Tuesday after we returned from New York my house was sold. The people who were buying it had already sold their house in Portsmouth, Rhode Island and had to be out by January 31st. They had to move quickly to purchase my house. So, we had less than two weeks to move out. We moved all the furniture into my Dad's second garage and moved in with my parents until we found a house. My parents had four bedrooms, so there was room for everyone. When I received the proceeds from the sale of my house, I repaid *Pépère* Sevigny the $1,000 loan he had given to Bob and I that had made it possible for us to purchase the house.

During our stay with my parents, Jerry had his second hernia operation. He was six. I continued to drive him to Fall River to Head Start at St Jean's. This was good for him as continuity was important and he had many little friends there. I felt a new step-father and the temporary move to my parents' home was enough disruption in his little life for the time being.

On weekends, Russell and I went house hunting. It was a hectic schedule for the three-and-a-half months we stayed with my parents. In April, we found a house on Thurston Street in Riverside, Rhode Island. It was newly-built and close to the school. It was in a quiet neighborhood with very little traffic. We moved in around May of 1967. I registered Jerry for first grade and Larry for kindergarten which would begin in a bit more than three months.

So began my new life with a new husband in a new house in a new state.

Part III

CHAPTER 25

The next ten years (1967-1977) after we moved to our new house on Thurston Street were somewhat easy ones now that I reflect back on them. There were a few small roller coaster rides but nothing really bad happened. We finished the basement area, built the shed, put up the fence and started camping in a used pop-up camper we had purchased. I think Melissa was around four when we first started camping at Brialee Campground in Connecticut. I say we finished the basement and built the shed, but really all that work was done by *Pépère* Dube, my Dad, and my carpenter. The boys all learned to ride two-wheel bikes, joined Cub Scouts® and later went on to Boy Scouts®. They attended St. Brendan's for their CCD classes. That's Confraternity of Christine doctrine classes to prepare for First Communion and later for Confirmation.

Melissa had been born on June 6, 1969, eighteen months after our marriage and just three weeks after Jerry's First Communion on Mother's Day of 1969. I had not even dared to hope it would be a girl and had the name Eric chosen for what was sure to be another boy. Lo and behold, it was a girl after all. Russell was disappointed though as he had two girls from his first marriage and really wanted a son to carry on the family name.

Roger started half-day kindergarten the following September after her birth. Now, I only had Melissa at home during the day. I really enjoyed her, as I had only one at home while the others were at school. This was different than when the boys were all born in a row and there wasn't much time to spend individually with any of them because back then I literally had three babies to look after.

Roger was sure mad at me when Melissa was born since I had told him I was going to "buy" him a new baby brother. In fact, my mother had to take him home with her for the first few weeks after I came home with Melissa. He was that mad at me. Jerry was eight-and-a-half when Melissa was born. He was a big help with her, except of course, that time I had her on the changing table and told him to watch her for one minute while I went to the bathroom for a clean washcloth. He turned his back on her for one second and she rolled off the table right onto the floor.

Thankfully, she was not hurt, just startled I guess, but she sure yelled her little lungs out.

Jerry regularly read to her and when she was old enough to sit at the table when he did his homework, she was right there getting her "homework" assignments from him. He had to give her "papers" to do to keep her busy. Translation: he made her copy pages of the encyclopedia, which she did with zeal, even down to drawing the pictures. If he didn't keep her busy, she would pester him and he couldn't get his homework done. I think this helped Melissa tremendously, as she was reading at age 3 1/2. When she started kindergarten, she was way ahead of her classmates. In the third grade, she was the one student chosen from Meadowcrest School to enter the newly-started Gifted Child Program at Waddington School in Riverside. She was in that program for her fourth, fifth and sixth grades.

Larry was the one who helped me potty train Melissa. She would not go on the potty for me, but when Larry came home from school I would ask him to sit with her in the bathroom and flip through her picture story books, letting her tell him a story. She would go on the potty for him, but the next day when he was at school she wouldn't potty for me. We kept up that routine of him taking her to go potty when he returned home from school for quite a while before she finally forgot about being "her little obstinate self" and became less choosy about her potty coach.

I kept in touch with the Sevignys and we always got together at Christmastime for the family's traditional "Santa's visit" party. There was also the annual summer clam boil where the whole clan (extended family) was in attendance, and birthday celebrations, so the boys grew up knowing their Dad's family. We did get together as much as schedules permitted. The Sevignys were always good to Russell, making him feel welcome and buying him a gift at Christmastime.

Mémère and *Pépère* Sevigny took Jerry with them on a trip to Maryland and Washington D.C. one year (I think it was 1971 or 1972), and they paid for two weeks of summer camp for the boys another year. They generously gave them U.S. Savings Bonds for birthdays, Christmas and special occasions like First Communion. These were all saved for them and never used later on to pay for college tuitions. They had those bonds when they started their adult lives. They were good to my daughter also, treating her like she was indeed a true granddaughter. At Christmastime and for birthdays, Melissa was treated equally well.

When Melissa began talking and we would visit *Mémère* and *Pépère* Sevigny, she began calling them *Mémère* and *Pépère* too, just like the boys. I recall that when I tried to explain to her that her *Mémères* were Grandma Brenton and *Mémère* Dube, and that *Mémère* Sevigny was the boys' grandma, she did not understand. *Mémère*

Sevigny piped in and said, "Let her call me *Mémère* like the others do. It doesn't bother me." How kind she was to my daughter. She even knitted beautiful little sweaters for her, just as she had done for the boys. Melissa always thought of *Mémère* Sevigny as her grandmother. She used to say that she was lucky because she had three grandmothers.

We also visited *Mémère* and *Pépère* Dube regularly. I especially remember the little contests my mother would come up with to keep the kids and adults amused if it was a cold or rainy day and we all had to stay inside. Someone would have to get up and sing a song, recite a poem or tell a joke in order to get a surprise. I remember singing the "I'm a little teapot" song to get my prize one time. I'm sure the kids all have their own special recollections of those memorable afternoons spent at *Mémère* and *Pépère's* house on Hortonville Road.

After Russell had gone on strike twice in three years, and he was not able to collect benefits, the funds were getting tight and the bank account was dropping rapidly. I had been working at a part-time job nights for about a year when working full-time became the only option to build up the saving account for any emergencies. I returned to work full-time in 1973. Our neighbor across the street, Mrs. Capaldo, took care of Melissa. After she started half-day kindergarten the following year, she cared for her in the afternoons until I returned from work. The three boys could be left alone for a few hours after school, since by then they were 11, 9 ½ and 8. Of course Mrs. Capaldo was right there if they needed her.

Mrs. Capaldo was more than a day-care provider; she was truly an extra grandmother for Melissa. She had sort of adopted me when I had first moved to the neighborhood. She had instinctively sensed I was lonely being in another state away from my family and friends and she became a surrogate mom to me. I loved her dearly because of her countless kindnesses to me and mine. Sadly, she passed away in 2000. Mrs. C also took care of her niece's daughter, Martha, who was the same age as Melissa, so Melissa had a play friend to spend the whole day with.

Originally, I had returned to work thinking it would be temporary. When Jerry began having difficulties with math and English at Riverside Jr. High (seventh and eighth grades), after he had been a straight A student through all his elementary years, I realized that he had to be transferred to a private school. He began his ninth grade at St. Andrews in Barrington, Rhode Island in September 1975. Full-time work for me would become permanent from that point on.

CHAPTER 26

Larry had difficulty with school right from kindergarten. At all the teacher conferences I was assured he would catch up. Year after year he advanced to the next grade even though he could not read. At the end of his third grade I insisted he repeat the grade as I saw no sense in *socially promoting* him when he couldn't read. I thought that maybe he needed that extra year to catch up. It was against school policy to hold back kids, and I had to sign a paper saying that it was at my insistence that he repeat that third grade.

He didn't catch up after repeating that third. Teacher conferences continued to be a joke. They labeled him lazy, not attentive, a class clown, and said: "he doesn't try." They showed me IQ tests that indicated he tested in the average to above average range, yet he could not learn to read. His inability to read affected his performance across all subjects. I searched and searched for an answer hoping to find the missing puzzle piece to explain his school and reading difficulties. I sent him to Mr. Farnsworth in Warwick for help "re-patterning" his brain through various exercises, like learning how to how to crawl again and things like that. I took him to an eye doctor on Newport Avenue in Rumford for eye exercises. I purchased a "Hooked on Phonics" course and a set of flash cards. I tried everything. Still, he was making no progress at learning to read.

At the end of his sixth grade when I met with the school staff, I expressed my concerns about him being promoted to Riverside Junior High for the seventh grade. He still could only barely read on a first grade level. I begged for resource help and asked that his teachers there be made aware of the fact that he had difficulty with school and could barely ready a first grade book. I asked that he not be called on to read aloud in class as he was laughed at. They assured me he would receive the resource help and again they said, "Don't worry, he'll catch up."

Well that "resource help" for Larry was a joke too. Twice a week, for one hour, he met with a reading resource teacher who tried to help him to learn to read. Two hours a week was nothing compared to what he really needed, I later learned. His teachers there were <u>NOT</u> made aware of the fact that he could not read. He was

142

called upon in various classes to read aloud. He was laughed at and teased by the other kids. He was the class clown, as they had labeled him, because he wanted the kids to laugh with him and NOT at him. What a humiliating first ten years of schooling he had experienced; including kindergarten through eight grades, with a repeat in the third grade, he had experienced ten years of frustrations and failures.

After struggling through the seventh grade they again promoted him to the eighth grade in spite of my strong objections. Whenever I went in to speak to the principal and his teachers at the Junior High, they continued to label him a class clown, said "he doesn't try," or he "doesn't pay attention" . . . and so on and so on and so on. Just before he began his eighth grade I had requested a meeting with the Special Education Director at the administration office. She was really of no help either. She made the usual promises of more resource help for his eighth grade. Again, that was a drop in the bucket compared to what he really needed. I remember she said that if I had him evaluated by a psychiatrist and he was certified as emotionally disturbed the school could then offer more help. I told her I wouldn't do that to him because he was NOT emotionally disturbed.

I clearly remember sitting with him at the kitchen table trying to help him with homework. Melissa would, of course, be sitting there too doing her second grade homework assignments. She would blurt out the answers to the questions I posed to Larry and I would scold her for doing so. It was a difficult situation, one who had so much difficulty with school and his baby sister who was ahead of the curve. How humiliating this must have been for Larry, yet Melissa was just trying to be a little helper and got scolded for it. He did try. I KNOW that, in spite of the school repeatedly telling me "he doesn't try."

By mid-October 1976, the second year he was at Riverside Junior High, Larry came home crying every day because of his increasing frustrations with school and his daily humiliations. The teasing and ridiculing he endured at school on a daily basis were taking their toll on him. I remember being with him at the kitchen table and him asking me how old he had to be to quit school. He said he was a "dummy," and he hated school and wanted to quit. I told him he wasn't a dummy and that quitting school wasn't the answer. We had to keep trying until we found the answer to the problem. I tried to explain to him that it was like a missing puzzle piece. We just had to keep searching until we found that missing piece. He kept saying, "I can't do it." I kept pounding my fist on the table saying, "I don't want to hear you say I can't. Instead, you say, I'll try." Oh, how those words came back to haunt me many years later but that's a story for later.

I was always on the lookout for articles about education. Right around the time Larry kept asking about quitting school, I read an article about a learning disability called dyslexia. I don't recall what magazine that article was in. It may have been *Parents*. Basically, dyslexia is a misfiring of brain signals that causes problems with letters being reversed, such as seeing a "b" as a "d", or seeing numbers reversed, like 36 and 63, or even seeing whole words reversed, like "was" and "saw" or like "god" and "dog." It is a specific learning disability that is neurological in origin characterized by difficulties with accurate and/or fluent word retention, poor spelling and decoding abilities. Managing dyslexia is a lifelong effort. Dyslexics don't outgrow their problems. Reading and writing usually remain a problem for life.

These are just a few of the many indications of dyslexia. There are hundreds of others. I eventually learned that that no two dyslexics are alike. Each has his own set of weaknesses and strengths, that it happens more to males than females and that the exact cause is unclear. It may be partially caused by an inherited gene. Many years later while discussing Larry's school problems with his grandmother, Bob's mother, she told me Bobby had always had difficulty with school. She would help him memorize things and help him with his homework, but he had difficulties all the way up until he graduated from Morton Jr. High, at age 18, after which he quit school. Had Bob, Larry's father, had a dyslexia problem back in the 40s and 50s? It could very well be. Back then, dyslexia was a problem with no name.

Anyway, some of the famous people identified as dyslexics in that article were: Nelson Rockefeller, Henry Winkler (Fonzie in the television show "Happy Days"), Albert Einstein and Charles Manson. The article went on to say that some dyslexics who received no support could turn to a criminal life due to their frustration. Those that succeeded did so because of supportive families and because they received tutoring help through their difficult school years. Nelson Rockefeller had a private tutor who attended all his college classes with him to take notes. His parents could afford this astronomical expense. The article also said that the earlier the problem was identified, the better the success in educational areas. A few other famous dyslexics are: Richard Branson (Virgin Records and Virgin Atlantic Airways), Charles Schwab, who virtually created the discount brokerage business, and John Chambers, CEO of Cisco.

It went on to list a number of clues or identifying markers to discern if dyslexia could be the problem. Among these were two that really hit home: inability to learn to read and being labeled a class clown or a "dummy." There were other things listed but, wow, did those two jump out at me. I asked myself, "Could this be Larry's problem?" The article mentioned a clinic in Rochester, Minnesota where they administered various tests to determine if a subject was dyslexic. I think the name of the director of that clinic was a Mrs. Osgood. After so many years, I have forgotten the name of that clinic.

After Larry had asked to quit school yet again I decided to call that clinic mentioned in the article I had read. This was sometime in early or mid-November 1976. I called long distance, no small expense back then, and spoke to Mrs. Osgood at the clinic for more than one hour. I told her I had just read the article where the clinic had been mentioned. I told her all about Larry and the last ten years of his schooling. I asked her many, many questions. She told me she could not diagnose on the telephone. If I couldn't find anyone locally to administer the battery of tests to determine if he was in fact dyslexic she suggested I fly out there to have Larry tested.

During that conversation I asked her about special schools equipped to teach dyslexics as she had said that if he was dyslexic, and ten years of public schooling never identified him as such, he would need one-on-one tutoring in a residential school setting utilizing the Orton-Gillingham method, the recommended method successful in teaching dyslexics. She gave me the names of schools and which state they were located in, but warned me that the majority of them had waiting lists for admission of, at the minimum, two to three *years*. She did agree to mail me a longer list of specialized schools, with complete addresses and phone numbers that very day.

I immediately called my mother and asked her to pray. I needed to contact as many of these schools as I could, and I NEEDED one with an opening right away. I just had a gut feeling that his problem was dyslexia and that come hell or high water I would find someone to administer the tests that would confirm this. I needed a miracle. After receiving the list, I immediately sent inquiries out to schools in Texas, Virginia and other states in the Midwest, and one to a school in Wisconsin. Locally, I began to research where in my area I could have the tests administered that would confirm he was dyslexic. My instincts told me this was the problem, but I knew that this had to be confirmed before he could be admitted to a specialized school. Within a few weeks, I received a call from Pinewood Academy in Eagle River, Wisconsin, run by Mr. and Mrs. Soroosh. Talk about putting the cart before the horse. Larry had not yet been tested to determine if he was in fact dyslexic. That truly is the sequence of what happened.

Total enrollment was thirteen boys, no girls. There was one teacher for each boy. Mrs. Soroosh explained to me that they had one boy who was not adjusting well to the school and that this boy would not be returning after Christmas break. They had an opening for January (1977) if I was interested. I explained to her that Larry had not been officially diagnosed as dyslexic and I was not having any luck getting him tested and diagnosed locally. She advised me not to delay getting that crucial testing done and to make an appointment at that testing clinic in Rochester, Minnesota as soon as possible. She was familiar with this clinic and their work. She also told me that a school visit and interview would be required prior to their making a decision on admission. It was late November. If I wanted to lock in that spot for January admission to Pinewood, I had to move quickly. This roller coaster ride began to accelerate.

I immediately called Rochester and explained all that happened since our last phone conversation and that I had already heard from a school in Eagle River. I made an appointment for the first week in December to have Larry tested. Mrs. Osgood said they usually do these tests over a two-day period but she would arrange for the testing to be done all in one day, as she appreciated the fact that time was of the essence. She, in turn, was familiar with Pinewood Academy, which was less than 300 miles from Rochester. I called Pinewood back and advised Mrs. Soroosh about the clinic appointment for testing and made arrangements to visit the school right after that testing in Rochester. If it all worked out perfectly (testing, school visit and actually being accepted there), he would be admitted just three weeks after our visit to the school. More novenas were ordered up. On top of all that, I still had no clear idea of how I would pay for that private residential school. One step at a time, I told myself.

I recall vividly the day I finally explained all these plans to Larry. His reaction was, "You just want to get rid of me because I'm a dummy and I cause so much trouble." He rebelled at the idea of possibly going away to boarding school (as he called it). It took a lot of talking and explaining to get him to calm down and to trust me.

I explained to him that was not the reason. He had to understand that public schools were not meeting his needs and he couldn't keep going on the way he was. Quitting school was definitely not the answer. I asked that he at least trust me to get the testing done in Rochester and to visit the school in Wisconsin first before he made up his mind about all of this. I reminded him that maybe we had finally found the missing piece to the puzzle I always talked about and had searched for, for almost ten years. One step at a time, I told him. That truly became my mantra.

Talk about a roller coaster ride. This was of the high-speed variety and one I would never forget. It was now December. I made the flight arrangements for sometime during the end of the first week of December. Larry and I flew to Chicago, took a connecting flight on to Rochester where I rented a car and drove the few miles to Rochester, heading directly to the clinic for the testing. If I recall correctly, we arrived around 10:30 a.m. Central time. Because of the time difference we had been able to depart from Providence very early, take two flights and still arrive at the clinic mid-morning to get the testing accomplished that very day.

After our arrival at the clinic he was immediately taken to the testing area. The interview would follow when the results of the test were available. It took all day with just a short break for a quick lunch right there at the clinic. Mrs. Osgood told me at the end of that long day (around 4:30 p.m., I believe) that he was a dual dyslexic, meaning that two of the three main pathways of learning were affected. One was his visual perception. He saw letters and even whole words in reverse. Second was his auditory discrimination. He heard the sound of a "b" sometimes as a "d" and *vice versa*. This did not mean he was hearing impaired. It was due to misfiring of brain signals that caused him to hear the sound of "b" like it was "d" or *vice versa*. Larry began to participate in the discussion of the results and asked many questions. She answered him and I truly felt that he now began to understand that he was not a "dummy" and the puzzle I had talked about was now close to getting solved.

She further informed us that his IQ tested a little above average. In dyslexics, there is no dominant side of the brain. Larry being right-handed should have had left-sided brain dominance, but this was not so. Sometimes the signals came from the left side of his brain; other times those signals came from the right. Thus, he did not consistently see a "b" as a "d". He was NOT retarded or brain damaged. It was just a quirk of nature. Hey, Albert Einstein was a dyslexic, and he sure was not brain damaged or retarded, was he?

Before the term dyslexia came to prominence, this learning disability used to be known as "word blindness." The term dyslexia is often used as a synonym for a reading disability. However, many researchers agree that there are different types of reading disabilities, of which dyslexia is one. Common indicators of a reading disability include difficulty with phonetic awareness—the ability to break up words into their component sounds, and difficulty with matching letter combinations to specific sounds (sound-symbol correspondence). A reading disability can affect any part of the reading process, including difficulty with accurate and/or fluent word recognition, word decoding, reading rate, prosody (oral reading with expression) and reading comprehension. Boy, I think I could write a short book on what I learned about dyslexia. If anyone reading this book is interested in learning more on this subject I suggest they go on the Internet and Google "learning disabilities." Another excellent source of information is the website for The International Dyslexia Association.

She also told us that Larry was emotionally stable in spite of his ten frustrating school years. That, she said, indicated to her that he had received a lot of encouragement and support at home. THAT comment made me feel great. The suggestion made by the special education director of having him labeled emotionally disturbed flashed through my head. Another comment Mrs. Osgood made at that time that I never forgot was, "I am appalled to hear that your son has been in a public education system in this country for ten years and no one ever told you he was dyslexic." Now, after ten years, I had finally put my fingers on that elusive puzzle piece I so often referred to in my search for a reason why Larry could not learn to read and was the cause of all those difficulties in his schooling.

Now the speed of that roller coaster ride sure accelerated even more. From the clinic in Rochester we grabbed a quick bite from a fast food restaurant then I drove that rented car towards Wisconsin. We traveled for about three hours heading north to Minneapolis-St. Paul, then east towards Wisconsin on Routes 61E and 8E. I found a hunting lodge that had not yet closed for the winter season (no Internet reservations back then; no Internet, in fact) and rented a room for Larry and me for the night. Upon leaving Rochester, the goal had been to get as close to Eagle River as we could. The following morning, we were up and on the road by 6:00 a.m., stopping at a hunter's food stop a short time later for a good breakfast. We were back on our way in less than forty minutes.

I drove that rented car on unfamiliar highways, not super highways like Interstate 95, but mostly state highways like Route 6. If I recall correctly, we followed Rt. 8E to RT. 51, then continued on Rt. 10E which took us right to Eagle River, WI. Eagle River is almost on the state line of Michigan. It snowed only lightly on and off, thanks to the Lord! This was the first week in December 1976. I forget what time we arrived in Eagle River, and I can't recall how many actual miles we had driven, but I think it was around a little more than 300 miles from Rochester, MN to Eagle River. I think we arrived just after 10:30 a.m. Mrs. Soroosh had understood when I explained to her that I couldn't give her a specific arrival time, as it depended on the road driving conditions and not getting lost in unfamiliar territory (no GPS back then, either).

Larry and I first received a tour of the school, which was actually an old hunting lodge constructed with humongous logs. Additions had been added to the side and the back when it had been converted to a school. It was in the middle of nowhere and Carpenter Lake was right off the back porch. After entering the front door, to the left was a giant fireplace and in the far left corner was a grand piano with a bear rug draped over it. To the right of the entrance area was a long dining room table (monastery style) and behind that was the extra-large kitchen, an addition to the original hunting lodge. Classrooms were tiny and were both on the first and second floors of the lodge. They were tiny because 95% of instruction was one-on-one, one teacher with one child.

All twelve of the boys (students) were already on their Christmas break, so we did not get to meet any of them, but Mrs. Soroosh told Larry a little about each of them—what states they came from, their ages and adding that they were all dyslexics like Larry. If Larry would be accepted he would be the only boy from the east coast. We then sat with Mrs. Soroosh at the long dining table and the conversation (in actuality this was the interview) revolved around Larry's school experiences and his family. Larry felt comfortable and answered any questions posed to him; he also asked a lot of questions himself. I sensed he was very interested. I truly felt the idea of possibly going away to school was now becoming more acceptable to him.

After a few hours, she told us that she would review all the results from the testing in Rochester, which she expected to receive within a day or so, having already spoken with the clinic on the telephone that very morning. She would then discuss everything with her husband who helped run the school. A decision would be made within just a few days as the January semester was beginning in less than three weeks. She said she would call me first and then formally notify me of their decision in a letter.

We left there, drove to Rhinelander which was approximately 20 miles south of there, dropped off the rented car, took the first plane to Chicago and then boarded the final plane back to Providence. During our two flights back Larry couldn't stop talking about the school. It had a "homey" feeling to it. It was not what he had imagined when I had first brought up the idea of possibly going away to school. I think he was thinking of a military-type school back then and this "homey" school was a pleasant surprise to him. It really impressed him. He said to me, "Mom, they have to say yes. I want to go to that school." Silently I thanked God for answering another prayer. Larry had trusted me.

Within a day of returning home, I received the call from Mrs. Soroosh. Larry was accepted for the one opening they had for January admission. All those novenas had borne fruit. He would be the 13th student. That number "13" turned out to be a lucky number for him.

Again, that roller coaster ride accelerated. Things were now moving at a speed of warp 10. A check had to be mailed by the end of December to cover the full semester from January to June 1977. That first half-year cost approximately $8,000. Thirty years ago, that was a lot of money, believe me. The cost for that half year of specialized, residential schooling is much higher when you figure in the additional costs of several round trip plane fares and all the required supplies, equipment and heavier winter clothes he needed.

I had less than three weeks to get it all together. Besides needing heavier winter clothing, he needed skis, ski boots and ski apparel and a large trunk for shipping. All his clothes and belongings had to be labeled with his name. My mother helped out a lot. She paid for the trunk and some of the clothes I had to buy. She helped label everything. *Mémère* Sevigny also helped with extra winter clothes like thermal underwear, warm socks, flannel shirts and warm sweaters. I went to Crossed Sabers Ski Store in Barrington and purchased the required beginners ski package, which consisted of boots, bindings, poles and some ski clothes. This alone cost more than $500. At this point, I began referring to Larry as my "million dollar baby," and putting "more water in the soup" became mandatory all the time. Somehow the check was sent, the required items were purchased, labeled and packed in the big black trunk and his plane tickets were bought.

I made an appointment with the special education director at the East Providence School Department. I informed her of Larry being identified as dyslexic and of his acceptance at the school in Wisconsin. I made the formal request to have all his school records and transcripts sent to Pinewood Academy in Eagle River. The director asked me how much this school would cost and I told her. With a visible smirk on her face she said, "Well, you can't possibly afford to keep him in that school for more than a few years so he'll be back in the East Providence School system eventually." I looked her straight in the eye and replied, "There is no such word as impossible in my vocabulary. Where there is a will there is a way, and Larry will be back in this inadequate school system that failed to meet his needs over my dead body." I'd love to meet up with her today and make her eat her words, "eat crow" as they say and give me credit for doing the impossible.

Obviously, she had no idea what a true stubborn Frenchman (lady) I was. Yes, I'm stubborn, French and a lady too! I do believe all of my children have inherited a bit of this stubborn gene from me, although I really prefer to call it "the gene of determination." *Say "thank you" to Mom you guys and gal!*

I was more terrified than he was about him taking those two planes all alone to get to Eagle River right after New Year's. I rehearsed with him the airport scenarios from Providence to Chicago and then from Chicago to Rhinelander. He would be going alone. He had been in all of those airports when we took that trip earlier for the testing at the clinic and then back from the school visit, but he could not read. Words and numbers were still a jumbled mess 95% of the time. If there was a change in flight plans, he would have to ask for assistance (no cell phones in those days to call home to Mom).

When we arrived at T.F. Green airport on the day of the flight, (early January, right after New Years but I forget the actual date), we learned the weather in Chicago was bad. An ice storm had messed up all the Chicago flights. Larry's plane ticket had to be changed. He had to fly to Connecticut first to make a connection there for a flight to Chicago. Now there would be very little time to make his connection in Chicago to get to Rhinelander, where the Soroosh family would be picking him up.

This was NOT according to the planned scenario I had gone over with Larry. Off he went. I was a basket case. Right before arriving in Chicago, he had the smarts to tell the stewardess that the way his earlier flights had been changed he wouldn't make his connection to Rhinelander. The stewardess had the pilot call ahead to the airline that serviced the Rhinelander airport, to tell them he had a student passenger that had to make that flight. They agreed to hold the flight for him.

When they arrived in Chicago Larry was allowed to leave the plane first ahead of even the first class passengers. He ran to the other terminal and made his flight to Rhinelander. I received the call after midnight that he had finally arrived safely. His luggage had not made it due to all the rush and flight changes but it would be delivered to the school the next day. Mrs. Soroosh assured me that one of the boys would lend Larry some clothes and they had extra new toothbrushes on hand. He would be just fine until his luggage arrived.

That had to be one of the longest days of my life after one of the fastest roller coaster ride I had ever experienced.

His journey to learn to read and succeed in school had now begun. He was 14 years old. It had taken ten years of frustrating school years to get to this point. Now in spite of all the past obstacles and with that solo flight that got detoured, giving me more gray hairs in one day than you can imagine, he was finally settled in a school that would help him and meet his unique needs. I say unique because as I previously related, no two dyslexics are alike. They used the Orton-Gillingham method of teaching which utilizes a multi-sensory approach. He would be sounding out sounds of letters first, then small words, while writing them and hearing them simultaneously. This means the three main pathways of learning which are hearing, speaking and kinesthetic are employed together or simultaneously. This approach would be used to teach all subject matters, not just reading. He literally had to start school all over again as if he were in the first grade. It had been explained to me that it would take a few years to actually learn to read and to fully catch up. It was not going to happen in a year's time. It's a very interesting method to read about in more detail than what I have briefly tried to explain here.

After settling in at his new residential school, which he did with no problems, he called home every Sunday telling me all about the past week. He was enthusiastic about the school and the teaching methods he was experiencing. He was comfortable there and felt no pressure. He was learning to ski. He never once asked to come home. I sensed he was happy in his new school setting.

At home it had been difficult for him all those years as his brothers and little sister had no difficulties with school. I can understand how he really felt like he was a dummy. Not that any of us deliberately made him feel that way, but I did have to be encouraging to his siblings when they did well in school and this must have been hard for him.

CHAPTER 27

Soon after Larry was settled in the new school in Wisconsin, I contacted a lawyer to address the East Providence School system. In the fall of his eighth grade, when I had requested to see his school files at Riverside Jr. High, I had discovered a crucial document dating back to Larry's kindergarten year in which the testing indicated a possibility of a learning disability. That was the first time I had seen this document. That was the foundation of my argument with the East Providence School system. I was never informed of that test or of the possibility of a potential learning disorder. Further, had I known of the existence of this crucial indicator back then, I could have taken action to further identify the true nature of his learning problems and obtained the much needed specialized teaching he desperately needed right away. Instead, the school system had put this testing result from kindergarten in his school files, never informed me of it, then labeled him a class clown, and repeatedly said, "He'll catch up."

Apparently, no teacher in all those years had reviewed his files thoroughly. If they did, no one did anything to follow up on that early warning that he had a learning disability. I had been promised all kinds of remedial help which barely materialized and when it did, it was just a drop in the bucket compared to what we now knew was a dyslexic problem which the East Providence School system had failed to identify and, in my opinion, was not equipped to address at this late stage of Larry's education. I had been told that children with learning difficulties did not come under the Federal Handicap laws. Even so, if the school did not have the resources they should have made me aware of this critical testing from the get go. I then could have sought out a more definitive explanation of his learning problems. I certainly could have and would have paid for private schools way back then had it been recommended. I felt strongly that there was negligence on the part of the school system.

The lawyer took the case on a contingency basis. But after just a few months of meetings and hearings, the school system offered an $18,000 settlement to avoid going to a trial. I didn't want to accept this offer as one full year at Pinewood costs $14,000, plus plane fares and special clothing, etc. As my lawyer had taken the case on a contingency basis, he wanted to settle. He was a young lawyer just starting out. If I didn't accept what was offered, he would require $5,000 up front to continue the case to trial with no guarantee that if we continued I would win the case. There was no precedent in the State of Rhode Island at that time for this type of case and, as I said before, I had been told that learning disabled children did not yet come under the Federal Handicapped laws.

A few years later I found out more about the laws on learning disabled children. The Rehabilitation Act of 1973, Section 504, did not actually come into effect until May 1978. This legislation now guaranteed certain rights to people with disabilities, especially in the cases of education and work. The Education for all Handicapped Children Act (EAHCA) became law in 1975 and was renamed The Individuals with Disabilities Act (IDEA) in 1990. This is a Federal Law that governs how states and public agencies provide early intervention, special education and related services to children with learning disabilities. It defines the rights of students with dyslexia and other specific learning disabilities. These individuals are legally entitled to special services to help them overcome and accommodate their learning problems. Such services include education programs designed to meet the needs of these students. What's the catch?

In 1975, the EAHCA was a Federal Law (later renamed the IDEA), but learning disabled children did not come in under the handicapped children umbrella. This happened when in 1978, section 504 of The Rehabilitation Act of 1973 was changed to include the rights of learning disabled students under the EAHCA. The catch is that law did not take effect until May 1978, almost a year and a half AFTER I had Larry transferred to that private, residential school in Wisconsin.

I couldn't afford to pay my lawyer $5,000 to continue with the suit and still have enough money to pay for the next full year at Pinewood, as well as keep Jerry in St. Andrews. I had no choice but to accept the settlement. After the lawyer took his fee, I was left with less than $14,000, which almost paid for the next full year Larry spent at Pinewood, his ninth grade. I would have to find a way to keep him in a private residential school for another three years after that. One step at a time and one day at a time, I reminded myself.

When Larry went to Wisconsin for that first half year, Jerry was already in his second year at St. Andrews in Barrington. Private school tuitions were beginning to take their toll on family finances. Somehow, I managed pulling many aces out of the deck many times.

Jerry continued to do extremely well at St Andrew's. He loved that school. Roger was doing fine as an "A" student in Riverside Jr. High (seventh grade, '76-'77), so I kept him there until the tenth grade when I transferred him to St. Raphael's private high school in Pawtucket for his last three years of high school. By the time Melissa was chosen to enter the gifted child program at Waddington School for the fourth grade (school year '79-'80), Jerry was a senior at St. Andrew's, and Roger was starting his eleventh grade at St. Raphael's Academy. Melissa continued in the gifted child program for the next three years. We enrolled her at Bay View Academy for the seventh grade. No way was she going to attend the local junior high.

In the interim, I was searching for a school for Larry that was closer to home. We visited Pine Ridge Academy in Burlington, Vermont during Easter break 1978 of his second year in Wisconsin. This also was a school for dyslexic children but it was co-educational, had almost one hundred students enrolled and was only 300 miles from home which meant a savings of all those round trip plane fares four times a year for the Wisconsin school. After the interview and a tour of the campus Larry again expressed interest in that school and he hoped they would accept him for the following September admission which would be the beginning of his tenth grade. Another novena was called up.

Again, against all the odds, we were notified that he was accepted at Pine Ridge School in Williston, Vermont for the school year beginning in September 1978. Their impossible waiting list had been surmounted and against the odds Larry was one of those chosen to fill the few open slots they had. Oh, the power of prayer and novenas! Again, I somehow managed to meet those huge tuition payments twice a year. He adjusted well to the new school and made slow but steady progress in learning to read.

I recall him calling home one Sunday mid-way through the second year in Vermont, which was in his eleventh grade. The first thing he said to me was, "Mom, I can read." That was a million dollar moment for me. He had climbed the tough mountain to undo all the damage and neglect of his early school years and now the "puzzle pieces" were all falling perfectly in place. In retrospect, I think a lot of small miracles were involved in Larry's long educational journey.

There is more to tell. During his eleventh grade in Vermont, he decided that he wanted to attend mechanics school after high school graduation from Pine Ridge the following year.

During that summer of 1982 we visited Rhode Island Trade Shop School in Providence and pre-enrolled him for the class that would begin in September 1981 following his graduation. I explained to the school personnel about Larry's dyslexic problem. They agreed to let us take all the text books he would be using for his course studies. They agreed to this because there would be no resource help available to him. He would have to make it through those mechanics courses on his own.

He then took these textbooks with him when he returned to Pine Ridge for his senior year. The school used all of those textbooks for his senior year, incorporating them into his IEP (Individual Educational Plan) and using them for his math, English, and reading studies. By doing this, he was able to get familiar with the courses he would be taking at RI Trade Shop School the following year. He would have the advantage, at least, of being able to more easily decipher the new words in a mechanic's vocabulary and trade terms as well as having a foundation of whatever math mechanics needed to ply their trade. That worked out great. Remember, he had been told when he enrolled at RI Trade Shop Schools there would be no resources or individual help available. He would have to get through all his courses on his own.

He graduated in June 1981 from Pine Ridge, worked a summer full-time job at Aid Maintenance cleaning offices at night. The very next September he began his auto mechanics courses at RI Trade Shop School. He then switched to part-time work at Aid Maintenance to help with expenses. He graduated in June 1982 with a 93% average. He was so proud of himself and so much more confident.

I must tell you a brief story about his home studies while at RI Trade Shop School. He had difficulty memorizing definitions or answers to questions that would be on the tests. I recall Melissa "tutoring" him. She made him repeat, over and over again using little rhymes, an answer that was crucial and in particular that he was having some difficulty remembering.

One question was: Name the two types of piston ring materials. The answer was: Nodular Iron and Chrome-Molybdenum. Melissa's rhyme worked. To this very day, thirty years later, he can rattle off that answer. He says he will never forget it.

Melissa was in her sixth grade at Waddington School, the last year of the Gifted Child's Program she had started in the fourth grade. They would sit and do their homework together at the kitchen table. Whenever she could, she helped him by suggesting little tricks to remember what he was studying. The one I related earlier was just one he really never forgot. She was his primary home tutor. She was seven years younger than him.

I'll get back to continuing with Larry's education journey. I digressed there a bit.

Before finishing RI Trade Shop School he came across a brochure at school about diesel mechanic training. He expressed a strong interest in pursuing that course of training to become a diesel mechanic. Again, I made flight arrangements for both of us to fly out to Cleveland, Ohio to visit the Ohio Diesel Technical Institute during his spring break from RI Trade Shop School.

After our visit, which included the tour of the training facilities and an interview, Larry made up his mind and he was enrolled for the next class beginning in September 1982. It was a twelve-month program. This, of course, meant more watered down soup. I'll tell you a secret. Sometime during all those years, I began to stretch that soup even further, adding a cup and a half of water instead of just one. I got away with it because I don't ever recall the kids saying the soup was watery. Every little bit helps, they say!

Jerry, his older brother, drove out to Cleveland with him early in September, in the old Nash Rambler that *Pépère* had bought for him, and got him settled in the motel room which he shared with another Ohio Diesel student. This was the housing offered by the school. He would be doing most of his cooking on a hot plate. He would manage as best he could. Jerry then flew back to Boston to start his senior year at Wentworth Institute of Technology in Boston.

During his stay in Cleveland, Larry got a part-time job on weekends at a car wash to help defray some of the living expenses, like gas for the car and food for the week. In a later chapter, I will recount a cute story about his time there.

He graduated from Ohio Diesel Technical Institute (which became the Ohio Diesel Technical College in 1995, and was then accredited to confer Associate Degrees), the same day Jerry graduated with his Bachelor's Degree in mechanical engineering from Wentworth Institute in Boston on September 3, 1983. Larry understood that I couldn't be in two places at the same time, so I went to Jerry's graduation in Boston. Roger also completed his eighteen-month Associate's Degree program in electronic technology, receiving his diploma within the same month that Jerry and Larry graduated.

Right after graduation diplomas were handed out, Larry had his little car packed up by 4:30 p.m. He also had a passenger to make the trip back to Providence from Cleveland. Andrew Bendigo was also a student who had completed Ohio Diesel and he lived in Providence. I really felt comfortable with Larry driving back as he had someone with him. I was still anxious about his brain signals misfiring and imagined he would take a wrong turn somewhere *en route* and end up in "East Chepachee" or some other location in the middle of nowhere. Dyslexia is never cured. Larry had been taught to read, yes, but how would he deal with that misfiring that still surfaced erratically. I worried needlessly. They didn't get lost. After driving all night, stopping only for gas and bathroom breaks or food, he arrived home early the next morning around 7:00 a.m., having dropped Andrew off in Providence.

Within one week of returning home he had been hired as a diesel mechanic by Schmidt Equipment in North Swansea, Massachusetts. This is a John Deere dealership not seven miles from our home. He has been with that company for

25 years and, after starting out as their road guy on the service truck, he worked himself up to the position of shop foreman. He still goes to school (John Deere Training School) to learn new diagnostic systems for the newest machinery that John Deere develops.

I find it so ironic that he, of all of them, who so hated school in those early years and wanted to quit in his eighth grade, is still getting schooling after all these years. He doesn't mind though, as he realizes he must stay at the top of his field and getting certified on all the new machinery is a must. He has never failed a course for certification on anything. I am so very proud of my "million dollar" baby who I now refer to as my "million dollar" mechanic.

Reflecting back on Larry's education journey I realize, as he does, that I made the right decision when he was transferred to the first residential school for dyslexics in Wisconsin. That was when he began to experience success with his school work.

All those novenas said by me, my Mom and dear Cousin Cecile for so many years, and especially that special one I asked my Mom for in November 1976, were all eventually answered. I know some of those earlier novenas just gave me the determination to keep searching for that missing puzzle piece. I often think of that poem "Footsteps" when I think of all those years. The Lord had carried both Larry and me those first ten years of his education and when the Lord deemed it was the right time, He led me to that article where I first read about dyslexia. That led to my call to the Rochester clinic, which in turn led to obtaining a list of special schools and then the call from Mrs. Soroosh about a January opening at Pinewood Academy. How about the fact that the Rochester clinic was in relatively close proximity to the school in Eagle River? I didn't get a call from a school in Texas or one further away from the clinic, did I? That Larry was so enthusiastic about going away to a residential school after our visit to the clinic and Pinewood was not a coincidence either. To top everything off, Larry was indeed chosen to fill that January vacancy.

The odds of all that actually happening were not astronomical. They were, I dare say, miraculous. I do believe all that transpired in that short period of time was not mere coincidence. It was destiny in the making, and it was all part of God's Master Plan. That destiny was shaped and made possible through faith and prayer, and specifically with all those novenas.

You all had better believe in the power of faith and prayers, but also remember that my prayers and all those novenas were not fully answered for more than ten years. So never give up! Hang in there!

CHAPTER 28

The years from 1967, when Jerry began first grade at Meadowcrest Elementary School until June 1991, when Melissa graduated from college represent an almost twenty-five-year time span. This includes the year Jerry attended Fall River Head Start from September 1966 to May 1967, after which we had moved to Rhode Island, which counted as his kindergarten year. He had been enrolled in that program because St. Jean's in Fall River had no kindergarten class at that time. I was almost 50 when Melissa graduated from college. A good part of my life had been spent being totally involved in their educations and juggling the finances to pay for private schools and private college for sixteen of those almost twenty-five years.

Jerry attended St. Andrews High School for four years and Wentworth Institute of Technology for four years. He graduated in September 1983 with a Bachelor of Science degree in mechanical engineering.

Larry attended Pinewood Academy for the last half of his eighth grade and for ninth grade. He attended Pine Ridge School for his tenth, eleventh and twelfth grades, graduating in 1981. From there, he attended RI Trade Shop School for one full year, graduating with a certificate in auto mechanics. Next, he attended Ohio Diesel Institute for a one-year program in diesel mechanics, receiving his certificate of course completion in September 1983.

Roger attended St. Raphael's Academy for his tenth, eleventh and twelfth grades, graduating in June 1982. Since he started his first semester at New England Technical Institute in January 1982, he actually completed his last semester of high school at the same time as completing his first semester in college. He graduated from the eighteen-month associate's degree program in electronics in September 1983.

Melissa started at Bay View Academy in seventh grade. She graduated elementary school there and continued on for four years of high school, graduating on her eighteenth birthday in June 1987. She attended Simmons College for four years, including completing the second semester of her junior year at the Institute d'Études Européenes in Nantes, France. She graduated from Simmons with honors in June 1991.

Looking back, the worse two full school years, financially, were 1981-1982 and 1982-1983. These were the years when I literally always put more water in the soup to stretch the food budget. My kids can tell you about the breakfast-for-dinner Fridays, "Pancake Fridays", when we had pancakes or scrambled eggs for supper. Melissa recalls some of their friends being invited to share our "Pancake Fridays" and of the pancake-eating contests. I recall that Keith Reed, Larry's best friend, won those contest nine times out of ten. She says she now realizes I always tried to make it all fun for them. She now knows that I fed the whole gang, including the guests, for under $10.

I obsessively crunched the numbers every six months. I recall sitting at my kitchen table, figuring, calculating and planning how I was going to meet the next tuition obligations, which were due every September and January.

The actual total cost of those sixteen years of private education was nearly $225,000. Of course, with all the scholarships that Melissa received for her college years, the actual costs covered by the family budget and the kids' part-time jobs reduced that to approximately $175,000, with $6,000 of that paid for by Melissa's father as part of the divorce agreement ($1,500 annually for each of her four the years at Simmons). Believe me, $175,000 was a lot of money back in the 1970s and 1980s!

The Social Security survivors' benefits the three boys received through the end of college, and the extra part-time job money I earned all went for education costs. I "made do" on clothes, skipped vacations and delayed major purchases as long as possible, taking every opportunity to stretch the almighty dollar. Anticipating the next six months of financial needs and finding ways to stretch a dollar truly consumed my life.

My kids all remember the official graduation outfit. I bought that outfit for Jerry's graduation from St. Andrew's in 1989, and I wore it for all the graduations that followed, except for the very last one in 1991. For Melissa's college graduation, I splurged on a new outfit. At Melissa's graduation party, the kids insisted I put on that outfit for an official photo. The last graduation would not be official until that outfit made an appearance. After that day, the outfit was officially retired and never worn again, at least not by me. In fact, it was recycled, so to speak. I passed it on to my cousin Cecile who wore it for a few more years. You can just imagine how much money was saved by using that same classic-styled outfit over and over again for all the graduations! It was a pale peach suit with a jacket and skirt. I wore it with a blouse that had peach flowers in various contrasting peach tones and dark and light green leaves on a soft-beige background.

Jerry often said to me, "Mom, some day you have to show me how you pulled so many aces out of the deck. I never saw anyone with so many aces in one deck." What I described above is how—along with a good dose of plain old common sense and determination ("Where there is a will, there is a way"), making do with whatever I could and making many little sacrifices along the way. Instead of going out to Friday lunch with the girls from work, I brought my lunch and ate in the cafeteria, resulting in a few meager dollars saved. I made do with the same winter coat for many years to save a few extra bucks. All those little sacrifices, along with the kids' sacrifices, like not going to the movies or roller skating or not getting a new bike, and the money from their small part-time jobs all added up. That's truly how the aces materialized. No magic tricks were involved. Jerry has called my determination "stubbornness." I bet they all remember me saying, "There is no such thing as impossible in my dictionary," or "Never say I can't. Say I'll try." Persistence always wins. It wasn't stubbornness. It was just plain determination on my part.

All four of my children finished their schooling with no student loans to pay off, except for one $2,500 student loan that Melissa took out during her last year at Simmons. I paid that loan off within a couple of years after she graduated. The only reason she took that loan was because we didn't want to use up the last of what we had left in savings. I had no other outstanding loans to pay off either. How many parents with limited means can say they accomplished getting four kids through private high schools and colleges with only one $2,500 student loan? It was truly a team effort. All four of my children gladly did their share to stretch those dollars to pay for their educations. I might again add that not one of them ever complained about my watered down soups.

Now that was some long roller coaster ride—one that lasted a long, long time and, I dare say, was the most expensive roller coaster ride of my life. This is how I like to look at it today. That sixteen-year period of mind-boggling private education costs were my investment years. I invested in my kids' education and in their futures. If I had invested only one-half of what was spent on education in the stock market instead, it would be interesting to see what it would have grown to in investments. I chose the education investment route instead and I will never regret that decision. Today, I am reaping the dividends and interest on that education investment.

*   *   *

I can't possibly recall everything from my twenty-year marriage to Russell, but a few things will be said concerning that phase of my roller coaster life.

My children were all raised in the house we purchased when we moved to Rhode Island just four months after our marriage. Melissa (who we called Missy when she was growing up, and Mel in her college and adult years), the only child born after I re-married and moved to Rhode Island, has really known no other home. Roger was 3 when I moved there, so he doesn't have memories of Kennedy Street although Jerry and Larry do.

Within two years of our marriage, Russell went through the first strike at Electric Boat and then another one, which lasted eight months, right after Melissa was born. This was tough, as Russell was still sending support checks for his two daughters, Doreen and Holly, from his first marriage. While on strike, he did not collect any benefits so money was certainly a problem. We had some savings that helped us get through those two strikes.

I had no intention of continuing to work indefinitely when I returned to work first on a part-time basis and then, in 1973, as a full-time bookkeeper. It was supposed to be temporary.

Well, it became permanent. I always worked outside the home from then on. I had stayed home more than ten years, from 1961, when Jerry was born up until 1972, when I took that first part-time job. I feel I was home and there for my kids in those critical first years of their lives. Then the extra paycheck helped to do improvements in the house and yard. We were able to buy new cars when we needed them and take little vacations to New Hampshire. We could afford to buy bikes when the boys all graduated to two-wheelers and we could build up the savings account.

When the problems with Larry's schooling in the public school setting surfaced and continued to get worse, I had made the decision that for their high school years all the kids would be enrolled in private schools. So, now part of that extra paycheck was put aside for the education fund. Jerry had been transferred to St. Andrew's for his ninth grade which began in September 1975. After Melissa was transferred to Bay View Academy for the beginning of her seventh grade year in September 1981, it was private schools for all of them from then on, until they finished college.

Even though we both worked and I still had the Social Security survivors' benefits for the boys, there were some tough years financially, mostly because of those astronomical private tuition outlays. Russell supported his two girls until 1980. By then, Doreen was over eighteen.

Sadly, Holly died in a terrible head-on car crash on March 13, 1981. She was just 21 years old. Russell surely must have experienced a lot of stress over his loss but he kept everything inside. He didn't even want to attend her wake and funeral. I was the one who had to convince him that he had to be there. He was her father. We also helped to pay for part of her funeral expenses as there was no life insurance.

Years later, after much reflection, I came to the realization that whenever something bad happened Russell "blocked it out" or at least he tried to. My mother, too, passed in 1981. I know I experienced a lot of stress especially during the last month of her life. The morning my Mom died my Dad and my two sisters and I were at her bedside. I recall calling Russell at 5:30 in the morning from the hospital in Fall River to catch him before he left for his drive to work in Connecticut to tell him my Mom had just passed. He said he'd see me when he got home. I told him he couldn't go to work. I needed him to take care of the kids getting off to school, and to make the flight arrangements for Larry to return home from Vermont for his grandmother's funeral. He had to call the school and tell them what happened and ask to speak to Larry so he could be the one to tell him about his grandmother. I had to stay with my father to make all the funeral arrangements and all the calls to Canada.

He had never once visited my Mom in the hospital during the three weeks she had been hospitalized prior to her passing. Again, years later, I realized that he always "blocked out" things he had difficulty dealing with. When I reflect back in time now, I realize that our marriage first started on its slow, downward spiral after Melissa was born. Not having a son to carry on his family name, Russell began to resent the fact that the boys would always carry their father's name. I think he regretted agreeing to that when we had that conversation about adoption even before we were married. He never came right out and said it, but I know now that Melissa's birth triggered a change in him.

When Larry started in those special schools, I got a second, part-time job as a waitress on weekends, working from 10:00 p.m. to 2:00 a.m. on Friday and Saturday nights to generate even more funds for education. There were other financial obligations to meet—car loans, orthodontist and dentist visits for four kids were just a few among many others. I worked at that part-time job for five years.

This also put additional stress on the marriage as I also asked him to do more around the house with me working the two jobs. Also, I couldn't go family camping as we had been doing since Missy was about three or four. He would not give up regular camping. If he had settled on a few weekend camping trips, it sure would have helped the finances. He still went with the kids, but sometimes only with Missy because either the boys didn't want to go or Jerry was working on weekends at the Squantum Club in Riverside. The boys were old enough to be left alone at home at night on the weekends when he went camping and I worked that part-time job as

I didn't start that job until 10:00 p.m. Remember, we were actually supporting six children through 1980.

Russell was the "silent" type. He let things fester rather than talk things through. He began squirreling more of his paycheck into his profit sharing and retirement fund at Electric Boat. Without my knowledge he even bought a new camper one year, had it registered to his mother's address and had it delivered to his seasonal campsite. He also had her address on his loan from Electric Boat for that "secret" camper. I never knew about this until the divorce when I saw the list of assets he submitted to his lawyer. I never saw his pay stubs as he would hand me whatever cash he could spare after meeting his secret obligations and salting more dollars away in his retirement plan or the EB Credit Union. My name was never on that credit union savings account. For a long time I could sense our relationship was in trouble and I eventually convinced him to go to marriage counseling with me. This was in 1982 or 1983. That was a fiasco. I soon found out he distorted everything so he would appear to the "good guy" and me the "witch." Sometimes, he would just be silent for the whole counseling session. After six months I gave up on counseling. If he couldn't be honest during those sessions there was no hope to heal the wounds of our relationship.

He began calling me at work on Friday afternoons telling me he had a retirement party to go to that night and he would be staying over with Billy instead of driving home from Connecticut later on. When I asked who Billy was he just said it was a co-worker. Billy never had a last name nor did he have a telephone, or so Russ told me.

Well, let me tell you—and Kathy, one of my best friends who worked with me during this time could verify this—he had more dang retirement parties to go to in six months than most of us attend in a lifetime. Kathy tried to convince me, "Gertie the Sleuth," to do some detective work. She suggested that we leave work early one Friday, drive to Electric Boat and wait outside the gate. When Russell drove out, we would follow him to see where the latest retirement party was being held. We never did, because I truly believed he just needed some space. Later, after the divorce, I did find out where he was actually going, but this was much, much later.

At this point, I was much stressed. The faltering marriage, the private schools expenses, working two jobs while still trying to cook decent meals and take care of my little family and the loss of my dear Mom, all took their toll on me. Finally, Kathy convinced me to see a counselor. I think it was sometime in late 1983. I attended group sessions with several other women who were in crisis situations. In the end, after much talking and revealing aspects of Russell's behavior and the rocky status of our marriage, I realized that his "silent treatment" was a form of abuse.

I also came to realize that trying to make things better between us and saving our marriage was just a one-sided effort. I think this is when I totally gave up on the marriage. I hung in there as long as I could, mainly because of Melissa. I was concerned about her college education which would begin in just about four years. A few more years passed.

In March 1985, I went to a school in Florida for a six-week course in the airline/travel field. I wanted to change jobs and needed to get some training. This was after the three boys had all finished college or their post high-school years and I had a break before Melissa would begin college in 1987. My Dad paid for the school tuition from the money he received when he sold his home in Swansea after re-marrying and moving to Canada. Dad did, after all, pay for some of my higher education.

I had discussed these plans with Russell and told him I realized he would be alone with the kids to fend for himself for that six-week period of Florida schooling. He said there was no problem. I went and did well at the school but when I returned home I found out my daughter had been rushed to the emergency room by her friend's parents a few weeks earlier with a severely twisted ankle, and her father was nowhere to be found. They had to call her Grandma to get a permission slip signed before the emergency room would even agree to treat her. They had kept all this from me for two weeks; I had called home to check on how they were doing at least every other day. They always said everything was fine and gave me pep talks to get me through my schooling. When I returned home, Melissa was still on crutches. That's when I heard the whole story.

Additionally, I found out that all the time I was gone, Russell had been hardly home. The two boys still at home, Larry and Roger, who were now working full-time, along with Melissa, who was almost 16, had literally been on their own. Jerry was temporarily living with *Mémère* Sevigny in Fall River. He had landed a full-time job at Raytheon after he graduated from Wentworth. Of course, the boys were in their twenties and Melissa was almost sixteen. I had cooked and frozen many meals prior to leaving for my schooling in Florida and there was money to buy additional food and whatever else they might need because I had put Melissa in charge of collecting the room and board money from Larry and Roger. These funds were available to her to use at her discretion.

That emergency room incident was the "straw that broke the camel's back." On top of all that Russell had kept his paycheck and never paid one household bill all the time I was gone. I had almost $1,800 worth of unpaid household bills (six weeks worth) to deal with. Now it was over.

I called a lawyer and filed for divorce. Melissa had managed the room and board money well. She used it sparingly for milk, bread and other food items. She had saved a few hundred dollars over that six-week period that I was away at school in Florida. That sure helped to get me through a week because I had no job. Shortly after that first week I took a temporary full-time job doing office work until I could find permanent employment. Trying to land a job in the travel field was out of the question as I would have had to take a large cut in pay. I had to return to what I was qualified for in order to earn a decent paycheck. I then took two other part-time jobs, one doing medical transcription at Bradley Hospital two nights a week and the second as a night cashier at the Heartland grocery store three nights a week. Eventually I found a permanent full-time job, again as a bookkeeper. I continued to work three jobs for almost a year to catch up and get on my feet financially.

Russell didn't fight the divorce but he wanted a one-half share of the house. It's a long story about that long and bitter struggle to obtain the divorce and keep the home I had raised my children in. It took more than a year to finally get what I felt I was entitled to. The divorce was granted in late December 1986 and was final in the spring of 1987. I did get to keep my house along with the balance remaining on the mortgage. He kept his new camper, his new GMC Jimmy and his EB Credit Union savings account.

As part of the divorce agreement, I did get Russell to agree to contribute $1,500 per year for each of Melissa's four college years. This, along with him trying to get half the house, was part of the delay in the divorce being granted. He didn't want to commit to any financial help for Melissa's college. He finally agreed to everything after I relinquished my rights to part of his future pension from EB.

Jerry, my oldest, was married on June 22, 1985 to Sheree. This was just a few short months after I had filed for divorce. They were married in Salem, Massachusetts and later purchased a condo in Merrimack, New Hampshire after Jerry left Raytheon and had taken a job with Kollsman.

I felt so guilty that I hadn't tried to hang in there a few more years as there was still Melissa to get through college. She was scheduled to start her freshman year of college in September 1987, not quite six months after my divorce would be final. All through the long divorce negotiations, which took more than a year and a half, I had asked myself how I was going to manage to help Melissa with her college education costs as a single parent.

*   *   *

If Russell would have kept in touch with Melissa after the divorce, maybe today she would have a relationship with her Dad. Any other man would be so proud to call her his daughter. I remember saying to him on the day the divorce was granted, "Russ, I'm sorry things didn't work out with us, but we did have some good years. I want to thank you for Melissa, our beautiful and intelligent daughter. Without you, I would not have her. She is so precious to me." He said nothing, just walked away from me to catch his plane back to Idaho where he was living. After the divorce, he did keep in touch with Melissa through the next four years and did attend her college graduation. But a few years after her college graduation, he just stopped keeping in contact with her.

Did I mention that he remarried even before our divorce was final? Although the divorce was granted in late 1986, it did not become final until six months later, in April 1987. In fact, he had to have a second marriage ceremony because the first one was invalid. Technically, he was a bigamist for that caper. Later, I found out that "another retirement party" was really meeting up with "D" at the campground where he had that secret new camper stashed. "D" became his new wife. She was 22 years younger than he was and just a few years older than his oldest daughter, Doreen.

In retrospect, when I reflect on those twenty years of marriage to Russell, I do realize that we had many good years. The first ten were definitely good years as we shared some great times as a family. I do feel that from the time Larry was transferred to the private residential school in Wisconsin our marriage started to really deteriorate. My whole paycheck from the full-time job and the extra I made holding down the part-time job then went into the education fund to meet the private tuition bills. The boys' Social Security benefit check covered all their clothing, dental and medical needs and, if there was anything left, it too went into the Education Fund. These were the "pit" years as money was now tighter because of the commitment to all that private education. I guess all those "pit" years were taking their toll on Russell, but he never talked about it. He withdrew into his silent shell more and more.

Now, more than twenty years after our divorce and my reflections of the twenty years before the divorce, I can now say life is funny with all its twists and turns and it's up to us to learn from our own mistakes. I hope I have and I also sincerely hope Russell has. He still calls me from time to time from North Carolina where he now resides. He and his wife adopted a boy, so he now has a son to carry his family name. That was very important to him. His son is now 21; Russell is 76. Time has not been to kind to him; he has had heart by-pass surgeries and has other health issues. His wife is a diabetic and doesn't work. Last I heard he was still working part-time as a security guard to supplement their income.

*   *   *

When Melissa began visiting the college campuses she was interested in during her junior year at Bay View (I had just filed for my divorce), we were overwhelmed with the tuition requirements. I recall Melissa saying that she could always attend a local community college or state college to save on the room and board. She could commute from home so that meeting the college costs would be easier for us. I told her to just apply to all the colleges she was interested in, no matter what the costs were, and we would just have to wait and see how their individual financial aid packages worked out before we could make a decision about a college. That was blind faith on my part, since I really had no clue as to how I could possibly manage to pull yet another ace out of the deck.

She was accepted to Simmons College in Boston in the spring 1987, as well as two other private colleges. She was most interested in Simmons, but we agreed that she would go where she got the best financial aid package. We had been assured by the admissions and financial aid staff that they would come up with a very good financial aid package for Melissa, but we had no idea of how much we would need to come up with for September when the first tuition payment was due. I had faith that God would provide and He did.

Because of our financial situation and her excellent academic standing, she qualified for many grants and scholarships, both from the colleges and those private scholarships that she applied to on her own. Also, Simmons had just instituted a new Honors Program Scholarship that would be an award of a $10,000 per year renewable for four years if the student maintained her excellent academic standing.

I was prepared to raid my IRA retirement account or to refinance my house, if needed, to make the tuition payments. I was determined Melissa would not be saddled with student loans for her four years of college, yet I was not sure I could pull another ace out of the hole for four more years.

As it turned out, Melissa was awarded a Simmons Honors Scholarship. Was this a miracle? Yes and no. It was Melissa coming up with her own "ace in the hole." That was not a miracle. Her excellent academic standing and her hard work through all her pre-college school years were bearing fruit. She had really solved the dilemma of paying for a prestigious college education herself. As it worked out, with the Honors Scholarship, the smaller private scholarships and grants she had been awarded, the $1,500 from her father, and her own contribution from her savings (that paycheck from McDonald's part-time work was saved weekly), my share of the costs for that first year was approximately $1,500. The first year's total cost for Simmons which included tuition, room and board, books and other related expenses was $16,000. My $1,500 share was a bargain.

Remember the question: Was this a miracle? I just gave you the reason why it wasn't a miracle. Now I'll give you the reason why it was a miracle, too. The miracle was that this Honors Program Scholarship had just been started. It did not exist prior to Melissa's freshman year of college. The miracle was that Melissa was in the right place at exactly the right time.

Each year, her scholarships were renewed and she continued to work at McDonald's on school breaks and during the summer months. We shared my car when she was home on break and during the summer. This was to save money to be able to meet the balance of the college overall costs and expenses each year. I don't have the exact figure but to the best of my recollection my outlay over her four years at Simmons was about $8,000. Considering the actual total cost for those four years was more than $60,000, you could say that my share was "the deal of the century." Melissa's work at McDonald's for four years generated close to $8,000, almost all of which went towards college. She worked hard to receive that education, by excelling all those years prior to her college years, earning her that Honors Scholarship, and she saved the majority of what she earned at McDonald's, during four years of high school and all through college (and after). She sacrificed, too. She could have insisted on getting a car after high school graduation. She shared my car instead and eliminated the added expense of car insurance. Her education was her priority.

During all her years at Bay View and college, we never purchased a prom dress or a special dress for any occasion at the school. She borrowed all the dresses she wore. Some of these were from Sheree, my daughter-in-law, who had made many of them and worn them herself during her high school years. Just imagine how much money we saved not having the expense of prom dresses.

I have many great memories of her years there. I especially recall the Mother-Daughter weekend held during her senior year of college. This is when I met Anna Pacheco, Lisa's mother. Lisa was one of Melissa's best friends at college, and they are still close friends to this day. Anna and I also remain friendly to this day.

Melissa came home to live after college so she could save money to buy her first car and to make plans to share an apartment in the Boston area where she worked. She commuted from East Providence to Boston, fifty miles each way, by train every day for six months to get to and from that first job. What a trooper! Within a few months she had saved enough for the down payment on a new car, a "no frills" Blue Ford Escort LX (with no cassette player and no air conditioning). She also had enough to pay her car insurance for one year thanks to help from her brother Roger who loaned her $1,000.

The economy was bad. She was lucky to land that first job in her field. The starting salary was $16,500, less than the cost for the last year of college tuition (not that she had paid the full amount), so she also kept her weekend job at McDonald's where she had worked all through high school and college. She took the first full-time job offered to her at the PR agency where she had interned her last semester of college. Four months later she landed a better-paying job at The Stride Rite Corporation. That was enough to fund her move to Boston. She moved into an apartment with two roommates in Brookline, a suburb of Boston, in February 1992. We all helped her to get settled there, supplying hand-me-down furniture, extra pots, pans, dishes and linens and whatever else all of us could spare.

I will mention here that all through her four years at college, her brothers helped out with money, sometimes just passing her an extra $20 when she came home for the weekend. Before college graduation, when she began interviewing for her first job, it was Jerry and Sheree who took her shopping and paid for all her appropriate business outfits. They knew Melissa's funds had totally been depleted and that mine were close to being depleted too.

CHAPTER 29

The ten years of my life, between 1987 and 1997, were the years of intermediate, more enjoyable roller coaster rides.

I had met Walter in spring 1987, just a few weeks before my divorce from Russell was final. I won't go into a lot of detail here, but will just say that over that summer he moved in with me. Melissa would be going off to college in September. Roger and Larry were still living at home, but were working full time and paying room and board. We did not marry. I did not want to hear of marriage. I had just ended a twenty-year marriage and wasn't about to jump out of the frying pan into the fire, as they say. Walter and I got along well, we enjoyed the same things and we were both satisfied with our arrangement.

We enjoyed going out on his boat, camping in a tent on some weekends and eventually he sold the boat and we became full-time campers from April through mid-October. He later purchased a used motor home which we used to travel going to different campgrounds almost every weekend. After a few years, we decided to go as seasonal campers and he purchased a used tag-a-long camper unit. In the fall and winter, we took many weekend trips to Cape Cod and to Canada to visit my Dad.

We also went to France for ten days in May 1990, while Melissa was studying in *Nantes* during the second half of her junior year at college. French was her second major. She was able to see a lot of Europe during her weekend travels using her student Euro rail pass. This was very frugal traveling as she had limited funds. She can tell you stories about sleeping in youth hostels and even a convent, of sleeping on the train while traveling to her next destination, and of traveling light with just a backpack of bare necessities, wearing shirts inside out when they got dirty to save on laundry costs.

A few months prior to our departure for France, I had a gall bladder attack that almost resulted in having to cancel that France trip. I was put on medication and although my doctor advised against the trip, I decided I was not giving up my dream of seeing France after all the sacrificing I had done to pay for it. Having been interested in genealogy for many years, and having successfully traced my roots back to France, taking that trip was a must. I had certainly used that old trick of putting more water in the soup to come up with the $1,500 I needed for that trip. I said a special prayer, asking my Mom to intercede for me, and to let me take my trip with no gallbladder attacks. The trip was great! Besides going to Nantes where Melissa was attending school, we visited the *Normandy* and *La Rochelle* areas and spent the last two days in *Paris*. I had no gallbladder attacks. Believe me I was extra careful as to what I ate since the doctor had warned me about eating rich foods. I have a large album of photos and mementos of that France trip and I often relive all the happy, good memories of that trip.

Four months later, in September 1990, I had to have laparoscopic surgery to remove my gallbladder. No big thing. It went well and I was able to return to work after only five days. In October, Germaine, Dad's wife was hospitalized and diagnosed with cancer. It was very quick, as the cancer was well-advanced. She died one month later, in early November 1990.

A year later, in September 1991, my very first mammogram at age 50 detected the big "C" in my right breast. A lumpectomy was performed and, afterwards, I underwent twenty-five radiation treatments. At this time, with the recommendation of my surgeon, I changed my primary care physician to Dr. V, an oncologist, so that I could be checked regularly for the possibility of that cancer showing up again somewhere. My younger sister had had breast cancer two years earlier. I was able to return to work in a very short time. The next six years were event-free, medically speaking.

Larry, who was still living at home, met and married Mary in August 1992. Mary had one son from her previous marriage. Michael was three when Larry and Mary married and I became an instant grandmother. As Jerry and Sheree had not yet started a family, Michael was sure a bonus. I was just about to give up hope of ever being a grandmother. Three years after they were married, Larry adopted Michael and he became an official "Sevigny."

Roger was still living at home. In 1993, I decided to cut the apron strings. He had been living at home since finishing his associate's degree at New England Tech ten years earlier. He was almost 30 years old and it was time to leave the nest. I told him he had to go out on his own. I explained that if anything ever happened to me, I had to know he was settled and able to survive on his own. He would never learn to fend for himself or become independent if he stayed living at home. I helped him with the paperwork to get pre-qualified for a first-time homebuyer's mortgage and went house hunting with him. We found a small two-bedroom house in Warwick, Rhode Island. He obtained a mortgage and moved to his own little place in late spring 1994.

Walter and I were alone after being together for seven years. During the next three years we continued with our routines of camping, trips to Cape Cod and to *Québec*. I worked every day, and he ran the errands, did the grocery shopping, took care of the yard work and kept busy. He was retired on disability due to a back injury some ten years earlier. He was financially well off as he had three pensions, plus savings from the sale of his house when he divorced. His children were all grown and on their own, so aside from giving them a helping hand here and there, he had no financial obligations. Life was pretty good for the two of us.

In the summer 1996, Jerry and Sheree came to spend the day at the campground where we had a seasonal site and camper. It was on that day that Jerry said to me, "Mom, remember when you told me to never come home with a package?" At first I didn't get it. Then the light bulb lit up and I said, "Jerry, don't tell me you're pregnant?" He replied, "No, mom, but Sheree is." Talk about a surprise and a shock. They had been married twelve years and I had just about given up on the two of them producing a grandchild. Andrew was born January 6, 1997. Jerry was so proud to have his son. The Sevigny name would carry on.

Melissa, who was married in September 1995, is godmother to Andrew. Unfortunately, after eight years of marriage, she divorced. I won't go into the details, but I will say when it doesn't work, it just doesn't. That's a fact. She did not rush to get a divorce. She really tried to make her marriage work. Eventually, she met her true soul mate and remarried in 2008. Phil, my new son-in-law, is an English bloke and a true sweetheart. Melissa officially took his last name but retained her maiden name as her middle name. I know that in the future they will eventually end up residing in England.

In early 1997, Walter and I, after much deliberating and discussion, decided that after being together for ten years it was safe to get married. We knew each other well and got along so marriage was now acceptable to both of us. We had a very small wedding with fewer than fifty people, officiated by our local Justice of the Peace, on April 14, 1997. We only took a weekend trip to Cape Cod for our honeymoon. Camping season was starting the very next week and we didn't want to miss any part of that whole season as we both enjoyed it so much.

Life continued to be good! All my children had their own homes and were doing well financially. I had two grandsons, Michael and Andrew. I was looking forward to retirement in a few more years. What more could I need or want? At this point I felt like my life was truly like a bowl of cherries with very few "pits." That feeling was short-lived as I was soon to find out that I would be riding the mother-of-all-roller-coaster ride.

CHAPTER 30

Hang on everyone . . . you're about to join me in reliving my scariest and longest roller coaster ride, the one that is now officially referred to as the "mother-of-all-roller-coaster ride."

When I went for my annual mammogram on September 4, 1997, I asked the technician if she could get compression films of my upper chest area, right-front shoulder and underarm areas. I explained to her that for almost a year I had felt a pulling, tightening sensation in these areas. Although Dr. V had assured me on several visits it was "nothing" and probably an after effect from the radiation I had after that earlier lumpectomy, I was still concerned about what I felt.

My exact words to the technician were, "I'm not worried about that right boob, but this pulling does concern me." She said, of course, she could take compression films of those areas. I recall that when she did, it was five times more painful than when she did the routine compression shots of the actual breast. Tears were running down my face, but I couldn't move, not even slightly with a sob or a gasp, during that procedure, so I didn't dare cry out in pain.

Four days later, September 8, 1997, I received a call from Dr. V himself. He first identified himself as Dr. V and then right out of the blue he said, "How long have you had that mass in your chest?" After catching my breath, having heard those terrifying words, I said to him, "Dr. V, if you recall, I have been voicing my concern about that pulling, tightening sensation in my right shoulder and underarm areas for quite some time, and you assured me it was nothing and probably just a reaction to the radiation treatments I received after my lumpectomy six years ago." He said, "Well, that's neither here or there. You have to see a surgeon immediately."

I was so miffed—no, I WAS PISSED—at him. I silently asked myself why he had ignored my concerns all those times. I reprimanded myself for not seeking a second opinion when I first experienced that pulling sensation and did not feel comfortable with Dr. V's response to my concern. I had seen Dr. V in January 1997 for a large cyst on my chin. Years later I read an article that stated that infected cysts could be an indication of cancer. I again saw Dr. V in March 1997 for a bad case of the flu that kept me out of work for two weeks. I often wonder if my immune system was compromised back at that time because the cancer was growing in me, undetected. I saw him again in May 1997 for a urinary tract infection that, again, I had difficulty fighting. The history of those last nine months surely indicated my immune system was out of whack as I was having recurring infections that I had difficulty fighting; but I had not really analyzed those infections back then. So many things went through my mind. I mentally relived the horror of more than thirty years earlier when I heard those terrible words from Dr. DeVillers about Bob's cancer . . . "four to six weeks" he had said. All of this flashed through my mind at a speed of warp 10, literally in just a few seconds.

After telling me I had to see a surgeon immediately, I told him my former surgeon Dr. Dorman (gallbladder and lumpectomy,) had died, and I didn't know who to see. He said he would contact a surgeon from Dr. Dorman's practice and get back to me. Well, it wasn't fifteen minutes later that Dr. S's office called and told me I had an appointment for the next day, September 9, 1997. Now, you all know how long it takes to get a doctor's appointment. I wondered what Dr. V said to this surgeon that I was given an appointment for the very next day? Hmm, I wonder. And so, the mother-of-all-roller-coaster ride began with that fateful phone call from Dr. V.

Years earlier, my children had a big scare, especially my boys, when a lump had been discovered after my very first mammogram at age 50. I had a lumpectomy followed by a course of radiation. Now that big "C" was in their lives yet again. Their father had died at age 26 of cancer. They had a reprieve from fear of the big "C" for quite a few years after my lumpectomy, but now it was back. Lord, I can imagine what went through their minds when, eventually, I had to tell them that cancer word was invading all our lives again.

Melissa, my daughter, will have to be vigilant with the big "C." Both of my sisters have had breast cancer too. There is definitely a cancer gene on the Berube side of the family. Of the twelve children in my Mom's family, at least five died of some form of cancer, including my Mom, who died from multiple myeloma. Several of my first cousins on Mom's side also died of various types of cancer. Melissa has had mammograms since age 30.

Getting back to hearing those horrible words from Dr V, the next day, September 9, 1997, when I saw Dr. S, he did a needle biopsy right there in his office. When I returned for my second visit a few days later, he had the results of that needle biopsy. He confirmed that the cancer was back in that same breast as my previous lumpectomy. He told me I needed a mastectomy. The pre-hospitalization tests were scheduled without delay. I went in for the surgery on September 29, 1997.

I was released after a few days and told to see Dr. S in about one week to have the staples removed from the incision. At that office visit, he examined me and then told me he couldn't remove the staples just yet as my wound was not healing as well as normal due to the previously-radiated skin after the earlier lumpectomy. He then told me, "We didn't get it all." I stared at him and literally could not speak for almost a full minute. Then I asked about the pathology report. He told me it was a Stage 3 sarcoma in my chest wall above the area where he had removed the breast, including all my lymph nodes. He told me it was possibly radiation induced. Talk about shock! I really don't know how I managed to not pass out. Another appointment was made with him for the following week when the staples would be removed. In between those visits he sent me for x-rays, body scans and several other tests. When I next saw him to have the staples removed, he told me I had to see another surgeon immediately, repeating that they "had not gotten it all." I was living another nightmare. I remember asking him why he couldn't do the surgery and he said, "You have to see a thoracic surgeon." Hearing another surgeon was bad enough, but hearing the thoracic part scared the heck out of me.

He scheduled me to see Dr. G, the thoracic surgeon. Within two days I was at Dr. G's office. Again, I didn't have to wait three weeks or longer for an appointment. Dr S had seen to it that I would see the thoracic surgeon without any delays. I saw Dr. G who explained that the cancer was in the right chest wall, down to the ribs and a radical surgery protocol was needed. I believe it was he that first said that I was almost Stage IV. He also told me it was an aggressive sarcoma and agreed with Dr. S that it was most likely radiation induced. I was in fact Stage 3B. He explained the proposed protocol to me. They would go in to remove all the cancer-infested flesh and remaining muscles, along with at least three of my ribs. My entire *pectoralis major* muscle had been removed when Dr. S performed the mastectomy. A synthetic plate would be inserted in the area where the ribs were removed to cover and protect my lungs and right chest area.

That "insert" as Dr. G explained to me was not so accurate a description. Much later when I was reading the surgery notes (I had obtained copies), I realized they actually had to drill holes in my breast bone and side rib areas where the ribs had been cut to wire this plate over my chest wall cavity. I had to undergo endless tests prior to that surgery to determine if I was able to withstand this radical surgery which, at the time, he estimated would take six or seven hours. He further stated that I also had to see a plastic surgeon, Dr. E. He would have to graft skin from my right thigh and buttocks to cover the plate that would be inserted, after padding it with the *latissimus dorsi* (crescent) muscle they would harvest from my right back/shoulder area, rotating it to cover the chest wound. I saw Dr. E just a few days later on October 21, 1997. In retrospect, I realize these three doctors had been conferring about my case and planning the protocol from the very first day after the mastectomy, when Dr. S found "he couldn't get it all."

The preadmission testing, scans, breathing tests, etc. all took place over a period of just a few weeks. In this timeframe, I also changed my primary care physician and was lucky to have Dr. Vincent Armenio take over my case just ten days prior to the scheduled surgery. This was around October 20, I believe. He was also an oncologist as well as a hematologist. I found him through my friend Judy. He was her mother's doctor. I had good vibes when I first saw him. He spent well over an hour with me going over my history. He told me he would be consulting with my surgeons before my scheduled surgery. In fact, Dr. A told me the patient file and notes he had received from Dr. V's office, when I requested all records be sent to Dr. A, were of no use to him. He said they were incomplete and nowhere was it noted that I had ever complained of that pulling in my right shoulder, underarm and upper chest areas.

The surgery was scheduled for October 31, 1997, yup, Halloween. That should have been an omen to me.

The Department of Radiology at R.I. Hospital had been contacted by Dr. S, as they had administered the twenty-five radiation treatments six years earlier. At the time of one of my preadmission testing appointments, the radiation team, headed up by Dr. C, met me in the waiting area and asked to speak with me. We all proceeded to a small consultation room. She explained to me that they wanted to do brachytherapy in conjunction with my thoracic surgery.

They had already discussed this additional protocol with Dr. G, and he agreed it was a good idea. They explained it all to me saying that tubes would be laid out in the chest cavity area during surgery, after all the cancerous tissue, muscle and ribs had been removed. After the synthetic plate was inserted the catheters would be laid down leaving one open end sticking out and sutured to my underarm area. Five days after the surgery, a radiology team would come to my room and insert the radiation pellets into these implanted tubes through that open end.

Brachytherapy is essentially internal radiation. Since the patient can emit radiation which might endanger others, I was told I would have to be in isolation for 90 hours during this radiation phase of the protocol. They felt this approach gave me a better chance of beating this very invasive cancer, a sarcoma of the chest wall. They felt this was extra insurance in case all the margin areas of the cancer could not be completely addressed at the time of the actual surgery which they referred to as a chest resection. After consulting with my primary care physician, Dr. A, I agreed with their proposed internal radiation protocol and signed the necessary consent forms.

On October 31, 1997, Halloween Day, I underwent the thoracic surgery, brachytherapy catheter positioning and plastic surgery—all at the same time. In total, it took thirteen hours. It wasn't the original six-to-seven hours Dr. G had discussed with me. Besides removing the ribs (five in all) from the sternum to the side, and the remaining chest wall mass (muscles and flesh etc.), they also found the cancer was in the right vasculature area (blood vessels) in my right underarm. That is partly why that part of the surgery took longer than they expected.

Besides all that, the positioning of the brachytherapy lines took considerable time. The plastic surgery took up even more time. During the plastic surgery, the surgical team grafted skin from my right thigh and buttocks to cover the plate, since none of the old skin from my upper chest area could be saved because it had been damaged by the previous radiation. They also rotated a crescent-shaped muscle, the *latissimus dorsi*, from my right back/shoulder area to place over the plate, padding it so to speak, before covering it with the grafted skin. Is it any wonder that all this took thirteen hours?

I remember much later my kids told me it was close to midnight before the family received the call that the surgery was over and it was explained to Walter that the additional time it took was due to the fact that they had found a blob of cancer in some blood vessels of the axilla area. My family must have been basket cases. They never really told me what was going through their minds while waiting for that call while each hour passed after the six to eight hours that Dr. G had initially estimated it would take. I can only imagine their anxiety and fears, since it took thirteen hours in all.

Earlier I did my best to explain the thirteen-hour surgery of October 31, 1997. I realize that explanation is totally inadequate. What follows is what was actually done in the words of each of the surgeons and the brachytherapy team. I have copied all of this from the actual operating record notes that I obtained later on, way after my surgery.

From Dr. G's operating notes, thoracic surgeon

Resection of right chest wall was done with an elliptical excision from the sternum down to the axilla. This incision involved the resection from the previous operation (mastectomy) as well as all the tissue over the chest wall; this now exposed the entire muscle mass over the anterior portion of the chest wall. Of note, during anesthesia a double-lumen general endotracheal anesthesia was used therefore, the right lung was deflated during this surgery. After removing the chest wall mass, ribs T2 to T6 were partially resected. It was also found that the mass was also involved in the vasculature in the right axillaries region. This was removed with proper hemostasis and surgical ties on the veins and lymphatics in that area. After removal of the mass, methyl methacrylate chest wall reconstruction (the "plate") was done with placement of no absorbable sutures through holes made with a drill. After placement of this methyl methacrylate, chest tubes were placed as well, both inferiorly over the diaphragm and superiorly in the apex. After further removal of as much of the recurrent mass AS POSSIBLE, the radiation therapy surgical team was called in for placement of after-loading catheters into the tumor bed.

From Dr. C's operating notes, radiation oncologist

The tumor bed measuring 8 x 5 cm was located on top of the neurovascular bundle beneath the right *pectoralis* muscle which had been resected (removed). Identification of muscles, arteries, nerves and veins in the region of the operative bed was made and the tumor was clipped superiorly, inferiorly, laterally and medially using single clips by Dr. G's surgical team. These clips represented 2 cm margins around the area at risk. The tumor bed was without evidence of gross visible disease as the tumor had been previously resected by Dr. G. A single plane implant was decided upon with a 2 cm margin around the area at highest risk. Having first outlined the approach with an inked pen with spaces placed at 1 cm, using a curved trocar along the lateral aspect of the wound, closed after-loading catheters were placed threading the catheters through the trocar and suturing them into the tumor bed with 2-0 chromic sutures. A total of six after-loading catheters were placed then secured to the skin using half moon plastic buttons followed by stainless steel buttons. They were then threaded over the after-loading catheters, crimped and sutured to the skin with silk sutures. The case was then turned over to Dr. E.

From Dr. E's operating notes, plastic surgeon

Chest wall tumor had been resected by thoracic surgeon and they had reconstructed the bony portion of the right chest wall using (plate) methyl methacrylate and mesh (MM). The patient remained with a large skin and soft tissue defect, as well as exposed MM which needed coverage. The defect extended from the mid-axillary's line to the sternum as well as from the clavicle down to the lower ribs. Patient remained in the left lateral *decubitus* (lying down) position. With a scalpel an incision was made from the mid-axillary's line at the edge of the wound, obliquely, back toward the area of insertion in the lumbar region on *the latissimus dorsi*, between the iliac crest and the vertebral column. With the Bovie, the underlying subcutaneous tissue was dissected and bilateral flaps were elevated on the plane of the latissimus dorsi (LD) fascia. The entire LD was exposed along its superficial fascia. Also with the Bovie, the origin of the muscle was then released off the iliac wing and side section was carried medially, all the way to the area of the lumbar vertebra. The dissection of the muscle was then carried superiorly to release the attachments from the area of the midline of the body. The deep fascia of the muscle was dissected to help elevate the muscle from the underlying tissue with care being taken to cauterize all the perforating vessels in this region. The muscle was elevated to inferiorly to superiorly. The superior margin of the muscle was dissected near the scapula away from the *teres* minor muscle. The *thoracidireal pedicle* was identified underneath the muscle as it was being elevated and care was taken to dissect this with scissors, all the way up to near its origin. The branch to the serratus was identified during the dissection and preserved. With the muscle then completely freed up inferiorly, it remained attached at its insertion on the humerus. This was then detached with the Bovie so that the muscle could be completely free to rotate on its pedicle, which was then performed. The muscle was then brought over to cover the anterior chest including the MM mesh. The muscle was then sutured around its periphery to the native chest wall so that the MM was covered, as well as several centimeters beyond. Next, the surrounding skin and soft tissue was advanced and sutured around the *latissimus dorsi* flap, down to the chest wall. An area under the axilla wall was closed using Monocril dermal sutures. Just prior to that two Jackson Pratt drains were placed in the back and sutured into place. Next, from the right buttock and right thigh regions split thickness skin grafts were harvested and were used to graft the *latissimus* flap. The grafts were held into position with staples. No air leaks from the chest wall were detected so the skin grafts were dressed with Xeroform and saline soaked cotton balls for conformity as well as dry, sterile dressings. The catheters which had been placed during the first half of the surgery were also dressed with Xeroform and dry, sterile dressings. Patient's right arm was then abducted and flexed at the elbow at 90 degrees and placed in a sling. Elastoplast tape was then used to hold the dressing over the skin grafts in place, as well as to hold the right arm in the position mentioned previously.

*   *   *

I will just say that, in layman's lingo, they SURE DID A NUMBER ON ME.

My oldest son told me later (much, much later) that he had been calling Walter every half hour after the first six or seven hours had passed. He kept asking, "What's taking so long?"

I imagine none of them got to bed before 1:00 a.m. and even then falling asleep must have been very difficult for all of them.

Larry told me that he and Walter did come to the recovery/intensive care area early the next morning. I still had a tube down my throat and couldn't speak. I tried to scribble what I wanted to say on a piece of paper. He said I complained that my throat was sore. He said he was shocked when he first entered the area and was afraid he would collapse right there. He had to leave and go out to the hallway to get his wind back. He said he didn't know if he could go back into the room as I looked like hell. After a few minutes he did return, but they didn't stay long as I was still drifting in and out of sleep with the strong meds. I do not even recall seeing him and Walter then.

Mid-morning, I was transported to the first floor of the Jane Brown Unit, a temporary room because they were waiting for another room on the second floor to become available. I remember all my family were there waiting for me, and I recall they had to carry Roger out from the room because he almost passed out when he saw me. Of course I looked like hell; I had just been through a thirteen-hour surgery on Halloween.

Within a half hour, I began to experience more and more pain. That epidural catheter that was dispensing the pain meds was obviously not working. It must have been dislodged when they moved me from the recovery room. I recall that I almost rolled off the gurney to the floor when they plopped me on that gurney. Dr. G was immediately called and removed that and substituted it with a morphine pump. I could now press the button at intervals to administer the morphine.

Later that afternoon I was moved to the nursing unit on the oncology floor. My room was the second after the nurses' station. The nurses' station was opposite the elevator doors. My family was called back to the hospital that night, because I was doing so poorly.

A few days later I was moved to yet another room, one designated for the radiation protocol. It was surrounded by brick on all three outside walls of the old Jane Brown Wing and was at the end of corridor after the left turn you took at end of the long hall to the left of where my first room had been.

I don't recall much from those first four days after my surgery; not surprising as I was so heavily medicated. I do recall my friends Annette and Stanley visiting me the day I was walking in the corridor with assistance from Walter. This had to be day five because I know I was not ambulated until the fifth day. That day was also the day that Betsy Isaacson, the physical therapist, taught me how to get in and out of bed alone without any assistance. On the sixth day, November 6, 1997, the radiation team showed up all suited up for protection from the radiation, including lead aprons, head coverings and plastic face shields. They had brought their little "pig." This was the lead container on wheels that contained the radioactive pellets, Iridium 192. Don't laugh. That's what they called it. After hooking me up to some kind of computer monitor and doing other preparations, using long thongs, they loaded the pellets into the catheters tubes that had been positioned inside my chest during the thoracic surgery, through the open end in my underarm area. They were using the monitor to guide this positioning.

Once the pellets were inserted my isolation time of 90 hours began because I was now radioactive. A big poster was taped to the outside of the door to my room. This was a graphic of large skull and bones with a giant X across them. Entrance to my room was forbidden except by the assigned hospital nurses and staff for each shift who could remain in my room for no more than a few minutes at a time. Well, that was no picnic. With the trauma of that major surgery, the extreme discomfort of that plate that limited movement in my chest area (the slightest twisting was painful), combined with the condition of my right arm, still in a sling with severe edema, and the extreme soreness of my right leg and buttocks where they had grafted skin, I WAS NOT in the best shape—and that's putting it mildly. I was a frightening sight to behold—and I was on my own.

Getting in and out of bed to use the bathroom required assistance before this isolation period. I would now have to walk alone to the bathroom and I had just been ambulated the previous day. I was far from being strong. Betsy had taught me, just the previous day, how to roll over to my left, swing my legs over the side, hang on with my left hand and get out of the bed, careful not to tip the little step stool, step into my slippers without bending and without falling just to get to the bathroom or the sink to wash myself. I would have to do this alone with no help during all the isolation period, almost four full days.

Trying to wash myself as best I could was difficult as I had only one hand to hold the washcloth, wring it out and soap it up. I couldn't reach all parts of my body with that whole right side affected. Getting back into bed was also difficult and I had to use the "grip" tool Betsy had brought me to pull the sheets and bed covering over me.

In this severely incapacitated state, for the total isolation period from November 6 through November 9, I was so miserable and so depressed. I cried often. No visitors were allowed and only the designated nurse for each shift could come in to give me meds and change the dressings on my leg, the dressings on my chest and take my vital signs while wearing a special lead apron and remaining in my room for no more than a few minutes at a time. My food was cut up for me outside my room and the tray delivered by the designated nurse. I was left to deal with everything as best I could.

The most difficult part was getting up from the bed to get to the bathroom. When I did manage to finally get to the bathroom on my own, pushing the IV pole ahead of me, I had more difficulties. I had to maneuver that dang IV pole through the door and position it to the front of the toilet. The toilet area was very narrow (this was an old wing of the hospital) and the wall on the side of the toilet was on the right, my bad side, not three inches from the side of the toilet seat. I had to be careful not to bang my right arm or right leg on that wall and cause excruciating pain. I did that just once and the pain was so bad that I never repeated the same mistake. I had an IV line in my left arm. Try to imagine the challenge to wipe yourself after using the bathroom when using your right arm or hand is not possible and you have that damn IV in your left arm. I dreaded those necessary trips to use the bathroom. I also could not wait until the last minute as it took me forever to manage this routine always conscious of Betsy's admonition that I think and follow each step she had taught me so as not to fall from the bed.

I was so lonely with no visitors and minimal contact with nurses or doctors. I could talk to the kids and Walter on the phone and that was literally my salvation. I could watch TV, but daytime TV sucked. The morning shows weren't too bad but the afternoon ones were terrible. I am not a soap opera fan. I did watch the "Oprah Winfrey" show every day at 4:00 p.m. That hour watching her program was truly the high-point of each day in isolation. Thank you, Oprah!

That was the longest, most depressing, "hell-on-earth" ninety hours of that whole hospitalization, or so I thought at the time.

After those ninety hours were up, the radiation team came in all suited up again in their lead aprons and coverings as before, and removed the pellets from those tubes using their long, skinny thongs. They replaced these in the "little pig" from whence they had been captured four days earlier. They had some kind of machine hooked up to me again where they could monitor the location of the pellets on their computer screen to facilitate their removal. They had to account for each pellet that had been inserted.

I cried when my family was then allowed to enter my room. They had all been waiting outside my room knowing my ninety hours of prison time was over. This was November 10, 1997. I was so happy to see them. I cried, but this time they were tears of happiness. Now I couldn't wait to get home, which I hoped would be in a few more days.

I faced yet another hurdle before that was to happen. It turned out that the morphine, Toradol IM and other strong pain meds had a nasty side effect: constipation. How that issue was resolved just two days before I came home is a story all its own. Warning: it's pretty gross, but I felt I should include it, as it was funny, too, at least in hindsight—not so much when I was living through it though.

Melissa had been the one visiting me the night this happened. After she left, I rang for the nurse. I told her I was extremely uncomfortable as I had not had a bowel movement since my surgery ten days earlier. I told her I wanted two old-fashioned soap-and-water enemas to "get rid of my problem." I specified that I didn't want those small Fleet enemas because they just would not work. She said she would put in for the doctor's order the next morning. I told her I was not waiting another night. I needed relief now, and if she didn't call my doctor's service to get the order that night, I would scream and yell all night long and keep everyone awake. I was very loud and belligerent when I said these things to her. I wanted her to get my point. She knew I meant business.

She did not leave my room. Instead, she phoned the nurses' station and instructed them to contact Dr. G's service and put in the request for the two enemas, telling whoever had answered to ring her in my room when the order had been placed. It took almost a half hour before she was informed that they had been ordered, but the pharmacist had said it would be some time before he could put them together. Apparently, old-fashioned, soap-and-water enemas were rarely ordered up.

Eventually, a team of three nurses and aides showed up in my room and joined the one that had stayed in my room. They were all suited up in paper gowns, gloves and hats. After some preparation steps, they proceeded to administer the first enema; this was done right while I was lying in my bed. It didn't work. That's why I had initially asked for two, because I darn well knew that probably one alone would not do the trick. Before starting with the second one, the nurse who had been standing to one side, the one who had remained with me earlier, admonished me to try to hold it as long as I could because that was the last one they had.

I did, but still was not able to hold it for more than one minute. When I began to push to eliminate, it was worse than the labor and delivery I had experienced when I gave birth to my four children. Everything was obviously so compacted from those ten days. In spite of the severe pain, I continued to groan and push as hard as I could. I finally got the relief I so desperately needed. This is when one of the nurses said to me, "Mrs. B., I believe this is a first for this hospital. You have just delivered a five pound ball of chit." (Hmm, I wonder if I should try to get in the Guinness Book of Records! Surely, it was a world record.)

The day before I was released, Dr. G's team came in to remove all the staples from my chest. My sister Lou and Walter were present in the room when they did this which seemed to me to take forever. I remember the face and the beautiful blue eyes of the Italian resident on Dr. G's staff who did this. He was so handsome and young. He joked with me during the whole time easing my fears. My sister later told me there must have been one-hundred staples, at least, and that when they had removed the chest dressings to get to the staples, my chest looked like a piece of raw liver. After all the staples were removed they dressed my chest area.

The night before I came home, Larry was visiting me. I remember I had rung for the bedpan as I had to pee yet again. After at least five minutes I told Larry he had to get the bedpan from the bathroom where it was hung on the wall and he would have to help me as I could not hold it any longer. He did what I asked. When he stood by my bedside I told him to close his eyes, and to keep them closed until I said it was okay to open them. I lowered the bed coverings and told him to just follow my instructions. I then told him to feel for the edge of the bed and to slide the bedpan in until I said to stop. I was lifting my butt with my legs so the pan would slide in easily. I peed, wiped myself with a tissue and then I asked him to feel for the edge of the bedpan and gently slide it out from under me so he would not spill any of the contents and to wait just a few seconds longer before he opened his eyes. I then used my gripper tool to re-cover myself and told him he could now open his eyes. He then went to the toilet, dumped the contents, rinsed out the bedpan and returned it to the hook on the bathroom wall. How many sons would do that for their Mom? I was in a pickle, and he rescued me from having an accident in the bed.

The next morning, thirteen days after that thirteen-hour surgery, I was released from the hospital, on the 13th of November. Although I never associated that number "13" with all this until now when I wrote it out, I guess I could now say it was an omen of a very scary loop-da-loop coming up on the roller coaster ride I was on. Melissa was the one who came with Walter to bring me home. There was a delay in my release, as I had a slight temperature that morning. They debated whether to let me go home or not. I was released that day in spite of that slight fever. A registered nurse was scheduled to come twice a day to change my dressings at home and to check my vital signs.

November 17: Not even a full four days after coming home, I was rushed back to the hospital via rescue squad because I started fever spiking, my temperature getting to as high as 103.4 degrees. This meant serious infection, so back to the hospital I went. I was readmitted to the hospital and was diagnosed with presumed hospital—acquired pneumonia and a urinary tract infection, assigned a regular room and immediately pumped with antibiotics. A multitude of diagnostic tests and x-rays followed the next day confirming the pneumonia and urinary tract infection and to try to identify another infection and its source.

November 18: A chest x-ray showed right lower lung field vs. right lower lobe infiltrate. Clindamycin and ceftriaxone antibiotics were started. A bronchoscopy was performed with intravenous sedation.

November 19: My antibiotics were changed to Vancomycin. I continued to have fever spikes that went up to 103.6. Anaerobic cultures taken of the pleura also grew out Staph *Aureus* and *Enterococcus*. A CAT scan of the chest showed a loculated pleural collection beneath the right anterior chest wall. After surgical prepping, purulent appearing fluid was aspirated from this area. A psychiatry consult was ordered due to my anxiety and tearfulness.

November 20: A chest tube was positioned in between my remaining lower right ribs to drain the fluid building up in my chest cavity. It was repositioned a few days later. (You will read more details on this a bit later on.)

November 21: A right pleural drain and a central line were placed.

November 24: I had a repeat CAT scan which revealed a pleural cavity fluid collection. My white blood count was checked and I was transfused with two units of packed red blood cells.

The pneumonia was eventually brought under control, as well as the urinary tract infection, but they couldn't seem to get a handle on the source or cause of the other infection. While they were trying to figure it out, I was in and out of intensive care with the fever spikes. I would be moved from there to a step-down unit then back to my regular room. This scenario was repeated over and over again as my fever spikes climbed back up to 103.4 degrees. Twelve days passed and still they made no progress on identifying the source of the infection or getting it under control.

November 28: The chest tube became fully dislodged when a hospital worker accidentally stepped on it and pulled it out.

Dr. G was immediately called. He wanted me to give written consent to reinsert that chest tube. This had to be done while I was sedated, but not put under anesthesia. I refused, telling him that I experienced excruciating pain the first time they did that procedure after he had assured me I would be sedated. Then again, a second time, just a few days later when they had to reposition it, again I was not properly sedated and relived the horror of the first tube placement.

Bullcrap—excruciating pain is too mild a description. It was pure and simple torture. Attached to the end of that tube was a metal flange with a point on it. That metal pointed end is what they shoved in between two of my lower ribs. I almost went through the ceiling when they told me to hold my breath and shoved that tube into me the first time. I screamed in pain. I recall that when they sedated me prior to that procedure they had difficulty getting the needle in a good vein due to all the times I had previously been poked. Apparently, what they gave to sedate me (but not put me to sleep so I could follow their instructions about when to hold my breath), was not adequate, because I screamed when that point was shoved into my side. I was still screaming in pain when they returned me to me room. They had to give me extra morphine to calm me down.

I experienced the same horrendous pain when the tube had to be repositioned a few days later. Michelle, a student nurse, was with me when they repositioned it. I begged the doctor to stop as I was feeling so much pain but he plowed right ahead. I was sobbing uncontrollably through the whole procedure and, afterwards, Michelle herself transported me up to my room via the elevator. She was supposed to wait for transport but she knew I was in pain and needed more meds to calm me down. In fact, she told me later she had called her nursing instructor, Mrs. Roche. She met Michelle on my floor and initiated the order for additional medication and told the nurses she would have it signed later by a physician. They didn't dare argue with her because she was tough, having spent many years as a nurse in the armed services.

So, remembering all this, I refused to sign the consent form and told him he had better find another way to get those fluids out of my chest area because no way was I giving permission for a chest tube reinsertion.

November 28: Dr. G had no choice then but to take me back up to surgery, open me up, and to manually extract the fluid—drainage of chest wall abscess. When he did this, he discovered that the chest plate was all infected. Furthermore, when he removed the plate, he found it was infected on both sides. THIS was the cause/source of the infection that they failed to identify for eleven days. After removing the plate, they had to scrape the infected tissues to the bone and pack my chest wall with bleach-saturated gauze to kill that infection.

He left the incision unclosed, skewering me like a Tom turkey, because they had to open that cavity and change those bleach-saturated gauze pads packed in my chest twice a day for at least five days. They gave me extra doses of morphine before these twice-a-day procedures as they were all done in my room. I continued to have fever spikes. Gentamicin was added to the antibiotics I was receiving.

December 2: I continued to have high fevers despite irrigation of the wound. I was poked daily with needles, and I had only one good arm they could draw blood from. Now I had a bad right arm with the swelling and edema and pain and a sore left arm with all the black and blue patches where I had been stuck, further aggravated by the dang IV line. I was brought back to surgery for chest wall wound debridement and placement of a left triple lumen and subclavian catheters. This nightmare I was living was getting worse by the day. The roller coaster ride was getting scarier by the minute.

Aggravated by all the trips downstairs for x-rays and tests, disgusted with the every other day surgical preps and procedures and feeling like a true guinea pig, I became increasingly anxious and stressed. I know from what my children have told me that I was wallowing in a pool of drugs, belligerent, vitriolic and harsh with my words. I was a savage, cruel to them and on the borderline of true paranoia.

My family told me much later on that at one point they were debating whether to have me transferred to another hospital as they were unsatisfied with the way things were not progressing. They felt Dr. G was not giving them straight answers to their many questions. What was the condition of that chest plate when he decided he had to remove it? Was it in the same shape as when it was inserted at the time of the thirteen-hour surgery? Did the brachytherapy have anything to do with the infection, maybe causing the infection, damaging or warping the plate? They asked if he had ever done chest reconstruction with a plate insertion in conjunction with brachytherapy lines before this one. He never gave them a direct or satisfactory answer. Of course, I never knew of these questions until later after I had returned home.

December 4: I was taken to the operating room for a right neck exploration with internal jugular venotomy and clot retrieval, (I had a blot clot in the jugular vein), chest tube placement and more chest wall debridement (debridement means scraping the dead tissue that the infection was killing). After that surgery, Falgyl and Astreonam (antibiotics) were added to the Vancomycin and Gentamicin regimen. I still had fever spikes. After my primary care physician, Dr. Armenio conferred again with Dr. G, I was taken off some of the four antibiotics. Dr. Armenio was convinced they were battling each other. The fever spikes started tapering off after a few days.

December 12: I was back in the operating room for more debridement and the triple lumen catheter was changed over a wire. Dressing changes were continued using Sulfamylon and then later changed to Dakin's solution. I believe it was after this surgery that Dr. G told my children that if he had to go in one more time for debridement, there was a good possibility I would lose my right arm. Jerry said to him, "No way are you going to take her arm." They also left instructions for all the nursing staff and the doctors that I was not to be asked to sign any further consent forms unless a family member was present. Previously, when I signed consent forms I often just signed away never reading what the consent was for. My children knew I was on heavy meds, and they made sure I would not lose my arm because I had signed a consent form while drugged up.

December 16: I was back in the operating room for an omental flap transfer (belly fat and blood supply) for chest wound permanent closure. No more Tom turkey skewering. An abdominal and left chest skin subcutaneous transposition flap with split thickness skin graft from the left thigh and an omental flap were performed. The omental flap was necessary to put a good blood supply in my chest wound cavity as there was none left after all the debridement that had been done. This incision was from my mid-section starting right below my left breast mid-section down to my navel. After that surgery, I had persistent *ileus*, or "disruption of normal gastro-intestinal activity," which did eventually get resolved after they reduced my pain medication.

I was ambulatory, with the assistance of the G-mobile (named after my surgeon, Dr. G), off and on between all those surgical procedures. The G-mobile was a special walker equipped to hold the pump that was attached to that chest tube and to which the IV pole could be anchored so I could walk the corridors, always assisted by an aide.

After the December 16 surgical procedure, I could be out of bed for longer periods. The fever spikes eventually tapered off until they finally did not reoccur.

Those approximately first four weeks in the hospital after I was readmitted on November 17 were HELL. I was crying often, depressed, discouraged and more and more impatient with things not progressing. I remember one time my sister Lou was there one afternoon and I said to her in French: *"Je suis tanné. C'est plat."* Loosely translated it means I am so sick and tired of it all. My sister Lou just recently told me I had also told her to get the hell out of my room one time and never to come back. I don't remember that at all as I was always so drugged up.

I spent another six days in the hospital. I was getting stronger every day. I could walk further and longer each time I did. I still could not eat much of the hospital food. I survived on Ensure®, fruit salads, salad, toast, bread and whatever anyone brought me from the outside world. I couldn't even stand the smell of the food trays out in the hallways. Daily x-rays and blood work continued to monitor my progress and to be on the lookout for a reoccurrence of pneumonia or another infection.

Thankfully, all proceeded well, and I was released to go home on December 22, just three days before Christmas. I recall that the first very night home all I could eat was oatmeal. I recall taking the oral antibiotics that had been prescribed. I could not tolerate these and kept vomiting them up. After a few days, Dr. G said to discontinue trying to take them.

*   *   *

I remember when I had to get up during the night to use the bathroom. I had to wake Walter for him to help me get out of bed. He then had to reposition all the pillows supporting my right arm and hand as I couldn't do this alone. My sister Lou was temporarily living with Walter and me. When she got home from work, she helped distract me from what I was still going through. She was so good to me. We often played cribbage to pass the time at night when Walter went to his room to listen to his music tapes and rest his back. She is an expert cribbage player. I used to get so mad at her because I could never outsmart her moves. I still have trouble to this day to win a few games when I play with her.

She had to assist me in cleaning myself properly after a bowel movement and applying medication for my huge hemorrhoid, a permanent souvenir from that first hospitalization when I was constipated for ten days. As I couldn't twist to the side to properly cleanse myself, she did that for me, along with medicating my butt. I will never forget all the things she did for me, but especially that unpleasant task that she so lovingly accepted and did without complaint. I love her dearly.

During the day, when Lou was at work, Walter would leave me sitting in the recliner and run errands or go wherever he needed to go with his friend Tony. Sometimes he was gone for a few hours and I talked to Judy, Annette, Kathy or Pat "O" on the phone to pass the time. I literally couldn't do much of anything else. I was afraid to fall when I was alone and end up back in that dang hospital, so I stayed put in the recliner until Walter returned home or my sister Lucille returned home from work in mid-afternoon. The kids called daily, Jerry from New Hampshire and Melissa from Massachusetts. Larry stopped in every day as did Mary. Roger called, but did not come by as often as he really had difficulty dealing with how I looked. Larry and Mary were the ones who ran extra errands that Walter had not been able to get done.

Nurses came twice a day to change the dressings and check the Jackson-Pratt drains and my vital signs. A physical therapist came to try to begin to help me gain use of my right arm and hand. Walter had to do practically everything around the house, including laundry and cooking. He also had to help me take sponge baths sitting on the edge of the tub and to get dressed. I was not allowed to shower until almost the end of January when the wounds were healed up enough that those bandages over my chest area were no longer required and the Jackson-Pratt drains were finally removed.

The kids all helped out as much as they could. Whenever they visited me they always brought the fixings for our dinner and did all the work (cooking and cleaning up afterwards). They all had their own lives, jobs and families to deal with. Jerry lived in New Hampshire and Melissa was an hour away in Norton, although she worked in Cambridge, but they came every weekend to help. Roger was twenty miles away. Larry and Mary were next door, and they helped with whatever they could daily. Mary even came to shampoo my hair, yet another simple task that I was not able to do for myself.

*   *   *

Dr. Armenio, my primary care physician and oncologist, scheduled me to begin the chemotherapy protocol the second week in February. My chemo would last for seven months. I had to have a port-a-cath procedure at R.I. Hospital. This was done by Dr. Alban Albian just a week before chemo started. I remember him so well because he was very short in stature and had to stand on a high step stool to perform that procedure. This port-a-cath was necessary so the chemo could be administered through that port as my left arm veins had had it with all the needle sticks and IV's of that five-week hospitalization.

Before chemo started, my Dad came down from *St. Lambert, Québec* with Cousin Lucille and her husband Roland the last week of January. I think it was on January 21, the anniversary of my Mom's death, sixteen years earlier. He had to see me. He had only spoken on the phone to Walter and the kids all that time from Halloween through to Christmas when I came home. He had spoken with me on the phone after I came home just before Christmas, but he was so worried about me that the only way he would be satisfied was if he saw me in person.

When he came through the back door I called out to him that I was sitting in the recliner in the living room, but I couldn't get up to greet him. I was all bundled up in a blanket to keep warm. He walked to the doorway of the living room, looked in, and turned right around to go back into the kitchen without saying a word to me. I know I looked like hell, having lost almost fifty pounds. This certainly was a shock to him. Much later on, my cousin Lucille told me what he had told her about that first sight of me. He said to her in French, "I saw Imelda." Imelda was my Mom who had died of cancer in 1981. The last photograph of her when she was so sick was taken at Christmastime 1980, in her recliner chair, three weeks before she died.

She was sitting in a recliner chair just like the one I was sitting in when my Dad walked into see me that day. She was hospitalized on January 2, 1981 and died three weeks later. Of his three daughters, I have always been the one who most resembled my Mom, especially when we were both healthy. Now, I again resembled her in my recliner chair, looking like death warmed over, I imagine. I can easily see how he looked at me and saw my Mom and what a terrible shock that was to him. Cousin Lucille, Roland and my Dad just stayed for three days and returned to *Québec*; Roland had to go to work.

*   *   *

I started chemotherapy in early February. The schedule was five consecutive days (February 6-10) of chemo treatment followed by a break of three weeks. That is another nightmare I don't wish on anyone. I was sick from the first treatment. On the ride back from the chemo, I had to have a plastic barf bag at the ready as I would often vomit on the short four-mile ride home. When I arrived home, I immediately had to go to bed with a woolen hat, gloves and a heavy sweater. I was always so cold. Chemo week was bad, but for the next three weeks I was somewhat okay. I had to see the oncology nurse to have the port-a-cath flushed weekly during those three off-weeks from chemo. This routine continued for seven months.

*   *   *

In early March, I received a call from Cousin Lucille with devastating news. My Dad had been diagnosed with cancer of the stomach and esophagus. It was well advanced, so it was just a matter of time. There was no hope for a cure or remission. In late March, in between chemo weeks, Walter, Jerry and I went to *Québec* to see him. I had to see my Dad and talk to him. We stayed just the weekend returning home on Monday morning. Jerry was so devastated to see his dear grandfather suffering so much. My Dad was on liquid morphine and had lost considerable weight since we had last seen him in late January, just eight weeks earlier, when he came down from Canada to see me. I often look at the photo of him that I have that was taken that weekend he came to see me. He looked so good. No one would have ever guessed the big "C" was about to strike him.

He was being looked after by my dear Cousin Lucille and her numerous siblings, all my first cousins, who all lived in the same area as my Dad in *St. Lambert*. I knew he was in good hands. I would have stayed with him had it not been for my chemo. Five days later, around the first of April, he was hospitalized.

Both my sisters were able to go up to *Québec* to be with him during the last ten days before he died. They called me regularly to keep me informed about how he was doing. On April 14, my sister Dee called in the early afternoon. She told me they had talked with the nurses and the doctor. They all said that death was imminent, but they felt he was hanging on for some reason.

My sister told me she thought it could possibly be because I wasn't there with them. I was so weak from just having finished my week-long chemo. I had been to see my Dad just a few weeks before; I just couldn't be there now. Dee suggested she call me around 4:00 p.m. and have me talk to my Dad on the phone. She thought that maybe if he heard my voice, it would soothe him and, maybe, he would let go. I told her I didn't know if I could talk to him without crying. She said I'd be okay.

When she called at the agreed-upon time and held the phone to my Dad's ears so he could hear me, I spoke to my Dad in French. I asked him if he was ready. I didn't have to elaborate. He knew what I was saying. He said he was. I told him he had been a good father and husband, and I thanked him for everything he had done for me. I asked if he wanted us to pray together. "Yes," he said.

We prayed in French for five minutes at least. After that, I told him I was going to pray that Jesus come for him soon. Jesus knew he was ready, and Jesus was ready to welcome him with open arms. I could hear him faintly sobbing. I was sobbing too. I again told him I loved him and said good-bye for the last time. I received the call from my sister eleven hours later, at 3:00 a.m. on April 15, 1998 that he has just passed very peacefully. He was 86 years old.

His cancer must have been festering for quite a while, since it was beyond the point of effective treatment when it was discovered. Sometimes I wonder if the sight of me that day shocked him to the point where he really thought I would die before him. He was a fighter. Yet it's almost as if he truly gave up when they told him about his own cancer. He wanted to die before me. I don't think he could have handled my death after what he had been through with my Mom and then with Germaine nine years later, both of them dying of cancer. He had buried two wives in ten years. He didn't want to live to see me buried too.

I returned to Canada for his funeral. Luckily, I had just finished my week-long chemo treatment. Dr. Armenio reminded me of my suppressed immune system caused by the strong chemotherapy and that being in crowds, kissing and hugging everyone, I would be more vulnerable to infection. I literally had no reserves to fight an infection if I did get one. I told him I was going. There was no way I would miss my father's funeral.

In my weakened condition, I made two trips to Canada, eight-and-a-half hours each way, each time, in less than one month, first to see my Dad before he passed and then for his funeral. The first trip was during the last week of March; the second was made in mid-April for his wake and funeral. Between those two trips, I underwent one week of chemo. My son Larry rented a large car so I could stretch out in the back seat for that second trip with my legs over Mary's lap. It wasn't a comfortable trip for her, I'm sure. Walter and Larry took turns driving. I had a tough time when I went the first time in the small mini-van that did not have a long rear seat, but this trip for Dad's funeral was tolerated better.

Much later, a few years at least, when I did have the opportunity to see all my relatives in Canada, they told me that when they saw me at my Dad's wake and funeral, they all were so shocked. They truly believed that I would be next one laid out in a coffin. I truly looked like a walking corpse with my little grey wig, skinny as a rail. I had always been the "chubby" one among my sisters, so, of course, my weight loss was a shock to them. When they first saw me at Dad's wake, I had already lost my hair as I had three chemo treatments in February, March and April, so I wore a salt and pepper wig, which I hated. They had also been kept informed of my ordeal from day one when I had that thirteen-hour surgery. They never imagined I would survive all that. I said to them: "No way was that going to happen. I am a Dube and my father's daughter. We Dubes are tough."

*   *   *

I have thought about all my doctors and the sequence of everything that culminated with that big surgery and what followed. I guess I have to start with Dr. V. There is no doubt in my mind that he was negligent and incompetent. Enough said as I've said it all previously and you don't need to hear it all again.

I recall what happened after I first saw Dr. Armenio just prior to the scheduled big surgery. He had consulted with Dr. G about what protocol would be followed after the initial surgery for the breast removal. Since it was determined that they had not "gotten it all" with the mastectomy, Dr. Armenio had suggested to Dr G that I undergo a few rounds of chemotherapy before the radical surgery was undertaken in an attempt to shrink the "mass" in my right chest wall. Dr. G did not go along with this suggestion and Dr. Armenio deferred to him.

I often wonder that if the alternate protocol and course of action that Dr. Armenio had suggested to Dr. G had been tried first, a few rounds of chemo prior to the big surgery to shrink that mass, maybe a good portion of the complications that followed would have been avoided. Take my ribs, for instance. They removed five, yet the pathology done after they were removed revealed no sign of cancer in the rib bones. Yes, the cancer was in the flesh covering and in between these ribs, but the ribs were cancer-free. So, did I really have to lose five ribs? Would a few rounds of chemo before the surgery have shrunk the mass on top of my ribs, changing the plan to remove those five ribs?

Then there are the lymph nodes. Dr. S removed ALL of them when he did the mastectomy which, of course, resulted in my chronic problem with edema (swelling). Yet again, the pathology reports indicate the lymph nodes were free of cancer. Did they even think to remove a few closest to the affected area and test them for cancer cells while I was on the operating table? Had they done that, they certainly would have found them to be all clear and maybe no further lymph nodes would have been removed. That would have resulted in no chronic edema problem. I do know that today the protocol is to just take a few sentinel nodes and test them before going ahead with total lymph node removal.

Perhaps a second opinion would have revealed an alternative course of action, resulting in a less invasive and debilitating surgery. As they say, it was "my bad" for trusting so completely and not requesting a second opinion.

Always, always, always get a second, and even a third opinion. This is a lesson learned too late for me, but not for all of you.

I'd like to give this lesson to all doctors. They first received this same lesson in medical school. The lesson is: FIRST DO NO HARM. Truly, I feel that some doctors have forgotten that. Reviewing the facts of the pathology reports with the benefit of hindsight must present, at least, the possibility that the surgery was too radical. Perhaps, had they proceeded more cautiously, like waiting for lymph node testing and completing a few rounds of chemo to shrink the mass before surgery, maybe I would not be in so much pain more than ten years after the surgery. Same with the ribs; why not remove a piece of one and wait for a pathology report before going ahead with removing more. There was no cancer in my rib bones per the pathology report.

I recall the day I was discharged from the first big surgery on November 13, 1997. I had a slight fever yet they still discharged me. I had been asking for the bed pan all night long—a sure sign of a urinary tract infection, yet they still discharged me. Why? Why? Why? I often wonder had they not done so and the pneumonia was discovered and treated then, would I have continued to have fever spikes? Most likely yes; they then would have had to find the elusive source of the flesh-eating infection at that time. Instead, I was released. For four days the pneumonia became full-blown and, apparently the nasty, very bad, flesh-eating infection grew, too, although they couldn't identify it for nearly four weeks. It was allowed to progress out of control.

Of course that radical surgery where they removed five ribs and did so much scraping in the brachial plexus region, (the network of the last four cervical and the first thoracic spinal nerves supplying the arm, forearm and hand), and my shoulder area, (relocating the *latissimus dorsi* muscle to cover my chest), resulted in the extensive trauma to my right shoulder, arm and hand. (RSD, the result of that entire trauma, was only diagnosed two-and-a-half years later.)

Then there was the brachytherapy protocol that, in hindsight, I think may have contributed to the massive chest-plate infection. I strongly believe that the synthetic material of the chest plate was affected by that brachytherapy. I don't think brachytherapy had been done before in conjunction with, or at the same time as, a chest-plate insertion. These are questions I should have asked before agreeing to that protocol. I really feel like they didn't really know what effect that protocol would have on the plate. I feel the brachytherapy "burned" or caused that plate to change its composite make-up, causing the infection which then festered undetected.

I also feel that the length of that big surgery, thirteen hours, with my chest open all that time could have been a catalyst to infection. Three separate teams were required for the three phases of that surgery. The doors to the operating room had to open at least twice when the teams took over for the next step of the protocol. Could a microbe/germ have floated in and settled in my open wound? It may sound like silliness to you, but I really thought about this a lot and feel that anything is possible; nothing is impossible. Within four days of being released from the hospital, thirteen days after the surgery, I was back in the hospital with pneumonia, a urinary tract infection and that life-threatening, flesh-eating infection with fever spikes over 103 degrees that they couldn't seem to identify or get under control.

I strongly believe that if I had not refused to give permission to Dr. G to have that chest tube reinserted, they never would have discovered the infected plate until after it was too late, like at my autopsy maybe. I know God works in strange ways, and He made me stubborn for a reason. If I had not been "stubborn" in refusing to agree to that second chest tube being inserted, they would have continued what they were doing. I probably would have died from that infection because none of them ever thought to question if the plate had become infected, which is exactly what happened. At my creation, when God gave me the gift of a sense of humor He also gave me the gift of obstinacy. Yes, it was a gift because that obstinacy saved my life. God knew exactly what He was doing.

I recall two visits to the doctors for follow-ups after my chemo was completed. Dr. G and Dr. E, both said to me, using different phrases, but basically saying the same thing, "Someone up there is looking out for you. Do you know that you beat the odds?" The consensus among all the doctors and hospital staff and anyone who was part of the team effort to pull me through that long ordeal, especially that life-threatening infection, was that the odds of me making it were very slim. One of them told me that they had given me a 20% chance of surviving. When my daughter did the editing of this book, she told me they told them (the kids) that they gave me a 10% chance of beating that infection and surviving. WOW! Methinks that St. Peter has much more clout with the Lord than I ever imagined. You will read more on that thought a bit later.

I recall other things the doctors and hospital staff said to me during that hospitalization. One was, "You have a strong faith." Another was, "You have a great sense of humor." They also all remarked that I had a very loving, caring family.

Obviously, God intervened in all that happened. He spared my life. He had His reasons. He certainly knows how to beat the odds. The biggest reason I did beat those odds was that He and St. Peter conferred daily on my case. This was certainly only after dear St. Peter begged and convinced the Lord to move my name further down on the list yet again. Both were then in agreement that they were not ready to deal with me yet. "Let the poor souls on earth deal with her for a bit longer," they clearly concluded. Besides, I have a strong feeling that my Mom and Rachel Nicole were doing their part up there, so God would spare my life. I'll also relate more on those two a bit later.

So, despite taking the mother-of-all-roller-coaster ride, I'm still here. It's all up to God. Things will progress and eventually end when His plan for me is complete. It's been more than ten years now since that chronic, excruciating pain started. It's long enough in my eyes but apparently not in God's.

I have been to countless doctors and specialists, including the Spaulding Pain Clinic in Boston, associated with Mass General, for a month-long stay in spring 2003.

I've tried acupuncture, therapies, magnets and "healing water" from this jerk holy—roller preacher I saw on TV. After shipping me his healing water, he wanted me to send a donation. What a charlatan!

I've called doctors in California and the John Hopkins Medical facilities in an attempt to find an answer to controlling this pain.

You name it, Jerry has bought it for me: neck massagers, special pillows, cushions, gel therapies, etc. I don't think there is anything he hasn't tried to buy for me with the hope it would give me some relief. He even sent me information on Elliot Hospital in Manchester, New Hampshire, for pain management. He noted in the margin of the page, "I'll come and pick you up and bring you back home. This is not a problem for me." He lives 100 miles from me.

There is no relief. Since God is not yet ready to deal with me, I often wonder how much longer I will suffer with pain.

I can get relief. "Why haven't I done it?" you may ask. I'd have to become addicted to strong pain killers like morphine. At least that would put me in "la-la" land for most of the time. But even strong pain meds do not take away my pain. Sure, I could deal with the pain in that state, but would I be able to stay alone in my own home? Would I fall down and break a hip or something? I am so careful now. I never climb on a stool to reach something high up in a cabinet. I don't try to carry laundry baskets up and down the stairs. Also, would I still be able to drive my car? I don't go far, just to the market, the bank, the post office or to the hairdresser, all of which are no more than five miles from home; but my car is my independence. Taking strong doses of drugs, and it would be mega doses, since normal doses just don't do a thing for me would certainly make me more of a burden to my children and more dependent on them than I am now. In fact, narcotic pain relievers make RSD worse.

So, until I reach the point of "no return" where I can no longer deal with this pain, I'll stay off the strong meds. I pray God is merciful and comes for me in my sleep before I reach the point where I have no choice but to become a "druggie" just to get through each day or to end up in a nursing home because I can no longer stay alone. I must also never forget to end my petitions to him by saying, "Thy will be done."

I know He is a merciful God, and I count on that because there are still very bad days when it is difficult to cope. On those days I sometimes get very angry with Him. I know He truly understands though. I am human. When I regain my senses, I do always try to say I'm sorry for getting angry with Him. I do try to offer up all this pain. That has got to count for something. I trust Him and I trust in His never-ending mercy.

*   *   *

I do want to say a few positive things about that hospitalization. First there was Rachel Nicole, my own little precious saint, who I know interceded for me when I asked her to. Rachel Nicole lived for only seven weeks. She died of a defective heart condition on November 24, 1994. She was the first child born to my nephew David and his wife Laurie. She was my sister Lou's granddaughter. At her funeral, the Monsignor told us that she wasn't an angel as we had been referring to her, but that she was truly our own personal saint in heaven. She had been baptized and was free of original sin and, in her short seven weeks of life, she certainly had no sins to atone for. Thus, she instantly became a saint when she died.

During all those tests and especially when the "vampire" lady showed up daily to draw blood, I asked for Rachel Nicole's help. She never failed me. They had such a hard time finding a good vein in my one good arm that sometimes it took three tries. After a while, the phlebotomists began asking me who Rachel Nicole was because whenever they had difficulty sticking me, I would tell then to hold off a minute so I could pray to Rachel Nicole. I would ask her for a "bingo," meaning for her to use her charms on Jesus to help them find that elusive good vein for blood drawing. She never failed me. I still have my little notebook that the kids gave me at the hospital for me to jot down things I had to remember to ask my kids to bring next time they came. I also used this little note book to record some of the help Rachel Nicole obtained for me. I have Rachel Nicole's picture framed on the wall of my bedroom. I continue to ask for her help in getting through yet another day of suffering with this unforgiving pain.

There are also notations about thanking my Mom for her help in getting me through another day. When I said a few short prayers each morning, I would ask her to intercede for me to receive help from God to get me through another day. My Mom was so good. She passed her strong faith onto me. I knew she was in heaven. I had a lot of confidence in her intercessions on my behalf.

The hospital staff and workers who were especially good to me were also noted in my little memo book. Of course, there were some that were not kind or sympathetic. Those I chose to forget completely. I remember saying short, quick prayers to St. Rita of Cascia whenever someone from the medical team showed up for another bedside procedure, especially the one where they had to unpack and replace those bleach-saturated gauze pads in my chest cavity after the plate was removed and I was trussed up like a Tom turkey. I also asked her to help me stay calm and get through it whenever they had to poke me yet again for more blood or administer yet another test. She always answered my prayers. For those of you who are not familiar with her, St. Rita of Cascia is the female saint of the impossible. St. Jude is the male saint of the impossible.

I fondly remember the student nurse, Michelle August, who took a special interest in me and was so good to me. She told me she learned so much from my case and that she would never forget me. She came to visit me at home with her three small children for several years. The last time I spoke to her, she told me she was now working for Hospice care and specifically with cancer patients. I had been her first cancer patient when she was a young student nurse.

Betsy, the physical therapist, was always so upbeat when she came to my room for the therapy on my arm. She always went the extra mile to get me a neck-roll pillow, or the gadget that I used to grasp things with, like pulling the bed covering over me or retrieving what I had dropped on the floor. She also showed up with treats from the Au Bon Pain® bakery on the first floor. I used to call her Betsy Ross, my American Flag Lady, which made her laugh.

After I was taken off the morphine the nurses all told me how mean and nasty I had been (and vulgar too) under the grip of those strong doses of morphine and other pain meds and when I was delirious with the fever spikes. A few years later, when my kids could talk to me about what had transpired during my hospital stay, they, too, said I had been mean and nasty as the nurses had told me. When the morphine was discontinued and alternate pain meds were prescribed (only after the first four weeks of that second re-hospitalization), I was a totally different patient.

One of those extra special nurses was named Velma. She told me they actually then all fought to get assigned to me for the day when their shift started. This was the opposite of when I was on the morphine, when she told me they would say, "Oh no, Mrs. Barnes, another day of hell," if they happened to the unlucky one to get the assignment. Afterwards, off the morphine, they would come spend their coffee breaks with me, and I'd dazzle them with my sense-of-humor quips. When they went down to the Au Bon Pain shop on coffee breaks, they, too, would bring me back a treat. Velma said I had gone from being the patient from hell to their star patient.

I remember Mary telling me that her dad, Jack, was saying three rosaries a day for me. I know that my daughter called all her friends all over the U.S. to tell them to have me included for prayers in their individual prayer groups. I received many prayer enrollments/cards from family and friends. Everyone and their uncle were petitioning the Lord on my behalf. (I imagine that dear St. Peter was elated at all those prayers being said for me. There will be more thoughts on this again a bit later.)

I received so many get-well cards that every week they had to take some home to make room for the ones that still continued to come in. They were all taped to the wall facing my bed. I have a large plastic bag full of those cards. Every so often I take them out and read them again. Annette, Madeleine, Pauline, Maureen and Jackie T. from Missouri, all grammar and high school friends sent me cards on a regular basis . . . some were uplifting and inspirational, others were funny; all are so precious. Pat "O" sent me beautiful cards that she created on her computer. Many sent me Mass enrollment cards for prayers for my recovery. I could list at least 150 names of those that sent me get-well cards. Melissa's college friends sent me a beautiful lap throw to keep me warm.

I hope someone takes the time to read those cards after I'm gone or put them in a scrapbook to be saved for my grandsons to read later on in their lives. That's if I don't get around to doing it myself. This darn pain sometimes stops me from doing so many things. I have been so involved in this dang book and preparations for my 50th class reunion I haven't done much of anything else. I have many other unfinished little projects to complete like more work on my genealogy records and sorting through all the photos and albums I have.

Believe me, just typing all of text for "my story" was a painful undertaking. First, my right arm and hand really got aggravated pegging away at the keyboard with my old toothbrush held in my useless right hand, resulting in even more pain. Second, it was very emotionally painful to relive some of the memories. Those unfinished projects will, of course, never get completed without more pain but I'll work through it just as I did in the writing of this book.

Now back to some more good things I remember. I remember waking up one morning in the hospital around 6:00 a.m. Jerry was at the foot of my bed. He had driven down from New Hampshire, so he could catch Dr. G on his morning rounds. He wanted answers. He was not pleased with how things were not progressing. This was when they couldn't seem to find the cause of that nasty infection that was literally killing me. I also remember him driving down from work in Merrimack, New Hampshire one night. When he heard I had not eaten much from my supper tray he asked me what kind of pizza I wanted. He went out and drove all around central Providence looking for a pizza place. He should have inquired at the nurses' station as to where the nearest pizza shop was, but he didn't. After at least an hour and half, I got my pizza and ate three pieces.

I remember Melissa staying with me through whole nights when I was having the fever spikes, sleeping in the chair with her winter coat as a pillow, and then going home to shower and change and report in to work in Cambridge. No one else wanted the night shift. She told me that the nurses told her she couldn't stay the night, and she told them to call security because she was staying. Is she kind of obstinate like her Mom or what? After a few nights, they stopped making a big deal of it as she actually made their job easier. They didn't have to check on me as often as she was right there and would alert them if she saw a change in me.

I remember the visits with my grandson Andrew. He was so good. We would sit him at the foot of my bed and we would give him the disconnected telephone to play with. He'd sit there, like a little angel, not moving. If that had been Austin (Andrew's little brother, who was not born until six years later), we would have had to superglue him to the bed. I have a precious memory of that, a photo of me and Andrew in my hospital bed. All of the nurses, especially one named Frances, thought Andrew was the cutest and best-behaved baby. He was the star attraction during visiting hours. He was maybe ten months old. Gosh, how dumb was I? I could have charged admission to my room to all those who wanted to see him. I would have been well on my way to becoming a millionaire back then. Talk about a lost opportunity; that was sure one.

My daughter-in-law, Mary, would often stop in after work as she worked right around the corner from the hospital. She would first stop at the cafeteria downstairs and bring me a treat to eat. Then she could stay with Michael at night and Larry could come to see me after supper. My sister Lou would stop in after work too, almost every day.

Dr. Elizabeth, who was on Dr. G's resident staff, brought me frozen yogurt from the cafeteria when I could no longer tolerate that horrible hospital food. I could eat the cereals and fruits, but not much of anything else. I was literally surviving on Ensure, the treats that the nurses brought me and the food that my kids brought for me.

I remember the very first night I was hospitalized when I was brought in with the fever spikes. Maria, a young Portuguese girl in her early twenties who was on the housekeeping staff, finished her shift at 10:00 p.m. then came to sit by my bed to mop my forehead and face with a wet facecloth as I was perspiring profusely with the raging fever. She stayed with me through the whole night. God Bless her for her unselfish act of kindness and compassion. After that night she often stopped by my room to see if she could do anything for me.

I remember Cousin Leo staying with me one night until I feel asleep, which must have been after midnight. I remember asking him to sing to me. I remember he told me he couldn't sing, but he would tell me stories. I fell asleep listening to his soothing, calming voice. He had to work the next day, and I'm sure he was exhausted as he had worked that day before coming to sit with me in the hospital. He lived quite a distance away in Milton, Massachusetts. I love him almost as much as I loved his dear mom, my favorite Irish Aunt Julie. He's a keeper.

I never want to forget all the good things that happened and the good people that were there for me, boosting my spirits, encouraging me and praying for me. Those are treasures that offset everything else during that mother-of-all-roller-coaster ride.

CHAPTER 31

After I finished the final chemo treatment, at the end of the second week of August 1998, I began to eat better and gain some strength, although I still was on strong pain meds to try to relieve the pain. As I was not diagnosed with RSD (Reflex Sympathetic Dystrophy) until two years later no one realized that strong pain meds would do nothing for my pain. I went for physical therapy for the arm and hand twice a week and had full body scans every three months to check for any sign of the cancer returning.

In October 1998, I attended my 40th class reunion. I was slowly recovering my strength after the chemo. I still just had light fuzz and I attended as a "baldy," refusing to wear that ugly wig ever again. I was even able to put together a *Thévenet* school paper for that reunion with the assistance of my daughter-in-law Sheree.

I still was experiencing a lot of pain in my right arm, shoulder and hand. The edema was a constant problem. I was wearing a Job's sleeve and glove to help with the swelling. I had been fitted for this in early January 1998. I was able to go shopping and walk around the stores for short periods of time at least. I was now able to shower without any assistance from Walter. I still needed assistance tying my sneaker laces or buttoning a blouse. I began driving again, but only for short distances as I tired easily. Walter basically continued to do 95% of everything around the house.

Walter and I had camped all summer. When camping season had begun on April 20, after we returned from my Dad's funeral in *Québec*, I had completed three months of chemo. I had four more months to go. I was able to take short walks at the campground, but mainly I spent a lot of time napping, reading and sitting by the campfire, all bundled up in a blanket. I was always so tired and so cold. After the second week of August, I slowly gained strength and was able to walk further distances during our twice-a-day walks. What I missed was bike riding. That was now forbidden as even the slightest fall could be disastrous. I had no chest plate covering my lungs on the right side. In the fall, we shopped for a new larger camper for the following season. We looked at many models and Walter eventually purchased the one he decided on. It would be delivered for the start of the next new camping season in April 1999. After Christmas, we took a week to fly to Florida to visit his brother Tom and Anna, Tom's wife. This was in March 1999.

When I had started to feel better, I began to notice things had changed between Walter and me. I should say that I then became more aware of the changes. With hindsight, I now realize they had begun after I had come home from the hospital. Walter became more and more verbally abusive and would drive like a maniac, even though I asked him to be more careful. I was so fearful of having an accident with no chest plate to protect my lungs on the right side. I couldn't wear my seat belt as it cut right across my chest area where I had all that major surgery. I realized later, after much reflection on all that had happened since the big "C" made its appearance, I couldn't tell Walter what to do. He just got more abusive and drove even more dangerously.

At first when I returned from the hospital in December the previous year and during all the time that followed, including the chemo and up until this point, I had always made excuses for his behavior. I justified his behavior with the thought that he was the one burdened with me. He had to do everything around the house, plus assist me with bathing/showering and getting dressed. Before the big "C" had surfaced, I was the one waiting on him hand and foot and pampering him. He was the one out on disability because of that back injury. I told myself that as I got stronger, he would be less stressed.

He had never spoken to me in a rude or belligerent manner during the ten years we had lived together, or during the first few months of our marriage, which took place just four months before I had that radical surgery. We had now been together for twelve years.

This new behavior continued and got worse until I reached the point of no return one day in April after we had returned from our Florida trip. We were on our way back from inspecting the new trailer that was to be delivered to the campground in two weeks. This is when he said to me, "Shut the f—up. You're not my goddamn mother." This happened when we were in the car. He was, yet again, driving like a madman, tailgating, with me begging him to please slow down.

I was silent the rest of the way home. My thoughts were all over the place recalling all the incidents since I had returned home from the hospital fourteen months earlier. After he said that awful thing to me, it seems everything became very clear. He was not happy with the *status quo*. He was sick of waiting on me and doing the things I had previously been able to do. He was not happy with the role reversals. Now I guess he thought of me as an unwanted burden. I knew now that I couldn't talk to him. I finally realized he thought he was always right, and God have mercy on the person who criticized him or contradicted him. Who was I to tell him how he should be driving?

When we arrived back home after he had said that horrendous thing to me, I sat in the recliner crying and thinking back on everything since the time I came home from the hospital two days before Christmas 1997. I began to recall incidents where he was downright mean to me or to one of my children when they visited. I recalled making excuses to my kids and to myself about him being under so much stress with the situation like it was. Then, I realized that his past behavior was totally uncalled for.

My kids were helping as much as they could. If he loved me, why was he sometimes so rude to me? Using his being "stressed" to excuse this continuing behavior, which had now escalated to the point where he said that terrible thing to me, was no longer acceptable. The plain and simple fact was that he was not at all happy with our new situation. He wanted things to be as they were before with me in the role of the little waitress and him in the role of being doted on. Besides all these thoughts and analyzing my situation realistically, another thing struck me. When I sat in the recliner that day, he had gone directly to his waterbed and started listening to his 1950s music tapes. He did this frequently over the more than ten years we had been together as he needed to rest his back. He, too, suffered chronic pain with his back condition, and I always thought he needed to rest, but now I knew it was also his way to shut me out. I knew he could hear me crying in the living room, yet he never came to me and said he was sorry.

I now realized that his waterbed routine was his way of shutting me out and of giving me the silent treatment if something had happened or after I had said something that miffed him. Instead of clearing the air, he went silent on me and that had been his pattern of behavior from the very beginning. After the Big "C" changed the status quo, he was increasingly less able to keep silent, thus he had increasingly become verbally abusive culminating with that awful thing he said to me when I had yet again begged him to slow down while driving. I also realized that I had been isolated by him and this isolation began right from the start of our relationship in 1987. He never wanted to visit my friends or do what I wanted to do. It was always what he decided. He always used his back pain as an excuse to get out of agreeing to who I would like to visit or get together with.

I had received a strong wake-up call that day. After replaying in my mind everything that had happened since I came home from the hospital, I realized this marriage was over. Instead of things getting back to normal after I slowly regained strength, our relationship and marriage had taken a definite turn for the worse. Again, the plain fact was he was not happy with the *status quo*. Although he never came out and said so to me, his actions and words over the past year or more made that fact indisputable. I knew I could not live like this.

I made my decision that very afternoon that I was going to get out of this situation. I was going to follow my gut. I went into the bedroom and I told him I would be calling my lawyer to start divorce proceedings. His reply to me was, "Do what you have to do." Well, that sure reinforced my decision. He never said he was sorry for talking to me the way he had, or that he loved me and didn't want a divorce. In other words, he did want *out.* I had been right in my thorough analysis of the situation. I was not afraid of being alone. There are worse things than being alone. Ironically, this was April 1, 1999, April Fools Day, just two weeks before our second wedding anniversary.

I walked over to Larry's house next door and contacted Brian, my lawyer, and told him to start divorce proceedings. I didn't want to call from home so Walter could hear what I said. When I returned home, I told Walter that he could stay in the house for two more weeks until the campground opened on April 15 and his new trailer was delivered. He could move into his new trailer for the season and find an apartment when the campground closed in mid-October. Mostly, he had tools and personal items at the house and, of course, his precious waterbed, which I couldn't sleep in anyway. I had been sleeping in the spare bedroom with the big double bed, my right arm propped up on three or four pillows to reduce the edema. I told him anything he couldn't fit in his trailer he could put in a storage cubicle that could be rented out by the month.

He said "fine." Wow, was I right about him or what? He NEVER said, "Let's talk about this. Can't we work things out? I'm sorry for what I said to you. There is no excuse for my behavior." I now know that in his mind he was saying, "Fine with me, now I won't be stuck with you."

I say this because much later, after the divorce, my children began to tell me things about what had transpired while I was hospitalized and afterwards. Melissa told me that one very critical night, when I was fever spiking, all the family were waiting in the hallway outside my room while the nurses were in with me. The family was then allowed in my room. Melissa had a slight cold and Walter had said to her: "I don't think you should go in. She may catch something from you." She replied to him, "My mother may be dying from a flesh-eating infection and you're worried she will catch something from me? Get out of my way, or I'll knock you over on my way in." Larry said to Walter, "You had better get out of her way."

Melissa said she was so angry because it was her and her brothers that kept in constant contact with Dr. G to get information on what was going on. Walter never had any news as he was never there to meet up with the doctors on their early morning rounds nor did he place calls to Dr. G to have the doctor call him later in the day to inquire as to the progress or non-progress of my situation. Whenever they called Walter, he never had the latest news—saying he hadn't seen or talked to the doctor. They, she said, made sure they got daily updates. Jerry even drove down from New Hampshire, so he could be there by 7:00 a.m. to meet up with Dr. G on his morning rounds. Whenever I was brought back to surgery for any reason and especially for debridements, which happened at least four times, one or two of them were there when Dr. G. finished and met with them after the surgical procedure. Walter was not there when they were told I could lose my arm. They were the ones relaying the latest update on my condition to Walter.

My daughter told me about one particular incident in early 1998. I was sitting in the recliner, so when this actually was said I did not hear it. All the kids and Walter were in the kitchen. I don't really know what had been said prior to this, but he had said to Jerry and Melissa that he was the one stuck with me and they left him all alone to deal with it. Melissa had replied to his comment by asking him if he had not said "for better or worse" when he took his marriage vows. Melissa said he did not like that one bit and walked out of the kitchen and went off to his waterbed and music.

My sister Lou also later told me of his behavior when I was in the hospital. She said when she returned home after stopping in to visit with me at the hospital after work he was in his room with the door shut 95% of the time. When he did come out to speak to her it was about what he had done that day. One time she said all he could talk about was the Winnebago he had looked at with Tony. He never said he had spoken to one of my doctors or that he had some new information on my condition. He was in his own world. She said she fixed her own meals, watched a bit of television and went to bed. She recalled that he had actually fixed supper on only one night, the night he had invited his daughter Susan over for supper.

Many friends later also confirmed my realization that he had controlled me and had isolated me from my friends from the start of our relationship. Walter was never interested in getting together with my friends.

Walter moved out in mid-April 1999 and went to the campground. I was now alone in my condition. Although I was doing much better, I still needed a lot of help. My kids were there whenever I needed them, and I know they were all very concerned about me being alone with what I had been through. I had to purchase a car because when Walter left he took both his truck and the new Ford Crown Victoria he had just purchased prior to our trip to Florida. They were all his and registered in his name. He did offer to sell the used mini-van to me instead of trying to sell it to someone else. He had purchased the Crown Victoria to replace the Mitsubishi minivan. I said no thank you. He sold it to someone locally. He did give me $500 from that sale so I could buy a car. Whoopee! That was generous of him. After he left in mid-April, I shopped around with Larry and bought a brand new car in mid-May, a 1999 Honda Accord. Ten years later, I still have that car and it has less than 20,000 miles on it. That should indicate to you how far I have driven in a ten-year period.

The divorce went smoothly. He kept what was his and I kept what was mine. There was no hassling. It was granted in July and final in October. I wasn't afraid to be alone, but it was sure hard to adjust to actually being alone. This was the first time I was literally alone in all of my life. I went from living at home with my parents to living with my first husband Bob. After he died, I had my three boys. Even after I was divorced from Russell in 1987, I was not alone. I still had children at home. Now, I had to keep the television on all day, and I had to fall asleep watching TV in my room. I couldn't stand the empty, quiet house. I was so lonely. I also went through a severe depressive period that lasted for months; no, make that years. I cried a lot and I know this upset my children when they called me daily.

Cooking was a problem as my right hand was almost useless. I did the best I could, but honestly most of the time I would just heat a TV dinner or make a sandwich. I was always so frustrated at what I COULD NO LONGER DO FOR MYSELF. My kids supplied me with good home-cooked meals when they came to see me, filling my freezer with pre-cooked meals they had prepared. My therapist helped me to pick out some handicap tools from the catalogue.

After I had ordered and received them, some things were more manageable. I got a rocker knife which I could use to cut up meat and sandwiches and vegetables etc. I got a zipper pull that had a button hook on the opposite end. This made it easier for me to button my blouses and zip up my slacks. I purchased a pair of left-handed scissors.

I ordered a small, square cutting board with two prongs. I could place a vegetable on the prongs to secure it and use the rocker knife to cut it up for cooking or for salads. I could also pare a potato for cooking using that prong. It also had two sides that would anchor a piece of toast so I could butter my toast without it moving all over the place if I tried doing this with the toast on a plate. I got an under-the-counter jar opener that I could open pickle jars using just my one good hand.

I suggest that you who are reading this try placing your right hand behind your back and try to do all the things that one does around the kitchen, especially relating to cooking, with just one hand. I think you will then begin to understand my situation.

Melissa solved my problem of tying my sneaker laces. She bought me those curly, stretch laces that young kids use on their sneakers. I could now just slip my sneakers on. She also solved my problem of automatically reaching for a pot handle on the stove when I did do a bit of cooking. Being a right-handed person, I instinctively always reached for the pot handle with my bad, right hand resulting in dropping the pan with its hot contents, nine times out of ten. Besides creating a mess to clean up, it was dangerous as I could have scalded myself doing that. She came up with the suggestion that, whenever I was cooking, I simply tuck my bad, right hand behind me in the elastic waist band of my slacks. This would deter me from instinctively trying to use my right hand while cooking. That worked. Is she not a problem solver like her *Mémère* (my Mom) was?

This adjustment to being alone took many years, not days or months, but years. I still had a lot of pain, and I was so stressed from all that had transpired since I returned from the hospital. My Dad's death, the chemo, the change in my relationship with Walter and finally the decision to obtain a divorce had all taken a huge toll on me. I knew I had made the right decision about the divorce. I never regretted it, but I was emotionally wiped out at this point. I was in a bad depressive state. I cried at the drop of a hat and was angry with the whole world and took it all out on my kids whenever they called.

My kids were all concerned about me, but they knew what I told them about Walter's behavior was true because they had witnessed his behavior when I was hospitalized and especially during that crisis situation with the infection and fever. I only learned of this behavior after I filed for divorce and he was out of the house. My children kept a lot from me about his behavior when I was hospitalized and after I had returned home because they didn't want to hurt me or cause any problems between us. Now that he was out of the house, they felt they could tell me a few things. They had also often experienced his rudeness when they visited after I returned from the hospital.

Their main concern was how I would manage alone. I said I would. Of course, Larry and Mary lived very close, in my backyard practically, and I relied on them the most. The others came down from New Hampshire and Norton as often as they could to help me in whatever way they could. Life went on. There were many, many "snippy" days—days when my children had to deal with my depression, my nastiness, my obstinacy and my crying jags. It took me forever to accept the fact that I had to ask for help and not be so dang obstinate when they offered to do yet another thing for me. Looking back on it now, I realize that subconsciously I wanted to still be in total control. I didn't want to relinquish that control. I was too proud to admit I could no longer do some things for myself. My children scolded me for being so obstinate and, at times, I had to be treated like the child as they were then the parents. Eventually, but I'm sure not soon enough to their liking, I was more receptive to accepting and even asking for more help but that was just as hard as adjusting to being alone. I said eventually but truthfully it was more like five years.

I continued to see my doctors regularly. They all tried to get me relief from the constant pain I had in my arm and hand. I was referred to one doctor after another. I had blood work done every other month. They were monitoring me very closely in case that big "C" reared its ugly head again somewhere else in my body.

I especially recall one visit to the plastic surgeon for a follow-up visit after I had divorced Walter. I asked the receptionist to change the records so that the next of kin for emergency notification would be my daughter because I had divorced Walter. She said, "Good for you. He was so mean to you." Wow, that was a surprise. I never realized he was so abrupt with me when he accompanied me to those office visits. Apparently, she had noticed it. I wondered how many others had.

In late 1999, after getting a referral from Dr. G. my thoracic surgeon, I saw a neurosurgeon, Dr. W. She recommended exploratory surgery to see if she could release scar tissue in the brachial plexus area as well as in the axilla (underarm) area. She felt that pressure on the bundle of nerves from all the scar tissue could possibly be the cause of the unrelenting pain in my hand, arm and shoulder. My sister Lou was with me when I went for that first consultation with her. I did not make a decision then. I asked Dr. G for his opinion of her diagnosis and I discussed it all with my children. I then decided to go ahead with the exploratory surgery with the hopes that I would get some relief from the pain.

That surgery, or should I say butchering, was done in January 2000. She was supposed to try to release scar tissue to relieve pressure on the nerves and specifically the *brachial plexus* bundle of nerves. This leads to the shoulder, arm and hand. For some reason, which to this day is still not clear to me, she decided to remove a piece of my right clavicle. She claimed it was so that she could better access the scar-tissue areas. That missing piece of clavicle ended up making my pain worse, significantly reducing the support for my right arm, and I now had more scar tissue and more pain in the shoulder area. Many more "snippy" days followed that surgery.

Sometime in mid-2000, I saw Dr. B at the Pain Center at R.I. Hospital who prescribed a topical cream, Zanoflex, and other pain meds for relief of my hand, arm and shoulder pain. That was another dead end. I stopped seeing him after three or four visits.

In late 2000 I was diagnosed as having Reflex Sympathetic Dystrophy (RSD) by Dr. B, an orthopedic surgeon that Dr. G had referred me to. This is the cause of my acute chronic pain. It is not curable ever nor is it effectively treatable at this stage. It is a permanent condition. It is crucial that an early diagnosis be made within six months of the event that causes this syndrome. My event was all those surgeries from October 31 through early December 1997. That trauma was the direct cause of the RSD. If only that diagnosis been made soon after my surgeries, when I complained about still experiencing a lot of pain, it could have been addressed and controlled more successfully and possibly the pain would not be as bad as it is today. Almost two-and-a-half years had passed before I was diagnosed.

My daughter Melissa returned with me to see Dr. B. He had sent me for MRI's, scans and x-rays of my shoulder. I recall crying at that visit, too, just as I had cried at the previous visit. Whenever I had to talk about my pain and relive those hospitalizations because I had to answer questions on the forms or by the doctor, I just cried. I was emotionally a basket case.

The test results indicated an unidentified white streak on my shoulder. I also had a small tear in the rotator cuff which he said should not be addressed with surgery as I had had enough traumas to my right side. I was referred to an oncology surgeon for to follow up on that white streak. After that visit with Dr. T, I was immediately scheduled for a biopsy of that shoulder area where the white streak appeared on the films and also a biopsy of the bone marrow. This was done in out-patient surgery January 5, 2001. The bone marrow showed no sign of cancer and neither did the shoulder tissue, but they could not identify that white streak that showed up on the x-rays and other films. It was a mystery to all the doctors and remains so to this day.

My children were all relieved to hear about the good outcome of the biopsies. Much later, my daughter told me what Dr. B had said to her that day when he had given us the results of the tests. As I mentioned I had been crying and when we were leaving he held her back to tell her that that white streak was very suspicious and it could be that the cancer had returned in that area. He waited until I was a good way down the hall leading to the waiting room out of range of hearing him before he told her this. He didn't want to alarm me or further upset me as I was so stressed and tearful. He also told her that I should always be accompanied by a family member to any doctor visit. If I was to receive any bad news, I should never be alone.

In April 2002, I was admitted to the Spaulding Pain Center, affiliated with Mass General in Boston, for a month-long stay. I received physical therapy, psychological counseling, learned relaxation techniques and they gradually came up with a non-narcotic regimen of meds like Neurontin, Effexor, Zanaflex, Naproxsyn and Elavil which at the end of my third week there seemed to alleviate 90% of that pain in my hand. Opiods and any narcotic drugs only exacerbate the chronic pain of Reflex Sympathy Dystrophy, besides the fact that they are extremely addictive. I had a bout of pneumonia while at Spaulding.

I was so elated I called my children and others to relay the great news about my hand pain. I was discharged after the four weeks and told to contact Dr. N at Mass General with any problems and if the pain started to return, as they could adjust and increase the dosages, especially the Neurontin.

After only a few weeks at home, the pain started to get worse again. I called and got the Neurontin dosage increased. I was originally on 600mg, four times a day. I did this twice over the next month because the pain was now back as severe as ever, and I was experiencing some troubling side effects. The third time, when they wanted to increase the dosage yet again, I read up more on Neurontin and realized those mega doses were the cause of the troubling side effects. I had attributed my increasing mood changes, depression and anxiety to the fact that my pain had returned after I had been so hopeful that it was now controllable.

When I did more research on the Internet about this drug, I read that the drug caused cancer in rats and it was unknown if it caused cancer in humans. What really opened my eyes and sent up a red flag was that it increased suicidal thoughts and behaviors. I had been thinking about suicide off and on for some time, but since I began taking the increased doses of Neurontin those thoughts were occurring more frequently. I had even planned all the details and constantly reviewed these in my head. In retrospect, I don't think I ever would have done it for two reasons. I always thought about going to hell. I had been taught that taking one's life was a mortal sin in the eyes of God. Second, I knew I couldn't do that to my children. Whenever I reviewed my plans for suicide, these two thoughts always surfaced.

After I expressed my concerns to Dr. N and Dr. A, I was gradually weaned off the Neurontin. You cannot abruptly stop taking it as it can cause severe seizures. With the Neurontin taken out of the mix, the cocktail of drugs I was prescribed at Spaulding were doing nothing, so eventually I discontinued taking all of them except the muscle relaxant.

I was hospitalized again for pneumonia on June 8, 2002. My dear friend Kathy lost her husband the day before, and I wasn't even able to be there for her or attend Bob's wake or funeral. My son Roger went in my place.

I contacted John Hopkins University in July 2002. They referred me to Dr. B in the Neurology Department. I spoke to him on the telephone. Then he wrote me with his suggestion that I go to Mass General Hospital in Boston to schedule Selective Nerve Root Blocks after identifying the specific nerve roots in the *brachial plexus* region that were responsible for my chronic pain.

In late 2002, I went to the Neurology Department at Mass General with my daughter. They suggested I consider a spinal-cord-stimulator implant and gave me some booklets and a video explaining this procedure. I scheduled another appointment for one month later. When I returned with my daughter one month later, I was first examined by Dr. Propescu, who detected a *bruit* in my left carotid neck artery.

She explained what it was (a sound or noise) and recommended I see my primary care physician immediately for an ultrasound. So, back it was to see Dr. Armenio, to schedule the ultrasound and then hear the confirmation that the carotid artery was indeed blocked. I was immediately referred to a vascular surgeon who reviewed the results and told me it was a 98% blockage and scheduled immediate surgery. I was a sure candidate for a stroke. This was done in out-patient surgery in early 2003. My oldest son Jerry came down from New Hampshire to retrieve me from the hospital. (Was this another loop-da-loop on that roller coaster ride that began in 1997? It sure was!)

One month later, I returned to Mass General to see about the spinal-cord-stimulator procedure that had been put on hold while the carotid blockage was taken care of. I had viewed the video and read about the procedure in the booklet they had previously given me, but when the doctor explained the process in more detail to me and Melissa, I got thrown a curve ball. He explained that when the leads would be inserted into the spinal cord sheath I had to remain absolutely still. I would be mildly sedated to keep me calm, but I had to be awake. I also had to be prone on my stomach. This would be a problem as I had difficulty getting and staying in that position. The slightest movement at that critical time could result in paralysis and he specifically used the word quadriplegic. Oh Lord, I said to myself. He further went on to say this is rare but it is a distinct possibility. I explained to the doctor that I had involuntary jerks (either muscles or nerves) that did occur erratically and always happening without any warning. He told me that I would be mildly sedated, but that he could not guarantee that this would eliminate an unwanted nerve spasm or jerk from happening at a critical time.

With that, the spinal-cord-stimulator implant possibility was shot down. I could not even consider it with even the slightest chance that something could go wrong that would result in my becoming a quadriplegic. How could I chance that? I would then be a true burden to my children.

I had another bout of pneumonia in mid-2004 requiring another stay at R.I. Hospital. This was the fourth bout of pneumonia in less than three years. Dr. Armenio gave me the pneumonia shot after I recovered from that one; this shot is supposed to be good for ten years.

Also sometime in 2004, Dr. Armenio referred me to the Interventional Pain Management Center in Pawtucket. There I saw a woman neurologist about possible nerve block injections. She explained it all to me and that it would be done right there at the center. I told her I wanted to talk it over with my primary care physician and my children and I would call to schedule the nerve blocks if I decided to try it.

After I did so and I reported for my first appointment for the actual first nerve block injection, my gut told me to get the heck out of there. Why? I had been kept waiting for over an hour in the examination/treatment room while the doctor and other personnel were in their coffee-break room. I could hear them laughing and talking from my little cubicle.

When the doctor finally came to my room the first thing she said to me was; "Well now, what are we here for today?" Immediately an alarm bell went off in my head. I asked myself "What kind of question is that? Is she not prepared to proceed with the nerve blocks? Had she thoroughly reviewed my case history? Did she really know what she was doing?" Again, that first question of hers came back to me. My gut told me to leave and forget about trying nerve block injections. Guess what? I followed my instincts and marched right out of there and told her I would not be back.

I was really now in tune to listening to my gut and to the strong vibes I was getting, recalling my experience with Dr. V back in 1997. I had also educated myself over the past few years trying to understand my condition in more depth. I knew that the nerve block injections had a very slim chance of alleviating or reducing my pain because too much time had elapsed. These nerve blocks would have been a long shot at best.

I had purchased a *Gray's Anatomy* book as well as *Taber's Cyclopedic Medical Dictionary*. In December 2000, I had also purchased online, a book by Dr. Hooshang Hooshmand titled *Chronic Pain* about Reflex Sympathy Dystrophy—prevention and management. I will list some excerpts from this book.

"RSD is the pain that never stops."

"RSD is a form of complex chronic pain."

"Chronic pain when it is complicated is hard to control."

"The chronic pain is accompanied by anxiety, phobia, irritability, agitation and depression."

"RSD is the extreme prototype of disabling chronic pain."

Finally, I read. "The key to successful management of RSD is early diagnosis (within the first six months of the trauma)." Again, I was not diagnosed with RDS until two-and-one-half years after my surgeries.

The book by Scott Fishman M.D., titled *The War on Pain* was how I found Spaulding Rehabilitation Hospital in Boston in 2002. Other books I purchased and read that were helpful in understanding and dealing with my condition were: *Pain Free for Life* by Darrell Stoddard, *Meditation as Medicine* by Dharma Singh Khalsa, M.D. and Cameron Stauch, a book about activating the power of your natural healing force and *The Healing Power of Faith* by Harold G. Koenig, M.D., a highly readable book on the healing power of faith.

I had become a member of the American Pain Foundation when I was doing research online about my condition. I still receive quarterly newsletters with informative articles and new websites to investigate in my endless quest for new breakthroughs on RSD pain relief.

The *early* diagnosis that did not happen was the one crucial and important factor in not being able to control the chronic pain of RSD. It was, as I had read, literally the pain that would never go away. I remembered a lot of what I had read about pain and especially about RSD, which is now mostly referred to as Complex Regional Pain Syndrome, when I made the decision to follow my gut and walk out of that treatment room that day.

*   *   *

In May 2005, I decided to give my daughter's idea of writing a book about my life a try. In retrospect, I realize that this was my savior. I became absorbed in writing the book, trying to recall the events of my whole life and dwelled less and less on my pain. I worked through the pain. I believe it was around this time that I told my children not to bring up my pain when they called. It was no use rehashing it over and over again. If I didn't dwell on it or talk about it I could avoid getting discouraged, depressed and having my "crying jags" when I got into the "poor me syndrome" yet again. When I began to slowly accept the fact that I would suffer with it for the rest of my life, my state of mind began to gradually and noticeably change for the better, but this did not happen overnight.

In 2007, I was hospitalized with a bad infection in my right arm. This infection came about as a result of a small paper cut on my right-hand pinky finger. I have to be ever vigilant as I have no defenses to fight infections due in part to the removal of all the lymph nodes on my right side. Remember, I had four earlier bouts with pneumonia in less than three years.

I again tried some physical therapy in 2007-08. This is a special kind of therapy called manual therapy. This therapy is delivered by the hands as opposed to a device or a machine. A chance meeting with an old friend who told me my former therapist Paula was now accepting Medicare led me to my primary care physician to get a referral to start the specialized manual therapy Paula does. I had seen her almost six years earlier, but had to stop as my insurance wasn't covering it as she was not in a handicapped-accessible facility. My son Larry had been paying for all those therapy sessions, and I could no longer ask him to continue doing so back then. He never told me how much he had paid out but I estimate it was over $1,000. When I began seeing her again in 2007, Medicare would now cover this as she was in a new handicap-approved facility. I told her I'd settle for 50% less chronic pain, but she said she wouldn't settle for that; she was shooting for 100%. Besides being a well-qualified therapist (Master's Degree) she has a strong faith like me. We also discovered we both had a connection to St. Rita of Cascia. I was seeing her twice a week. We shared many stories of our faith and lives. I treasure her as a friend and as my super therapist.

Dr. Armenio said that he felt I had a change in attitude about my chronic pain condition. He's right. This was partially due to Paula's therapy. My children have said the same. I mentally deal with this pain much better now. Why? I guess it must be the Lord's doing primarily because He enlisted the help of Paula with her therapy and of my daughter in planting the seed idea for this book.

Unfortunately, Medicare will not cover indefinite manual therapy sessions with Paula and I had to stop the therapy yet again in 2007. A few words on Medicare are warranted here.

They don't really set limits on my prosthesis and the special bras needed to hold it. The "boob" cost over $500 and the special bras cost over $45 each. I am allowed to get six new bras each year, as well as a new prosthesis each year or every other year. I can no longer wear the prosthesis because one, I can't hook the bras up myself, and two, the weight on my bad, right shoulder is unbearable. So, I haven't gone for new bras or a new prosthesis in more than five years. I have saved Medicare all that money, yet they would not extend my manual therapy with Paula. Why can't they customize each patient's needs, making allowances and trade-offs, so the patient decides what is best for her? I would have gladly traded getting a new "boob" so that I could get more of Paula's therapy. I should go for new bras every year and replace my "boob" whenever it is allowed, then go on eBay® and sell these (since I can't use them) and make the money for more manual therapy treatments. I could cheat them royally if I were a dishonest person.

Now that I am almost finished with this book, I will see if I can resume the therapy with Paula. Unfortunately, as Paula had to move again and to a smaller, non-handicapped facility, Medicare will not cover this therapy but my children have told me they will help me with the costs. Paula and I both have a lot of faith and are not quitters. Maybe, in time, she can reduce my pain level for longer periods of time. Maybe St. Rita will bless us both for our devotion to her, intercede for us both, a real breakthrough will be achieved and I will experience just normal pain in lieu of this chronic pain. As I said before, Paula's goal was to get me 100% pain free. Honestly, I'd settle for less than just 50%.

I have also tried the Fentanyl patch, but had bad side effects like extreme slurring of speech and extreme lightheadedness. It did not reduce my pain level one bit, so I discontinued that after a few months. I have tried the Lidoderm patch also. My daughter has suggested I try spa treatments for relaxation telling me she would pay for this. One of these days, I will pamper myself with a nice spa treatment. I have done research on the net on biofeedback techniques. This too I may investigate further, although I accept the fact it will not cure my pain. It could possibly be another tool for dealing with it though.

Having looked into a multitude of possible paths for some relief from this chronic pain over the past ten years, I have now resigned myself to the permanence of my condition and realize it is up to me to find ways to cope with it on a daily basis.

I solved the problem of changing my earrings (pierced ears). I gave all of my good earrings to my daughter, and now I don't even wear any. If one became unfastened I had to wait for someone to show up and ask them to put a missing earring back on as I can't do this with only one good hand. I was often doing my errands to the bank, the post office or going to the doctor's office with only one earring and I just gave up on those because I was getting some strange stares.

Spending time on my computer helps to distract me from my pain and also beats doing housework. I am limited to what I can do around the house, but am able to do my "*popotte*" as they say in Canada. *Popotte* means daily little chores like tidying up or cleaning out a drawer, giving the bathroom a quick wipe down or wiping down the appliances in the kitchen. What I can no longer do is vacuum, or any kind of heavy work. I do my own laundry, but folding it aggravates my pain with the constant movement of my right arm. I now readily accept my children's help, no longer resisting because I want to be in control.

For more than two years after I divorced Walter, Melissa paid for Gisela's house—keeping services. She came once a week to do the weekly cleaning. After she had to quit because of her own health problems, I had Kim who came every other week. Melissa paid for that, too, for more than a year. Eventually, I did not have anyone from the outside to come to do housework. I came to realize that my daughter needed a break from all that expense. She never told me that. It was my own conclusion. I realized I could now do more for myself and they could do whatever was needed when they visited, which was often. That has worked out, albeit that the house is not always spotlessly clean. I don't let that get to me. I just go with the flow. It's not that bad as the Board of Health has yet to show up and condemn my house as unfit for human occupancy.

Now that my book is almost finished I can get back to my POGO games and play spades and cribbage. I have a regular cribbage opponent online. She lives in England and her name is Oriel. We have become good friends and exchanged photos, written each other and talked on the phone. After she sent me a photograph of herself my first thought was that she could be one of the Queen's lady-in-waiting, as she looked very classy and noble.

I can spend more time keeping in touch with my friends through emails. I have a few friends that don't have computers, believe it or not, and I write those letters using my computer then just print and mail them out. If I do get a short written note off to someone, I always try to print as at least that is more legible than my poor left-handed writing.

I can now get back to my original schedule of listening to my inspirational and prayer tapes. I can read passages daily in all the inspirational books I have received as gifts over the years. I can get back to EWTN (Eternal Word Television Network) regularly and at 3:00 p.m. daily join in the Chaplet of Divine Mercy devotion that I so love. I can join the sisters on EWTN nightly for the recitation of the rosary.

I love to read and I can get more of that in now that this book project is close to being finished. I intend to look into books-on-tape and eBooks because it is getting difficult to hold large books with only one good hand. My right hand is atrophying more and more. It is now in a permanent clawed position. I am unable to open three fingers on that hand. I have limited use of my thumb and the pointer finger but I am grateful for that as I do need them for certain things. In spite of the numbness in those two fingers, I do manage to get a bit of use from them. In the past, I honestly thought about having my right arm and hand amputated so I would be rid of this pain. So far I have talked myself out of that drastic idea.

Thoughts of suicide no longer pop into my head. My crying over this situation has practically disappeared. I do have bad days, but not as often. I would say that eight out of ten days are somewhat tolerable. It is really, as they say, mind over matter. When I do have a very bad day, I remind myself to get through that one day; I ask the Lord for strength to deal with the pain; I rest more either in my bed with the electric massager (a gift from my dear daughter) or in my recliner chair. I take this opportunity get more spiritual reinforcement with my favorite books. As I have previously said, I take it one day at a time.

The only meds I take now, and I do not take them on a regular schedule, are Tylenol PM to help me sleep and Flexoril, a muscle relaxant that helps when I get all tensed up on very bad pain days. I also take a daily baby aspirin because after the surgery for the blocked carotid artery my doctor told me to take one daily. I do have to get fitted for a new Job sleeve to help control the chronic edema in my right arm. I purchased a Joslin Arm Sling and the Swathe Immobilizer Strap to use with that sling. This helps support my arm and shoulder, but I don't wear it every day as I must use that arm even if I am limited in what I can do, just to avoid complete atrophy

Remember how I wrote about becoming a nun somewhere in this book? I think I may enlist St. Rita's help with that. If you read the story of her life, you will understand why. Go to her website, saintritashrine.org. Through her, I just may be able to find an order of nuns that will accept an over-the-hill, old lady with not much more to contribute than a willingness to spend the rest of her days on earth praying perpetually for those in need and for the most forgotten soul in purgatory. Having done some research on the Internet already, I know that most religious orders have an age limit for joining. Maybe I will just have to found my own order of religious, the "Over—the-Hill" Congregation of St. Rita Believers (chuckle). Hey, remember—never say never. It could very well happen. Who knows if that is not the last thread that the Lord is weaving in His plan for my life. Again, this is my sense of humor surfacing again. Truthfully, I would welcome the opportunity to join a contemplative order of sisters, one in which one has to take the vow of silence. Otherwise, they surely would give me the religious name of Sister Mary Jabberjaws.

My live-in boyfriends (notice that's plural) are Sir Reggie and Sunshine. They are my two cats, my faithful companions that I got about five years ago from my friend Clara who is a sucker for rescuing cats. They were going to be euthanized. She rescued them from the shelter and had them at home with five other cats while trying to find good homes for them.

I originally told her I would take one, but when I went for it and chose Reggie she told me Sunshine had to go with Reggie as they were a pair. Sunshine could not survive without Reggie. They had been rescued as kittens together. Reggie had taken over the dominant role and is Sunshine's protector. Sunshine had been severely abused and did not like physical contact with humans. To this day, I cannot pick him up, and he will never jump on my lap. Whenever I have company, he hides downstairs or under the bed and doesn't come out until everyone has left. Reggie, on the other hand, is Mr. Personality. Unlike Sunshine, who is a tabby, Reggie is a black and white long-haired cat; he actually looks like a skunk with his coloring. They are indoor cats and are no trouble. They are my companions. I imagine they feel like they are at the Ritz after being abandoned as kittens and living in fields and cellars. I can talk to them. We have nice conversations. They never give me any back talk. They always agree with me. What more can I ask for?

I'll end this chapter with a quote I came across by Brenda Peterson. "Because animals seem to dwell in the present moment, because their own presence is so instinctive, their attention so unwavering, they offer us a different kind of compassion than humans do. Anyone is lucky to have both human and animal contact in their lives."

CHAPTER 32

My nasty years were from 1999 to 2006. That is, ME being nasty. Those were the depression years when I dwelled on my constant pain 24/7 and my frustration at not being able to find an answer to this chronic problem. They were the "ups and downs" years of adjusting to being alone for the first time in my life. Divorcing Walter in mid-1999, less than two years after I survived that big scare with all the surgeries, followed by the horrendous chemo and, on top of all that, my father's death in April 1998, certainly all contributed to my nasty moods and depression.

It was definitely a humbling experience to need and accept help from my children, when I was used to being the one helping *them*. When they offered help, I resisted and was downright nasty about it. That dang pride of mine! I now realize that my children's countless acts of love and kindness did ease my burdens, especially during those nasty years. Somehow they all survived. I will also say they did so with grace, kindness and unwavering patience with me. God bless them.

I will share some recollections of my friends' and family's kindnesses and generosity to me in spite of me being nasty 95% of the time.

I will never forget my dear friend Annette's unending moral support and patience, especially during my divorce from Walter and the months that followed. She called me long distance almost every day to try to encourage me or cheer me up. I was in a depressive state more often than not when she called and was downright nasty to her. She never gave up on me and continued to call every day without fail.

Before that, when I was in the hospital for the five-week period for the infection, she had recorded herself singing Christmas carols and other memorable songs from the 1950s, our teenage years. She bought a small tape player with earphones and delivered her kind and thoughtful gift to me in the hospital. When I listened to these, it brought back fond memories of our years at *Nôtre Dame* School and JMA. Her voice was truly that of a special angel serenading me. It was as effective as the pain meds in distracting me from all I endured during that long hospitalization. Thank you, Annette, for all those daily calls, the tapes, all your visits during both my hospital stays, your countless cards and notes and especially for your precious friendship that I will always treasure. I do love you.

Thank you, too, for getting the word out to all our classmates and friends when I was hospitalized. You made sure they all prayed for me and sent me beautiful inspirational cards. You sent me a card at least three times a week. Some were funny to make me laugh, some were inspirational and others were about our special friendship. I often read your personal little notes written on the inside cover of those cards. Those and all the cards I received are so precious to me.

My friend Jackie T. in Missouri sent me beautiful letters, notes of encouragement and cards also. Madeleine and Pauline did as well, always adding a personal message and reminding me I was tough, that I would get through this and telling me I was always in their daily prayers. All of them spent loads of money on all those cards and postage stamps. Maureen, besides sending cards, heard I was finally going to be released from the hospital for Christmas and she sent me a big package from Michigan with kitchen towels, an apron with cats in the design, a beautiful door wreath she had made and a wall hanging she had made from twigs and artificial flowers. I wish I could describe it as it is truly beautiful. I still have it hanging on my wall.

Judy, my new surrogate sister, and I truly became such good friends during this period. We were friends from the campground, although we were not close friends while we camped together. She lived just four miles from me. After divorcing Walter, I reached out to her in my loneliness and depression. She never once said she was too busy to talk, or put me off when she could surely sense I was in another crying mood. She was ever so good at lifting my spirits and making me laugh with her "plans" for me.

Her outrageous suggestions helped to distract me from the bad mood I was in when I called her. A few times, I actually wet my pants because I was laughing so hard. One time, she picked up on my revelation to her that, when and if I was reincarnated, I wanted to come back as an Egyptian princess. She jumped right in and suggested that before I died, I give her permission to display me in her backyard shed, embalmed and dressed up as an Egyptian princess. I certainly would be a unique attraction, and she would be able to charge admission and generate some income for herself. She even went so far as to suggest I be sure to put this "permission" in my will, so my kids couldn't object.

Another time, when we spoke on the phone, to distract me from my pain and bad mood, she suggested she come over with her power tools. She would drill a hole in my head, give me a lobotomy and get rid of my dang pain once and for all. Believe me, I never let Judy enter my house with any kind of power tool, for fear that she just might have gone through with it. Judy's nicknames for me were "Jabberjaws," because she said my mouth never stopped, and "Lois Lane," because when we first met she had a hard time remembering Lorraine and she dubbed me "Lois Lane," as close to my name as she could remember.

She came over to help with whatever I needed, whenever I asked her to. I especially remember her coming over to wrap all my Christmas gifts every year. That was tough for me to do with only one good hand. *I love you, Judy. God rest your soul. I miss you so much.* Judy passed away on July 28, 2008 at age 59.

Now, about my good friend Kathy, I guess what best describes our friendship is Frick and Frack. Being friends for more than 25 years, I could probably write another book on all we have shared. We are complete opposites, so how we did become such good friends I'll never understand. I met her in 1981 when she came to work as the second bookkeeper at Jonette Jewelry where I worked as the accounts receivable bookkeeper. She also has had a roller-coaster-type life. She divorced her first husband when her two girls were very young because he was truly a "nutcase." Later, she remarried, but after just a few short years her husband died of a heart attack in his thirties. This happened not too long after I met her. Like me, she married for the third time in 1986, I believe. This last marriage to her "Bob" lasted sixteen years. Sadly, Bob passed away in 2002 from diabetes complications. He was not even 60 years old. Bob was the love of her life, like Bob was truly my first love and the love of my life.

Kathy's two daughters, Kelli and Kerri, refer to us a Laverne and Shirley. I'm Laverne. When they were small, they use to laugh at our interactions and said we reminded them of those characters from that 1970s sitcom. To this very day, her girls greet me as Laverne. Kathy's been through so much with me. She, too, is always ready to listen and offer help. She is the one that really helped me through the period right before I divorced Russell and then afterwards. She's the other half of the "investigative team" we formed to try to uncover the real truth about Russell's endless retirement parties.

With her too I was able to lighten up and chase the nastiness away. We spoke on the phone often and she reminded me of all the future plans we had made together over the last twenty years or so. We planned to go to Florida after all the kids were grown and on their own. We would become "bag ladies" and live under the bridges in Florida, where it is always warm. She hates the cold weather more than I do. We would definitely be classy bag ladies, because I saved all those designer shopping bags that have handles for this anticipated move to Florida. We would tote our possessions around from one bridge to the next, always looking like real classy dames. She helped ease my loneliness with all those silly conversations reminiscing about our future plans.

Another one of our plans was to check ourselves into Butler, a psychiatric hospital, for ten days of R & R. As neither of us could really afford a true vacation, this was the solution to that problem. Our medical insurance would foot the bill for this and, after ten days, we would check ourselves out. We knew that if you voluntarily checked yourself in, you could discharge yourself when the time was up. We figured we'd enjoy the day trips, arts and crafts, especially basket weaving, and that we'd get three square meals a day. What a deal! I love you, too, Kathy (a.k.a. Shirley) for making me laugh instead of cry. Our conversations were a big help chasing away the "blues" too. We are currently working on two more alternate plans. One is to somehow get into the witness protection program, so we can escape and start over somewhere new at the government's expense. The other is to advertise to expand on Gertie's Investigative Services, something we started years ago. I am in charge as Laverne and she is my assistant as Shirley. We have employed our sharp investigative skills many times over the years for various reasons. We figure that now we can make some good pocket money with these skills.

My old friend Terry, the young girl I became acquainted with when we both lived on Eastern Avenue, is another dear friend that I have cherished over the years. Remember, I told you earlier about bringing her tea and toast when she was so sick during her first pregnancy. We often talk on the phone and reminisce about our earlier years. We have so much in common having both experienced scary roller coaster rides. Ironically, we discovered only in the early 1980s that we had known each other when we both lived on Jenkes Street. She lived just two houses down from me and she recalls walking past my house on her way to the corner store to buy an ice cream bar and saying hi to me and my sister Dee. She said I was the friendliest one of the two. She had moved to Michigan not long after Bob had passed but after her divorce she returned to this area and now we can get together every now and then.

I must mention my dear Cousin Cecile. She always lent a shoulder for me to cry on. I had tapped her for novenas for all my needs over all the years. At one point she said to me, "I'm so sick of praying for you and your needs. Give me a break for a while." She often reminded me that she had changed my dirty diapers when I was a baby. She's 20 years older than me, the oldest daughter of one of my Mom's oldest sisters, *Tante* Marieanne. In fact, she was but ten years younger than my Mom, her aunt. She also had some tough roller coaster rides in her lifetime. Her prayers on my behalf, especially during my hospitalization and recovery, will never be forgotten. I love her dearly.

Pat "O' is another dear friend. She is now retired and lives in Newport, Rhode Island. I met her when I worked at J. Licht as a bookkeeper. She was always so helpful to me with the computer program I was learning. She was an ace on that computer. Even though I left that job only after a short time, Pat and I kept in touch and became good friends. I recall one time when we spoke on the telephone. She told me that she had my name put on the prayer-group list of people to pray for. She was working at LaSalette Shrine in Attleboro, Massachusetts at the time. We keep in touch with emails and phone calls now as she no longer drives, and she continues to send me beautiful computer-generated cards for all special occasions and even some in between for no special reason at all. She is such a thoughtful person. Her friendship is so precious to me. I love her dearly.

Many other friends have helped and sustained me over those tough years. I can't possibly mention them all by name. They know who they are and how I feel about them. God bless each and every one of them.

Dear Dr. Armenio, my primary care physician, is also a friend and not just my doctor. He has referred me to so many specialists and pain clinics over the last years. I think he got as frustrated as I did when yet another hope was shot down after one or two visits to the latest referral. It is not his fault that the missing puzzle piece to solve the question of how to find relief from this chronic unrelenting pain remains elusive.

As far as Dr. Armenio goes, he is the best. I thank the Lord he agreed to take on my case as my new primary physician and oncologist, just ten days before that big surgery on Halloween. I know that was God's doing. Pain control is not his primary medical discipline but he has tried over all these years to find the right specialist to address this unrelenting pain. He is ever-so-patient with me, always telling me I am his favorite patient, and I feel he truly has empathy for my pain dilemma. I love him dearly. He's a sweetheart and a keeper. I sometimes give him such a hard time as I am so often exasperated with this chronic pain. He never loses his cool with me and puts up with me. God bless him!

My dear *Tante* Jacqueline in *Amqui* always has the right words to say whenever we speak on the telephone. She instinctively knew when I was having a bad day. Her faith and wisdom boosted and sustained me. She was faithful in passing the news onto my other aunts, uncles and numerous cousins. I received many cards and letters of encouragement from all of them. I still speak with her frequently and she still always has an encouraging word and always gives me wise counsel. She, too, is a keeper and I love her dearly.

For my 66th birthday, all my kids pitched in to pay for a new recliner that I got to choose myself. My children often include gift cards along with my other gifts. I use these for things I need at the supermarket or just at the CVS, as I can never seem to get out of that store without dropping $20.

Larry, son #2, the one my mother said would be the closest to me all those years ago, cuts the grass, plows and shovels, paints the house, is here at the drop of a hat if I need him, is also my handyman, and is the delivery man for the Sunday morning treat of Dunkin Donuts® coffee and a muffin. He fixes the sump pump, deals with the dehumidifier and installs the portable air conditioner units every year in the spring and then removes them in the fall. He gave me a new TV set for Christmas one year and he paid for my new garage door with an electric opener. I could also fill many more lines with all that he does for me. I have never bought a quart of oil or an oil filter for my car. Larry takes care of all my car maintenance. I have valet service when requested as Larry carries the laundry baskets up and down the stairs for me. He carries up all the garments I put on clothes hangers and places them in my closet.

Whenever she comes over, Melissa brings meals with her, or cooks meals for me, and she stocks my freezer too. She is ever so generous in giving me "bonus checks" to cover unexpected expenses. She gave me a "One Day at a Time" pin and the "Footprint" crystal pendant along with numerous inspirational books to boost my spirits. Whenever she buys me a new outfit, it is just what I like. She knows my preferences and always chooses exactly the right thing. There are many more things she has done for me and generously given to me over these past years.

After I have visited them, Jerry and Sheree send me home with containers of food. They bring me *cretons* and French meat pies which I am not able to purchase locally. They also stock my freezer with delicious "stuffies." Jerry and Sheree gave me my VCR and DVD players. They have purchased special creams, supplements, herbs, vitamins, aroma therapies and meditation tapes. One of the books Jerry purchased for me was *Chicken Soup for the Surviving Soul* (for cancer survivors). Whatever new thing their unending searches found for pain relief, either on the Internet or in their travels it was promptly delivered to me. Jerry is his mother's son, never giving up. He still keeps trying to find something that will bring me some relief from this chronic pain condition. He really absorbed and practices what I used to say when he was growing up, especially, "Where there is a will there is a way." He's still a work-in-progress as far as being able to make those magic aces appear out of a deck when he needs them though, but he'll get it eventually.

Then there were Jerry's Friday trips here for the day with his cleaning equipment. He would shampoo a rug, spruce up the hardwood floors or do whatever heavy cleaning that had to be done. He'd vacuum thoroughly moving all the furniture to get in all the nooks and crannies as he knew I couldn't do this. Now that his two sons are involved with gymnastics and sports, he is chauffeuring them around most weekends and his precious days off are spent getting his own work caught up around his own little home.

Sheree, my dear daughter-in-law, is my own personal seamstress, my personal shopper—always choosing exactly the right outfit for me and, of course, an excellent cook who spoils me with lasagna and lemony chicken soup. As she was born and raised in Salem, Massachusetts, I sometimes refer to her as "Jerry's little Salem witch," but I mean this in a loving way as she is like the "Good Witch of the East" and in no way like the "Wicked Witch of the West." I am blessed to have her, truly, as a second daughter.

Roger, my occasional handyman, repairs my electrical switches, lamp switches, small appliances and telephones. He sometimes comes over on Sunday mornings to help me out. I have a "to-do list" ready for him which he does without complaint of it being too long.

There possibly could be a full book written about the story relating to his personal journey and our relationship as mother and son #3. For many years, he has been battling his own demons. Roger is an alcoholic; he now admits it. Although he has bouts where he stays sober for sometimes quite a few years, he inevitably falls off the wagon and resumes his self-destructive lifestyle. I have tried to encourage him to seek counseling for his addiction but he doesn't follow through on his promises to do so. For many years I hoped and prayed I could get through to him. Now I realize that he has to take the step of in-depth professional counseling himself. All my prayers and novenas won't help if he doesn't first try to help himself. It really is in God's hands now and whatever happens is in Roger's control. God does not control us, rather He directs us. I always say to Roger that God helps those who help themselves. I also tell him that God will direct him but that Roger has to ask for God's help and direction. God does not impose Himself on us. He waits to be invited.

There are many more "dividends" from those education investment years I spoke about in an earlier chapter. Believe me, I count my blessings and dare say that I could fill three chapters listing all that my children so generously do for me. Of course, all these dividends and interest from my education investments that I am now reaping are tax-free and don't have to be reported to the IRS. If I had invested those dollars in mutual funds, just think of how much *Uncle Sam* would be getting from my hard-earned investments. This way, the IRS gets zilch, and I get the maximum return on my wise investments. I thank God every day for bestowing on me the gifts of determination, as well as a sense of humor when he created me. I also thank Him for guiding me to make those wise investments. He knew, in His infinite wisdom, exactly what I would need to do as far as my children's education was concerned and gently guided me all the way. He knew how I would, in time, benefit if I chose to follow His guidance. How wise and generous is our God!

I can honestly say that without my kids and my friends, I would not have survived "those nasty depression years." Oh, I still have bad days but not as frequently. The full-blown nasty years are over and done with. Now there are just a few bad days here and there. I try to not dwell on that pain and, somehow, I manage to get through it, again . . . o n e d a y a t a t i m e. I know I've said that before, but I do have to repeat it often as it does somehow help me through yet another rough day. It will certainly help you, my grandsons and my readers too, if you just remember to remind yourselves of that phrase whenever you are experiencing a bad day.

I do know I am a survivor. Of the many blessings God bestowed on me, as I said before, (Hmm . . . I do repeat myself a lot; that's definitely a sign of old age.) I think the one that helped me most was my sense of humor. That sense of humor somehow got placed on the back burner during those "nasty years," but it resurfaced and it sure does help to laugh instead of cry.

I recall that from time to time during those tough years following my surgeries and my divorce I would be so discouraged I would say, "I can't." That's when the kids would remind me of my own words to them when they were growing up: "Never say never," "Don't say I can't, say I'll try," or "There is no such word as impossible in my dictionary." So be careful what you do say to your kids because those words just might come back to haunt you as mine did. They are now my teachers and I am the child. Larry especially tells me often not to say "I can't." He is training me to say, "It is difficult for me to (do whatever)," instead. The reason I eventually acted on the suggestion that I write a book was because of those words that came back to haunt me. I thought about all the times I had said to my children that I didn't want to hear them say, "I can't," and I realized I couldn't say it either. I, at the least, had to try.

PART IV

CHAPTER 33

"From the fullness of his grace we have all received one blessing after another."
John 1:16

When I began fighting that long battle with the big "C" and especially during that long hospitalization it never once crossed my mind that I would become disabled and not be able to return to work. I was wrong, of course. I am NOT often wrong. (lol)

I worry that I will fall off a step stool or down the stairs if I am not careful. Should I break a hip or something my situation would become worse. So, I don't carry anything up and down the basement stairs. I hold on to the railing. I don't get down on my hands and knees to retrieve something deep inside a cabinet as I have difficulty getting back up.

I applied for and received my Social Security disability pension which I began receiving in January 1998. I did not divorce Walter until the middle of 1999, so financially there were no problems at first. After we divorced, my financial picture changed. I could live on that Social Security benefit check, but I needed to withdraw funds each year from my IRA for property taxes. Thank God I had that good little nest egg. My problem was that I had to start withdrawing from those retirement funds in 2000, at age 59, so that retirement fund will not last as long as it was intended to had I been able to continue working until age 65. Besides that, the fund would have grown to an even better nest egg with at least seven more years of contributions. Luckily, my house was paid for, and I had no outstanding loans or credit card debt. If I am careful not to spend foolishly what remains in my IRA funds will last me a good number of years.

If I had to pay for car maintenance, yard work, snow shoveling, clothes and house repairs, cat litter and cat food and everything else my children take care of for me, my resources would be depleted in a very short time. The kids all tell me to just ask if I need extra money. They know I am trying to remain independent as long as I can. They also know I have been through rough times before and I'm good at making do with very little and stretching the almighty dollar and of course, putting more water in the soup. Nevertheless, if my IRA funds should get depleted sooner than what I anticipate, they assure me they will take care of the property taxes and any other expense I can't meet on my limited income.

How can I not count my blessings? I have so many. I will say it again. My four most precious blessings are my loving, caring and most generous children. I have three more precious blessings in my three grandsons. My dear aunts, uncles and cousins in Canada, but especially *Tante* Jacqueline, have to be added to my list of blessings. Judy was a true blessing. Kathy, Annette, Terry, Cousin Cecile, Oriel (UK) and Pat O. are just a few of my other dear friends who are all bonus blessings in my life.

"My cup does runneth over" and my blessings are numerous. Thank you, Lord. I acknowledge that You have been most generous in bestowing these blessings on me and all the other countless blessings not mentioned here.

CHAPTER 34

Several years ago I wrote a poem about being a very proud mom. It is certainly amateurish but it did, and still does, express how I feel about my kids. Here it is because I have to brag again about my super kids.

My Four Aces
By: "The Winning Hand Mom"

Let me tell you about "the super kid" . . . my daughter Mel.
Where do I begin? 'Cause there's so much to tell.
All the world's mothers should be blessed with a daughter like she,
Who strives always to be the BEST she can be.

Always a joy, a delight and a source of constant pride,
Achieving her goals, with some luck on her side.
Yes, she's lucky, but also bright and so very mature,
And don't forget, witty and charming, that's for sure!

I'm so proud to be the mother of Mel . . . my "super kid."
Lucked out and "hit the jackpot," that's what I did.
When God sent me this beautiful, intelligent, super girl,
Whose truly precious, a "gem," a perfect pearl!

All the wealth and riches of the world could never replace
My "super" Melissa . . . so I rest my case.
I'm already rich beyond measure I think you'll agree,
So not much richer do I ever want to be!

And, besides having Melissa who's only ONE ace . . .
I have three sons who hold equal place.
Each has achieved goals to make me so proud and "made my day"
So, four times blessed am I; that is what I say!

Jerry earned the "King Medal Award" honor of the year,
And he achieved a perfect "four-point-o" grade one year.
A true Number 1 son—a second ace—he turned out to be;
Married to a sweetheart who's so good to me!

Larry overcame so many frustrating years at school,
Achieving milestones . . . I KNEW he wasn't a fool.
The day he called from Vermont, excited, and said to me
"Mom, I can read!" I said to myself, Glory Be!

Roger's so bright . . . aced a college exam with no sweat,
He has much potential and new challenges to meet yet.
A "whiz" at electronics and math teasers you can see,
A future "robotics" ace . . . it could be he will be!

Jerry, Larry, Roger and Melissa . . . FOUR ACES . . . you see!
So tell me, how much richer could I ever be.
Because richer than most is this mother so proud,
And I'll brag about all four . . . OFTEN . . . and yes . . . LOUD!

*   *   *

I have made several references to becoming a nun at various times in the telling of this story. I like to joke about that. I know that was not my fate and destiny. I realize that if it had been my fate I would not have my children or my three grandsons. Just because of their existence I am so very happy that I never considered going into the convent as my dear mother would have so liked.

As a postscript to this, I will say that now that I do have my kids who are now all grown and on their own, there is no reason not to "enter a convent." If only I could find one that would accept me now.

*   *   *

Jerry

Jerry has always been a source of pride to me, but, the very special time he made my heart burst with joy and pride was graduation day from St. Andrews when he was named the King's Medal Recipient. His name is inscribed on the wall of honor in the assembly room at St. Andrews.

Another time I was his very proud mother was the day he graduated from Wentworth and *Pépère* Dube and Germaine came down from Canada to attend this momentous event. I recall *Pépère* saying he never thought or imagined that his grandson would be a college graduate or an engineer. It was a great source of pride to him recalling that he himself had completed only three years of formal schooling back in his day, attending school in a one-room schoolhouse that had a wood stove in the center of the room to keep everyone warm in the cold months. He showed me and my sisters that one-room schoolhouse on one of our visits to Canada. He bragged to all his family in Canada about his grandson, the engineer.

Jerry reminds me most of Bob around the home. His Dad was always a help to me with the boys and the house like Jerry is with his boys and with Sheree. *Jerry, do you remember when Mr. and Mrs. Laflamme wanted to adopt you because you were such a big help to them?*

Larry

Son #2 has come a long way from the frustrating school years when he felt he was a dummy because he couldn't read.

Larry taught me so much. He was the very first one to remind me of those words way back in 1979 when I said, "I can't." It was the time he wanted me and *Pépère* Dube to go skiing with him in Vermont when he was at Pine Ridge. He told me, "Mom, I don't want to hear you say I can't. Say I'll try." These were the very words I had repeated to him over and over again, year after year, whenever he became frustrated with not being able to read. Well, my words came back to haunt me and, yes, I went skiing. I prayed to every saint in heaven and made up a few new saints, too, just to get me off that mountain in one piece that day up in Burlington, Vermont.

Oh, and yes my Dad went skiing too. He was almost 69 years old and had never been on skis in his life. But that didn't stop him. Remember earlier in the book I related how brave and without fear he was when he immigrated to the U.S. not knowing one word of English? Well, at 69, 43 years later, he was braver and even more fearless. He hugged a few trees coming down that first slope and Larry had to rescue him from a stand of trees several times but it didn't deter him. He made several more runs with Larry.

I only made that one run because I was not fearless. I wasn't going to push my luck as I had already petitioned every imaginable saint to get me safely down that mountain on that first run. In fact had there not been a stack of firewood logs stacked up against the outside wall and below the large window of the lodge where my Mom and *Mémère* Sevigny were sitting watching us, I would have crashed through that window and landed in their laps. The logs saved me. They probably saved both of them, too, because had I gone through the window I could have impaled both of them with my uncontrolled ski poles. I stopped so abruptly that I was bent over the logs staring at my Mom and *Mémère* through the window. They were laughing their heads off at the sight of me. I was making the sign of the cross, over and over again, giving thanks to the Lord and His precious saints, over and over and over again, for my safe deliverance down from that mountain.

I recall saying to my Mom once that I wished Larry was all grown up and on his own because I was so exhausted from the school struggles. She said to me, "Watch and see. Later on, he will be the one closest to you." Guess what? She was right. I also remember him saying to me, "Mom, don't worry. When you are old and in a rocking chair, I'll take care of you." Guess what? He does take care of his old mom that spends half the day in her rocking chair with her arm elevated to try to relieve the chronic pain and persistent edema.

All my kids are close to me and very good to me, but Larry is literally the closest. To think he was such a little mischievous devil. (I wonder where he got that from.) He still is and can still catch me with his antics and practical jokes. I have to be on my guard constantly. Occasionally, I catch him with one of my own "capers." I think he inherited my sense of humor. The "crack-in-the-ass" story best illustrates his sense of humor and tendency to be the life of the party. You will read about this in more detail a bit later. In this way, he is most like his father, the life of the party.

Roger

Roger is so intelligent. I believe he has the highest IQ of all four, but he demonstrates very little common sense at times. He is a work in progress, I guess. I will never totally give up on him.

He aced a college math exam, the required college-level math class he had to pass to enter New England Tech. I was so proud when the school called me to tell me Roger had passed that math test, a requirement to entering the program in January while other students had started in September. He had aced it! No sweat! Like his father, he really has a generous heart. He'd give the shirt off his back to one in need.

That terrible disease is trying to control of his life. I have had to resort to some "tough love" with him over these many years. His journey has been a long series of spills and falls, of ups and downs and of wasted years. Hopefully, now that can he can admit to being an alcoholic and say it aloud, he will stay on course, getting the help he needs through counseling and AA and finally become the master of his life. I know he can do it if he persists. He is, after all, his mother's son and giving up is not part of my make-up. He just has to hold fast to that thought. He has to take charge of his life and be in control of himself. No one can do it for him.

All three of the boys are good workers, generous, always willing to lend a hand to one in need, and versatile in being able to do many things. They are truly their father's sons. I know Bob would be so very proud of all of them and I know that he is especially watching over Roger, protecting him in his long battle to conquer alcoholism. In a later chapter, you will read a special story about why I say that.

Melissa

Melissa never ceases to amaze me. She set her goals, worked toward achieving those goals and surpassed all expectations. Sometimes I'm her mom and sometimes it's the other way around. When she prefaces what she will say by saying, "Mom," I'm the mom. When she prefaces it by saying, "Mother," I had better pay attention because the roles are reversed and I'm the little girl. She is most like me in her creativity and all her other strong, good qualities. (chuckle) She is most like her father when she reveals that "damn Yankee" side of herself. She does this rarely, but it does creep in there at times.

Like with the boys, there are many, many proud moments to recall concerning Melissa. Again, one of those moments was the day she called me at work to tell me she had just received a Fed Ex package from Simmons College informing her that she had been awarded one of the new Honors scholarships. This was that $10,000 scholarship renewable for each of her four years, and the answer to our prayers.

At one time, all the awards and achievement certificates she received through high school filled both walls of the long hallway in my home. It really got to the point where there was no more room to hang another and, eventually, Melissa took them all down and placed them all in a binder. If I listed them all in this book I would fill at least five full pages.

I do believe I could write three more chapters on all the proud moments my dear children gave me but you would all soon begin to say I was a braggart. You are right! I am a braggart when it comes to my children and their accomplishments.

I may not have been the greatest mother but, rest assured, no mother loves her kids more than I do. I would have gone to hell and back to help them achieve their dreams and have better lives with less struggling than I had. If only we could go back and do some things over though. One of the things I would have done is kiss them and given them hugs more often when they were younger. I was so young, so overwhelmed with just surviving, that I neglected those hugs and kisses. I should have told them more stories about my childhood, stories that could have made an impression and taught more lessons on life. I used to say "Don't worry, I have another ace in the hole," but I really never showed or explained to them how I managed to do that. I have so many regrets, but that's life.

I'm certain all of them will someday have regrets about missed opportunities, words omitted, or words that should have been said. I hope they have learned enough from me to minimize those future regrets. My hope for all of them is for full lives with very FEW regrets and NO scary coaster rides.

* * *

Some More Favorite Memories of My Children

I remember trying to unsnarl Melissa's tight curls when she was little. We would be standing at the vanity in the bathroom looking in the mirror and one time she said to me, "Mom, look I'm growing up and you're growing down."

I remember planning a school trip to New York, when we had all of Melissa's outfits lined up in the kitchen. When Melissa's Dad asked about it, we told him she was going there to be a "street lady" for the weekend to make extra money, and he believed us (chuckle). I remember Melissa's tales of how she played hide and seek on a rainy night in Little Neck cemetery and she fell into an open grave. Her friends had a devil of a time pulling her out of the mud hole. Oh, and when she confessed to me, years after it happened, the incident of her episode at Colt State Park hiding under a car from the cops. She and her friends were innocently in the park after closing time and got caught. Melissa hid under a car thinking the policeman would not see her. Well, he saw her.

I remember when, as an adult, Melissa finally told me she had almost called the child abuse center on me when she was little. Apparently, I had never bought her a tutu, and she wanted to take ballet lessons. I told her she had never expressed interest in ballet lessons. If she had, I'm sure she would have taken them and worn her precious tutu.

I remember that *Québec* trip for *Pépère's* wedding. Jerry, Sheree, Melissa, Larry and I were in one room with two double beds. A few were sleeping in sleeping bags on the floor (I was stretching the almighty dollars then too). I had finally settled everyone down and turned off the lights. We had a long drive back to the U.S. the next morning. After all was quiet, maybe about fifteen minutes after I had shut off the lights, Larry pulled the caper of the century. He yelled out, "Ma, Ma, wake up. You gotta take me to the emergency room." I switched on the lights and asked what the matter. "Ma, you got to take me to the emergency room. I got a crack in my ass." I can still remember how we all couldn't stop laughing, holding our sides because they were hurting so much. It took more than an hour before we all settled down again and finally got to sleep. I think this was the very first time Sheree had met Larry. She had just started dating Jerry. What a first impression he made. To this day, Sheree laughs when she recalls that caper.

I remember talking to Larry on the phone one night when he was at Ohio Diesel Institute and he told me he hadn't worked much that week. He was working part-time at a car wash. It had rained most of the week. He didn't have much grocery money, so he and his roommate went to the park and killed a squirrel to cook up on the hot plate they had in their motel room. I felt so guilty. I rushed to get a postal money order for $5, all I could spare right then. Access to emergency money using the ATM did not exist at that time. I mailed it to him that very night. To this very day, I don't know if he was pulling my leg or if truly happened. He did come back from Ohio with a stuffed squirrel.

I remember when Roger bought his first used car, an orange Volkswagen bus. I went with him to get it because he didn't know how to drive a standard shift. He received lessons on the gears and shifting all the way home via Mink Road and the Wampanoag Trail. That was it. He was then on his own. He was a quick study. He managed to drive his pride and joy, his very first car, after that one and only lesson from me.

I remember Larry and Keith Reid skipping school at Riverside Junior High for more than half a year before they were finally caught. They had their "method" down pat. They knew that if they were not absent for three days in a row, the school would not call their parents to see where they were. So they would skip school two days in a row, go to school a few days and plan their next "bunking." This continued on for six months before Janet, Keith's mother, finally caught the little devils by accident.

I remember when Cappy (my neighbor, Mr. Capaldo) caught the boys playing with matches in the woods when they were young. He let me know what they were up to, and they were severely disciplined. Jerry "fears" picking up a book of matches to this very day. He never forgot the consequences of playing with fire.

I remember Roger and his friend Jason (who also called Roger's grandfather *Pépère*) helping *Pépère* on the roof. *Pépère* called Jason *mon petit noire,* (my little black one). Jason was almost six-feet tall at age 14 and he was black, but Pépère nevertheless referred to him as *petit* in spite of his tallness. They were *Pépère's* helpers for the day. I remember Roger and his two older brothers each taking a turn going to "work" with *Pépère* on Saturdays. I never wonder where they all got their work ethics. They all learned so much from their grandfather, my Dad, the carpenter.

Hopefully, my children will recall more of their own special memories and relate them to my grandsons.

* * *

I do feel the happy memories of my life outnumber the bad ones in spite of all the nasty and long roller coaster rides, and of course the big ones namely: Bob's passing at such a young age, the puzzle of Larry's school difficulty and all those years of that struggle, the private education years that would have bankrupted someone else but not this obstinate (not stubborn, obstinate is more delicate) French lady, and finally the big "mother-of-all-roller-coaster ride" of 1997.

Chapter 35

My Grandchildren

I'll begin first with Andrew and Austin. How I wish I was able to take them to the circus or the Ice Capades®. Oops! I think it's called Disney on Ice® nowadays. I hope later on, they will realize that with my unrelenting pain, it was not possible for me to be the doting grandmother I so wanted to be, spoiling them and enjoying outings with them. I was able to play with Andrew for a few months but when he was not even a year old everything changed as a result of all those surgeries. I have a few photos of those times when my right arm and hand were of use to me and I could change Andrew's diaper at least. Now, I'm useless. I enjoy seeing them. I so wish I was able to do more with them. I especially enjoy our early morning IM contacts before they get their breakfast and get ready for school and get on with their busy days. Andrew and I will exchange silly jokes and such, and Austin will pipe in when he gets the chance.

I remember one morning while on AOL and IMing back and forth with them. Austin asked me why I got up so early. I had told him I was up since 4:00 a.m. I told him, "The early bird gets the worm." He replied that he didn't like worms. I asked if he had ever tasted one and he said, "NO." He asked if I liked "gummy bears" because he liked those, but definitely not worms. Sometimes, we only get to spend a few minutes together on the Internet but those minutes are so very precious to me.

As my primary purpose in writing this book was for the benefit of my grandsons, what follows is written like I was speaking to them in person.

Andrew, I hope you will always cherish those two holy pictures I gave you, along with the two letters I wrote, on the day you made your First Holy Communion. I have already written two letters for the day when Austin makes his First Communion, and have two more old and special holy pictures for him too. The letters for Austin are in my strongbox.

Before I forget to mention it, I want to relate this especially for Austin. Before you were born, your mom and dad and big brother Andrew all tried to pick a name for you. Your brother Andrew definitely had a name he had picked out for you, and it wasn't Austin. It took a long time before you all agreed that you would be named Austin. Your father did not know it at that time but his father, Bob, who was your grandfather, had a best friend named Austin Belanger who lived in Westport. He would be in his seventies now if he is still living. Wouldn't it be something if your paths crossed somewhere and you actually got to meet him? He could tell you stories about your grandfather when he spent his summers at the cottage on Watuppa Pond in Westport.

Michael, my oldest grandson, do you recall the bionic granny story? You were eight years old at the time of my big surgery. I'll refresh your memory. You had obviously overheard your mom and dad talking about the seriousness of my condition and you had asked your mom, "Is *Mémère* going to die?" Your mom told me this at the hospital and was so worried about you. I told her to have you call me at the hospital and I would talk to you. When you called, I told you I was doing okay. It just was going to take a bit longer for the doctors to fix me up and that they were going to fix my arm so it was a bionic arm. Well, you felt better after I told you that, so much so that when you went to school the next day you told the teacher and all your classmates that you had a "bionic" *Mémère*.

Michael, remember all the camping weekends you spent with me. Do you remember me attending your pre-school graduation and awards day at St. Brendan's? Do you remember the time I was taking your father for a CAT scan (his back was out again)? You were very young and when you heard me say I was going to take him for the CAT scan, you thought I was going to have Harley, your cat, scanned. You had the idea that this was "bad" for Harley. You got scared and let the cat out, even though he was an indoors cat. You didn't say a word, but your Grandpa Hughes noticed you were troubled when he picked you up from school that afternoon and he finally got it out of you. Of course, we then explained what a CAT scan was. We found Harley and brought him home. We sure had some good laughs together over that one.

Michael you had many good times with *Mémère*. Be sure to tell your cousins Andrew and Austin about them. Tell them all about your camping weekends with me. They never got to do all those fun things with *Mémère*. They lost out on so much because of my disability and pain. I lost out on so much, too.

Now I'll relate to all of you, my dear grandsons, a few favorite old memories and some handy tips for your benefit. The weekly outings to *Pépère's* house in Swansea are very special memories. One of those memories is that without fail, whenever your fathers played basketball in the long double driveway, they always managed to break another window in *Pépère's* garage doors. He never got mad, always repairing the broken pane only for it to happen again on another Sunday. Should one of you ever accidentally breaks a window on the garage door you can use that bit of information to get you off the hook, reminding your dad of how many times he and his brothers broke their *Pépère's* windows. Michael this no longer applies to you. I assume that at your age you have outgrown "breaking windows."

I remember them hammering away in *Pépère's* workshop fabricating their "creations." I don't wonder why they are all handy with tools today. You should all always ask for permission to use your dads' tools. I know that they will teach all three of you a lot of things that they learned from their *Pépère.*

Andrew and Austin, I remember the "atomic Stench" incident. I still have that door poster your Aunt Melissa tacked to your dad's bedroom door. I will leave the full story of the atomic stench to be told to you by Aunt Melissa. You can also ask her to recount the time she got even with your father for teasing her yet another time, and what she did to his boat shoes. I also recall the furious call from your father when he was away at Wentworth after he discovered all his underwear flies had been sewn shut. He sure had a tough time taking a "wiz" between classes that day, and the next day too, as Aunt Melissa had sewn up each and every pair. Aunt Melissa never got mad at her brothers for teasing her, but boy did she ever find ways to get even.

I suggest that you write down those two stories I mentioned that your Aunt Melissa will relate to you in particular, for posterity. Someday, when you are married with children of your own, you can retell those stories and because you will have written them down, you will not ever forget important details.

I think about the "bad knees" your dad claims he has today because I made him kneel in the hallway for punishments. Ask your dad why he had to kneel in the hallway (along with Uncle Larry and Uncle Roger). In case he embellishes his answer to you, I'll tell you why HE says that. They all shared one room, and when it was bedtime they would all take forever to settle down to get to sleep. After several warnings to cut it out and get to sleep, they would again start with their antics. So, I would make them all get up and say to them, "Okay, you're not tired enough yet. Now, kneel down in the hallway facing the wall, and I'll tell you when you can get back in bed." Their little knees got sore. After fifteen minutes, they were allowed back in bed. What do you know? They quieted down and went to sleep.

They repeated their antics on many nights resulting in the on-your-knees-in-the—hallway punishment over and over again. Uncle Larry was the smart one. He always positioned himself in an area of the hallway where I couldn't see him from the chair I was sitting in. The others weren't so smart. Uncle Larry would sit on his legs and rest, quickly getting back to the kneeling position when I went to check on them after they complained that Uncle Larry was cheating. In case your dad forgets what the real reason is that he has bad knees, it was actually caused by all that basketball playing during his years at St. Andrews School and later through his college years.

Especially for you, my grandsons, I have included a few of my favorite poems some of which are in the "author unknown" category. You will find these in the Appendix section at the very end of this book, along with a few special notes to you.

My hope for all three of you is that whenever you are experiencing a difficult period in your life, like riding some little scary roller coaster rides of your own, you will derive strength from reading these poems. I also have many inspirational books. I hope that one of you takes charge of them later on. I am sure that as you browse through them, especially during tough times, you will come across a few that become very special to you. Whichever one of you takes charge of this little collection can be the head librarian, loaning them out to the others when needed.

Andrew, I am putting you in charge of my old toothbrush, the original one I used to peg away at the keyboard when I wrote this book. It's in my strongbox in a zip-lock bag. Whenever you or Austin are faced with a problem later on in life I hope you will take it out and recall that I overcame the problem of typing with just one good hand using that old toothbrush. I hope it gives you the courage to surmount any difficulties that you encounter in your lives.

When God does finally call me home to Him, I don't want you and the others to be sad. Be happy for me, as I surely will be happy that I finally heard my name called. There is a passage written by Max Lucado in his book entitled *Grace For The Moment, Volume II*. It's called "The Departure Date," on page 274. After you have read that passage, you will no longer feel sad when I have departed this world.

I have a special addition (surprise) to this chapter specifically for you, Andrew. I am so very proud of you and your talents. You are a top gymnast surely headed for the Olympics® someday. I brag about you to everyone. I know your storytelling and writing abilities came from the female side of your family, namely, your mom, Aunt Melissa and me. You may have inherited your math abilities from your dad, but give us gals some credit, too. I want to share this story with all those who read this book.

You, Andrew, wrote it for a school assignment when you were just about eleven years old. You received an A+. Now you can brag to everyone that your story was published in a book. The story you wrote follows here.

Rafting Down the Rapids
A Personal Narrative from the Point of View of Winfield May
By Andrew Sevigny

My name is Winfield May, and I am fourteen years old. I am a partially blind student from the Arizona State School for the Deaf and Blind. Last June, I and a group went on a five day white-water rafting trip on the San Juan River.

Our group, including me, consisted of two partially blind students, two completely blind adults, four guides, and six sighted students. Together, we went down the San Juan River, whooping and hollering through the rapids. The students who could see described the sights to ones who couldn't see.

The San Juan River flows east to west across the desert in Utah. At the beginning of the trip, the group rafted through dry open land. Gradually, the land turned into cliffs and we had to squeeze closer together. At that point we were going swiftly down the river. We stopped at a town called Mexican Hat and we picked up food and water.

After we stopped at Mexican hat, we kept on rafting. When we got to the calm stretches of the San Juan River, we threw buckets of river water at each other. We got soaked, but we needed it especially under the hot desert sun.

On the last day of our trip, the river got calmer and the canyon walls got wider. There was a strong wind blowing the rafts back like an invisible hand. Everyone paddled hard without stopping until we reached the river.

I enjoyed my first white-water rafting trip. We were all nervous at first, but then we got over it. The blind students actually did better than the sighted students. Usually when people see the big waves they get nervous. We would love to go again!

You did a super job on that Andrew! I am so very proud of you! Again, now you can truthfully say you are a published author.

*   *   *

My dear grandsons, here I will give you some immediate family information so you will have it all handy. This is important information on your extended family.

As you know, I have only two sisters and no brothers.

My oldest sister is Tante Dee Dee (Dolores) who was first married to Edward Zambic. They only had one child, a daughter named Donna. Donna is married to Wayne Funk and they have no children. Tante Dee remarried later to Armand Arruda.

Tante Lulu (Lucille) was married to Raymond Denis and had three children: Michael, Cheryl and David.

Those are your dads' first cousins.

Michael was first married to Christine Mello and had two daughters with her: Maeghan and Amanda. He next married Dawn Urban and had a son with her. His name is Michael Jr. He married a third time to Maura McCarthy and had two children: Madison and Mason.

Cheryl had four children: Samantha, Alison, David (who we always call D.J.) and Jennifer. David was first married to Lori Mello and had three children: Rachel Nicole, who died at only seven weeks of age, Leslie and Joseph. He married a second time to Francine Beaulieu and they have two children: Sarah and Shanon.

All together, *Tante* Lulu has thirteen living grandchildren and she has one great-granddaughter, Aubrey, who is the daughter of her granddaughter Amanda.

I guess my nieces and nephews inherited the same "fertile Myrtle" gene as I did. (Chuckle)

CHAPTER 36

What follows is the special story I referred to earlier about how I feel that Bob is especially watching over Roger from heaven. I call it the Headhunter Statue Story.

Bob had obtained the statue at a church auction before Roger was born and gave it to his father to place on his bar in the basement of his home on Grattan Street. There it remained for more than forty years until after *Mémère* Sevigny passed away. After her house was sold, Uncle Ronnie asked the boys to go over to pick out the things they wanted as souvenirs of their grandparents. Roger asked for that headhunter statue.

On January 21, 2007, during a visit with Larry to Roger's house to see his tremendous progress in getting the interior of his little house in immaculate condition, I noticed the headhunter statue sitting on top of the curio cabinet where he displays all his ceramic chess pieces. It looked so familiar to me. I asked Roger where he got it. He told me about clearing out stuff from *Mémère*'s house and asking Uncle Ronnie for it. He had always remembered that statue being on the back shelf of his grandfather's bar for as long as he could recall. That's when I put the pieces together.

"Do you know the story behind that statue?" I asked him. "No," he said. I told him the story of its origin and how it ended up in *Pépère*'s bar. I also told him that somewhere in my photo albums I had photos of that statue and that I would find them and write up the whole story about it.

What follows is the true story of that headhunter statue that I shared with him shortly afterwards in a letter.

*　　*　　*

Letter to Roger, Late January 2007

Back on Labor Day weekend in 1963, your Dad and I, along with Bernie and Roger Banville, went to Weirs (Laconia), New Hampshire for a mini-vacation. It was the first and only vacation we had taken since our marriage in 1960. I was four-and-a-half months pregnant with my third child. This baby would be born January 1, 1964. That baby was you, Roger.

You were named Roger, after your Dad's uncle Roger Lafleur, *Mémère*'s younger brother, who died at Pearl Harbor but Roger Banville liked to say you were named after him. *Mémère* and *Pépère* Sevigny babysat your brothers, Jerry and Larry, so that we could have this little vacation.

On Sunday afternoon of that weekend, we went to a raffle held at a local church that was hosting the raffle to raise money for the seminarians. Two of the seminarians were your Dad's first cousins. One was named Jerry. I forget the other one's name. It may have been Joseph. They were the two sons of Joseph Lafleur, *Mémère*'s oldest brother, who also was killed in World War II. Incidentally, these cousins eventually left the seminary and both got married. I believe they are now living in Florida.

Bob bid on that headhunter statue and won. I believe it cost $20. Bernie and I thought it was grotesque and asked why, of all things, he bid on that instead of all the other nice items they had up for bid. Bob said that was what struck his eye and that's what he bid on. We laughed and joked about it the whole weekend, took photos of it and dubbed it the "headhunter statue."

I'm not absolutely sure if your Dad gave it to *Pépère* Sevigny for his bar area, or if *Pépère* got it after your father died but, either way, it ended up on *Pépère*'s bar in the basement.

Isn't it strange that, not knowing the story/provenance of that headhunter statue, you asked for that item from *Pépère*'s bar? It struck your eye too. Imagine, 44 years after the statue was acquired by your father at that auction, you find out its true history.

My thoughts relating to how the story of the statue was revealed to you after all these years follow.

Since this discovery/revelation happened on the anniversary day of *Mémère* Dube's death, January 21, and 26 years to the day since her death, which also happened to be the age your Dad passed away, I feel strongly that both of them had a hand in this "revelation" to you. I feel that they both are looking out for you from heaven and that they sent this message about the statue to let you know you are never alone. I do believe it is so. Also, because it was on *Pépère* Sevigny's bar, in *Mémère* Sevigny's house, both of them too had a hand in the revelation of this story. They too are watching over you.

When I'm gone to join all of them in heaven, I too will still be watching over you along with all five of them; *Mémère* and *Pépère* Sevigny, *Mémère* and *Pépère* Dube and your Dad, Bob.

You might be asking yourself how *Pépère* Dube fits into this story. Well, the best explanation I can come up with is first, that he is your grandfather after all, and second, he was a carpenter, a woodworker. Perhaps, up in heaven, he is the one who was put in charge of all matters pertaining to "wood," especially works of art like the headhunter statue. Yes, I call it a work of art now. Truly, it is a work of art because of its history and the amazing fact that you ended up with it all these years later, not even knowing its history and relationship to your Dad, the Dad you never really knew.

Take care of it and cherish it, and be sure to pass it along to Andrew later on. Andrew will have an ever-so-precious memory of his grandfather Bob and of his Uncle Roger.

* * *

When I told Ronnie, Bob's brother, the story of the headhunter statue, he was amazed. Even he didn't know the true story of that statue. He remembers it always being on his father's back bar and always thought his parents had collected it as a souvenir during one of their various trips.

I don't think it was a coincidence that Roger ended up with the statue that his father had bid on in 1963, roughly four months before Roger was born. I really believe that Bob had a hand in making sure Roger ended up with it.

I also believe that Bob is still taking good care of all his boys—make that his "suns."

CHAPTER 37

In some previous chapters I refer to being obstinate and not being able to accept the fact that I was not going to be in total control. I stated that I had some difficulty accepting help from my kids sometimes giving them much grief and heartache.

I discovered "A New Beatitude" in the December 2006 issue of the *Liguorian*. This article hit the nail (and this stubborn Frenchwoman) right on the head as far as my obstinacy and accepting help were concerned.

The author, Victoria Bahr, relates how an ankle injury led to surgery involving the insertion of a plate and screws, which consequently led to her hobbling around during the Christmas season. She never imagined what a humbling learning experience this would turn out to be.

She had always been in control, multi-tasking and taking care of everyone. It was so difficult to accept, or even ask, for help when she was the one used to being the "helper."

Truth be told, this sentiment hit very close to home. In fact, it sounded like a true clone of me. I have had a similar experience. After my surgeries of 1997, I was downright obstinate about not asking for help from my children for anything. My pride got in the way and was bolstered by my stubbornness. My dear children can tell you countless stories of that period and believe me they are not pretty tales.

After reading that article in 2006, I finally realized I was wrong. Do you know how hard it is for me to even admit I was wrong? I pray you never get the opportunity to meet with any of my children because they will certainly put me to shame with their countless stories of mom being the personification of a true "stubborn Frenchwoman" for countless years.

In one part of that article, Bahr says, "These days, I'm trying to graciously accept the help I still need." She goes on to say that one of her children had a grade school assignment involving the creation of a new beatitude. She suggested: Blessed are those who can accept help graciously. She emphasized that we should consider how good it feels to be helpful to others, and that it does seem selfish and sad when we deny others that same pleasurable good feeling.

She further stated that, in hindsight, her broken ankle led to a great learning experience, further saying that it was possibly the greatest Christmas gift she had received that year.

My reflections on her article brought me to the realization that some things that happen to us are, as they say, truly blessings in disguise. Albeit it took nine years after my surgeries before I came across that article, after I read it I finally got it. Sometimes we have to let God and, yes, let others do what we cannot do—and be gracious about it.

*   *   *

One of my dear aunts in Canada sent me the following poem followed by related comments that I want to share with my grandsons. It is a source of inspiration to me to continue riding the roller coasters of my life. It is worth reading. It was either in her church bulletin or in a Senior Citizen Club Newsletter (*L'âge D'or*). Following is the translation from French.

Happiness at Your Door: (Le Bonheur a Vôtre Portée)

Happiness is a journey, not a destination!
Work as if you are in no need of any money,
Love as if you have never been hurt,
And dance as if no one is watching you . . .

We convince ourselves that life will be better once we are married and have a baby and then a second baby. Then, we become frustrated because our children are small and everything will be better once they are grown. We further become frustrated when they become teenagers and convince ourselves we will be happier when they have moved out of this stage.

We tell ourselves our life will be perfect when our mate or partner gets his or her act together, or when we have a nicer car, or when we can take better and longer vacations or when we retire. The truth is that there is no better time to be happy than right now. Our life will always be imperfect; it is preferable to admit this and decide to be happy right now in spite of everything.

One of my favorite quotations is by Alfred D. Souza. He says, "For a very long time, it seemed to me that my life would eventually start—my true life. But there were always obstacles along the way; a crisis to get through, a chore or project to finish, a debt to be paid. Then life would truly begin. I finally came to understand that these obstacles were my life."

This perspective helped me to see that there is no "road" to happiness. Happiness is the road, the journey . . . so cherish and appreciate every second of right now. More so, appreciate those seconds because you have shared them with someone special and remember that time waits for no one.

So, stop waiting for this or that to happen, stop waiting for the weekend to come, stop waiting for spring to get here or whatever before you decide that there is no better time than right now to be happy.

*　　*　　*

Here is another precious one I want to share with my grandsons, translated from the original French, sent to me by my Dad when he was living in *Québec*. It also had appeared in his parish newsletter. It is a reminder to me that I should always be ready to meet the Lord, our God.

I'LL SEE YOU LATER, LORD! (A Bientôt Seigneur)

When you come for me Lord, can I ask You to please knock at my door so I know You are coming? I remember that You said that You would come "like a thief in the night." That's really not necessary, Lord. You said that so that we would always be ready; thank you Lord! But you see, Lord, at home when I do my chores I am clumsy and often stain my clothes so I wear an apron. When a friend knocks at my door, I remove that apron so the friend doesn't see all the stains and the sight of me is agreeable to him or her.

Please leave me enough time to remove my stained apron to receive You, Lord. I ask this of you, but Thy Will Be Done. I know whatever you decide it will be for the best. I wanted You to be aware of this special request; this is permissible among friends. Isn't that so? Are You not my greatest friend, the one that never forsakes me and in Whom I have placed all my confidence?

Thank you, Lord.

CHAPTER 38

Here in this chapter I will remind my grandsons that God bestows on all of us special gifts with the purpose to help us in our journey of life. I'll jot down a few examples my sense of humor which I cherish as an extra-special gift from God because it sure helped me lighten up at times and definitely was an often-used coping mechanism.

That precious gift from God, my sense of humor, eventually kicked into high gear after my ordeal of those surgeries but not always or consistently as I still experienced many bad days. I have to relate a few incidents where my humor really did shine. (chuckle)

I recall when I told Jerry and some of my friends that I really only regretted one thing about the fact I had to lose my "boob." I told everyone that it really hurt to lose my Playboy® centerfold contract because, apparently, there, in fine print, was that disastrous, contract-killing clause: "must have two boobs." I said, "Oh well, kiss that $200,000 contract goodbye."

Another time I recall is when I set up a new "nic" for my POGO® games. My new "nic" was RDMPMEM. A "nic," for those who don't already know, is a screen name you make up for playing games online. My Internet friend Oriel, who lives in England and is a regular cribbage opponent on the POGO games site, asked me what that stood for. I told her it was an abbreviation for "Road Map *Mémère*" (RD MP MEM), because my body looked like a road map with all its squiggles and scars, and I was working on getting a contract from Rand McNally®. I figured a photo of a human map (my scar-ridden body) would certainly generate more interest and sales for Rand McNally maps. I only had to figure out a way to convince them of this so I'd get a nice, big, fat, lucrative contract. We had a good long laugh after I related my plan to her.

I remember relating to everyone my plan to get the last laugh. All I needed to know was the day and time I would die, but I needed to know this at least six months in advance. My bold plan had to be carved in stone, with no possibility whatsoever that I would get spared after that six months was up. I could then book a trip around the world, go shopping at Saks Fifth Avenue® and visit Maxime's® in Paris. I could hit Harrod's® in London, (they have the cutest red 50s-look coin purse with white dots), and also even order a special, custom-made Jaguar. I could lease a luxury yacht for a month and cruise the Caribbean or the Mediterranean.

Oh, I could think of a zillion things to buy and do before those six months went by. Of course, this would all be done using the multitude of credit cards I had applied for which I would max out. How else can I afford to shop at Saks Fifth Avenue, or buy a Jaguar? Have an idea folks! After six months my "time" would be up and I would happily depart this world having thoroughly enjoyed the "good life", albeit only for six months. My estate would be responsible for my debts. The last laugh is on those credit card companies. There is NO estate. I would die penniless, or close to it. You see, before beginning to use those lovely credit cards, I would have transferred all remaining assets to a trust for my children. Trusts are protected from creditors. What are they going to do? They can't dig me up to "face charges" can they? Hmm, maybe I should be cremated. It's hard to reconstitute "ashes" isn't it? Really, what I just wrote is but just another example of my sense of humor, because I never could be that dishonest and go through with such an outrageous scam.

I guess He knew what was in store for me during my life. He had the master plan after all. He specifically assigned me that great sense of humor. See how God gives us what we need? I do.

Earlier I mentioned RDMPMEM, I have to explain my main "nic" of MemDooby. When I got my first computer, my daughter-in-law Sheree was the one who sat with me to give me a few lessons. She helped me to set up my Internet account. When we had to choose a screen name, Sheree suggested I go with "MemDube". Believe it or not, it was not available. Someone else already had that one. So, Sheree brilliantly came up with MemDooby. Dooby was a variation in the spelling of my maiden name. Later, I found out why this name was not taken.

When my friend Judy showed me how to get into the POGO game site, I began playing games using that "nic" as my screen name. Some games can be played alone and others like Spades are played with a partner or Cribbage against an opponent and where you also chat while playing the game. Almost immediately, some partners or opponents would write in the chat area of that particular game, "Hey Dooby, pass me a joint." I ignored them, as I had no idea what they were talking about. Eventually, someone in the chat asked if I knew what a dooby was. That's when I found out it meant a marijuana joint.

I never changed the original "nic" that my brilliant and dear daughter-in-law Sheree had come up with. I continued using it and still do to this day. Now, whenever someone makes a comment about a dooby, I go right along with it. I tell them, yes, I am a pot-smoking old granny, explaining that the "Mem" part is for granny in Franco-American lingo and further, that I don't share my pot with anyone. Of course, I do not smoke pot at all, but they don't need to know that. I just go with the flow. I get a lot of "lol's." As for my daughter-in-law Sheree, I assure you that, afterwards, I thoroughly researched any name or suggestion she came up with if I was unsure of its true meaning.

I have told Sheree that if I get arrested because the "law" is monitoring that POGO site and they read my comments about being a pot-smoking granny, I expect her to bail me out of jail and hire the best lawyer she can afford to keep me from being convicted. Yes, if that should ever happen, she will be the one to pay for my defense and keep her sons' *Mémère* from becoming a jailbird. She wouldn't ever want them to go to school and tell everyone their *Mémère* was serving time for a pot conviction. For that reason alone, I know she will come up with her own ace in the hole and find a way to pay for the best criminal attorney for my defense.

Carol Indyck should pay special attention to this next part. I myself will try praying to St. Ichabod again. *How do you know, Carol, that he's not a saint?* The bible says, "Oh ye of such little faith." If you have read this story, Carol, you should know by now you should NEVER SAY NEVER. (Carol is Uncle Pete's better half, and Uncle Pete is really Cousin Pitou, Bob's first cousin.) One time, when I told Carol I had made a novena to St. Ichabod when I was searching for that missing puzzle piece regarding Larry's education difficulties, she told me she didn't think there was a saint by that name. I told her I was praying to every saint I knew and even to those that just might be a saint. So, St. Ichabod was on my prayer list of saints. Truth be told, there is no St. Ichabod as far as I know. My Internet search turned up nothing.

I hope some of what you read in this chapter left you all chuckling and helped to lighten up my sometimes depressing story.

CHAPTER 39

I suppose I do have to mention my faults. I've deliberately delayed writing about those, but I can't just mention some of my strengths or better qualities. As my primary purpose in writing this book about my life was for my grandsons and the generations that will follow, I wanted to give them courage to recognize and admit their own shortcomings by admitting to some of my own. Why? Well, it is because we cannot work on self-improvement unless we first recognize our faults.

Okay, I admit I have many faults, but I won't give you the satisfaction of admitting to all of them here. Besides, if I did, this book would be so dang long. I'll identify only a few that I am aware of and, yes, I'll sometimes give you excuses or an explanation in an attempt to minimize those particular faults. These are probably the ones that are the most annoying to my family and friends.

First, there is my pride, which causes me to brag a lot. I am so proud of my children's accomplishments that I boast about them. I think I'm entitled, so there! Enough said here about my pride.

Second, there is my constant tendency to interrupt people when they are talking. I guess it's really called "rudeness." My excuse for that is that my brain is overloaded. When I think of something to say, it just pops right out of my mouth somehow. I don't even realize I have interrupted whomever was talking until after that "pop up" is out. My dear friend Judy could have given you several examples of my interruptions as she had nicknamed me "Jabberjaws" in exasperation. I'm sure my children could also give you several examples. Their list would surely be at least ten pages long.

The next fault I will admit to is that "snippy" one or of having a short-temper. Believe me, my bark is worse than my bite, but I am aware that, at times, I come across as tough, unloving and "snippy." To be truthful, this should be re-labeled as my fault of unkindness. During those long days in the hospital, when I was wading in hallucinating pools of narcotics, residual anesthesia and other powerful meds that made me paranoid, trusting no one and angry at everyone, then later at home when the chronic pain and the daily frustrations of not being able to do something for myself were in control, I WAS UNKIND AND RUDE. During my depressive period after the divorce, I was constantly in that snippy mood and I was often unkind to my loved ones and dear friends.

When I say unkind, that also is not an accurate description of how I behaved. I was malicious, vitriolic, rancorous, harsh, heartless, ruthless, and savage. Even those words do not accurately describe my behavior. I'm sure my daughter could come up with the perfect word. I am ashamed to write what I have been told by my children of what actually transpired when I was hospitalized and afterwards. The list of "snippies" and "nasties" my children could write about would be a hundred pages long for sure and would not be at all pretty or enjoyable to read.

Being stubborn is the last fault I will admit to. I like to be in control and now, especially, with this chronic pain situation, I'm never in control, the pain is. I have to constantly work on that fault. The reverse side of that stubbornness though is my determination. Determination, after all, is part of the reason I got through all the roller coaster rides of my fate and destiny. About that pain—it may be in control of my life but it is no longer in control of me.

I wish I could afford to see a "shrink" to discuss all of my faults (I'd be in therapy for at least ten years), and have him agree with me on EVERYTHING after I have explained, with appropriate excuses, the reasons I developed these faults. So many people in my life have not always agreed with me, yet I know I am nearly always right. (chuckle) I guess that's another fault, that of thinking I am always right.

Looks like I still have a lot of self-improvement to do yet.

That's it! I will NOT admit to any more faults. If my ears start ringing I will know that those that know me personally are all adding their observations on my faults. Oh Lord, my poor ears are ringing already!

CHAPTER 40

In the next two chapters, I will tell my grandsons about two very special gifts I received from my children. The reason for relating those stories is to remind them to always be grateful and to recognize that some gifts they will receive in the course of their lifetimes will be extra special ones to be treasured for a lifetime.

My children surprised me for Christmas one year with the beautiful gift of my Mother's Ring. I have to write about that very special Christmas. Before I forget, I bequeath this ring to Melissa for her to eventually pass on to the very first great-granddaughter that is born. Michael, Andrew or Austin surely will produce one girl when they marry.

Before I opened the gift and knew what it was, Melissa gave me a poem she had written to be read first. That poem follows.

It's Christmas time again,
That time that comes but once a year.
And we, your "elfish" children,
Would like to take this chance
To spread some Christmas cheer.

Granted, cheer is something
That should be spread all year through,
But children are often forgetful
So we're making up for lost time
sending this greeting, with love, to you.

Merry Christmas, Mother,
From we, the children five.
Thank you for everything.
We love you, and we're
Sorry we had to lie.

You've told us many times
In the course of all our days
"Don't come home with a package."
Well, Mom, just this once
We had to disobey.

Yes, Mom, come home with a package
Is exactly what we've done,
But what makes it worse is
That all five of us are guilty
And not just simply one.

We know what you're thinking
Not a sound can you utter.
If you're thinking we're all pregnant
Take a deep breath then get
Your mind out of the gutter.

Let us simply say that the
Package of which we write,
Is our reminder to you of
All those long "fulfilling" nights.

Now you can't ever forget us,
Or the things we did,
And we won't ever forget you, Mom,
Because we love you.

Now open our package . . .

Aren't you glad, after all,
That you had kids*! (*this was a reference to my "nun aspirations)

After I opened the box with the beautiful ring in it, I was instructed to read the last part of what Melissa had written, which follows here:

Each stone represents a child all its own, each with fond memories and sad memories alike; but, together, this quartet represents you. It represents the hardships, the sacrifices and the joys of being a Mother. After all, Mom, we all have a little part of you in us, and now you will always have a little piece of us with you. Wherever you go, or wherever the path of life takes us, always remember that we do love you, and we do appreciate all you have done for us.

> *Merry Christmas with Love,*
> *Jerry and Sheree, Larry, Roger and Missy*

I remember welling up with tears. I was so moved by their gift, the poem and Melissa's final lines that I read after I saw the Mother's ring. I guess I don't have to tell you that these were tears of pure pride, joy and surprise.

CHAPTER 41

My children gave me my first computer as a birthday gift. I think it was in 1992.

They were so thoughtful and generous. I think they decided they were not going to put up with a "computer illiterate" mother. I had to join the soon-to-come 21st century because those "*Freddy Flintstone*" days were gone forever. That was such a precious gift. They took turns giving me basic computer instruction. I didn't even know what to do after I turned it on.

I prepared a special *Thévenet* issue (JMA school newspaper) for my 35th class reunion, held in October 1993, using that very first computer. Getting that *Thévenet* issue perfected, especially all the graphics, was possible only because of the expertise of Sheree, my dear, patient and talented daughter-in-law. Again, in 1998, another *Thévenet* was put together for our 40th class reunion, of course with Sheree's help. I was going through chemo at that time (finished in August 1998) but with Sheree's generous help, I was able to get this project done. I have a photo of myself at the reunion held in fall of 1998 with my somewhat bald head. My hair fuzz was just beginning to appear after finishing up the last chemo round in August. I refused to wear that ugly wig, so I attended as a "baldy." I think I looked cute and in fact a few of my classmates gave me so much credit for showing up bald. "You've got guts!" they said. By the way, with Sheree's help, I published a third issue for our 50th Class Reunion in October 2008.

Since then, I have become a bit more computer literate (although Melissa is still teaching me things), but I know enough to meet my needs. Should I need to learn more advanced skills, I'll tackle learning those as they come up. I have been able to keep in touch with many friends through emails and such. My handwriting is so bad now, because I can no longer write right-handed, that I can do letters and notes on the computer to friends that don't have computers or email. If I do feel a hand-written note is called for I will print with my left hand as at least that is legible.

I peg away using an old toothbrush held in my right hand for all the right-hand keyboard keys. It works out fine. I'm still a pretty fast typist in spite of having to use this method. I can communicate, via IMing on AOL, with my two grandsons in New Hampshire. Of course, this story would never have been written had I not had a computer. I play POGO games, mostly spades, cribbage and word games, to pass the time. This distracts me tremendously from my chronic pain.

Of all the beautiful and generous gifts they have given me over the years, the gift of my "first" computer ranks very high. Thank you all for my first computer and for everything. To everyone else reading this story I say see, those education investments were already starting to pay off.

CHAPTER 42

The law and my life crossed paths over the years and I have some definite thoughts about the law. There are valuable lessons to be passed on to the generations that will follow. Except for stealing that red juicy apple when I was about six years old, I don't think I've ever broken the law. I'm not counting speeding tickets here. My experiences having the law being on my side is what I am referring to. Our legal system is the best in the world, but in my case it leaves much to be desired. I'll explain that thought to you.

Case #1—Me vs. The Employer
Case never filed; lack of evidence

When my husband died at age 26, I was young and naïve. Had I agreed to the autopsy and gone against my father-in-law's wishes maybe the evidence would have been uncovered to prove that my husband's employer was culpable in a wrongful death suit. The doctors all thought that it was unusual that he was full of radiation. We now can conclude that he was overexposed to radiation while working in the "pill" (the reactor compartment of the submarines) as an outside machinist. The gauges that the employees wore must have been defective. I wrote in an earlier chapter how Red Scanlon who worked with Bob and later Red's son tried to pursue this possibility but they were stopped in their tracks because of the classified information "snafu." If we had the autopsy done would that have made a difference and could a wrongful death suit have been filed? Guess I'll always wonder and no one will ever know for certain.

Case #2—Me vs. The Public School Department
Case never went to trial

When my son Larry had all those difficulties in school I was promised all kinds of remedial help that never materialized or, if it did, it was just a drop in the bucket compared to what he did need. After ten years of my searching for the piece of the puzzle that was missing and after transferring him to a private school equipped to undo the extensive damage done over all those years, so that he could eventually

263

learn to read, I saw a lawyer to start legal action against our local school department. In my eyes, they were negligent in never bringing to my attention that crucial testing that had been done in kindergarten which had clear indications of the possibility of a learning disability.

Too bad I had a young lawyer just starting out who did not have the resources to pursue my case further. When the school department offered to settle before going to trial my lawyer recommended taking the offer. Why? He couldn't afford to go to trial on a contingency basis with no guarantee that the case would be won by us. He needed the money. Probably, it was to buy a decent desk for his office. When I consulted with him he had three cinder blocks stacked on either side with an old wooden door across the top. This served as his desk. He heated his humble office with a wood burning stove. He told me if I wanted to continue to trial he would require $5,000 up front. He knew I couldn't do that and still manage to keep Larry in the private residential school for the second year, with Jerry, the oldest also in a private local high school, St. Andrew's. I was not made of money.

I often ask myself what the outcome would have been had I gambled and taken out a second mortgage, taking my chances at trial. If only I was a gambler. I bet I would have won. *Why* would they offer $18,000 to settle if they felt they were on solid ground? The plain fact was that they were negligent in never bringing that early Kindergarten test to my attention. Hindsight is marvelous isn't it? This is sure a classic case of "could have, should have and would have." If only I had sought out another more experienced lawyer with a well-established large law firm. Oh, the significance of those little words *why*, *if*, and *if only*.

Case #3—Me vs. Dr. V
My trust and naïveté did me in, yet again . . .

My mother-of-all-roller-coaster ride—the big surgery, all the surgical procedures that followed and the infection is another example of my *naïveté* and trusting nature. Would I ever had to ride that scary coaster ride if my oncologist had taken me seriously when I mentioned to him that I felt that pulling sensation in my right shoulder? He repeatedly assured me it was "nothing to worry about" and that it was probably an after effect of the radiation. Guess what, it was an after-effect of the radiation. The pathology report after the mastectomy before I had the chest surgery for removal of the ribs, etc. clearly stated that the cancer was "radiation induced." I had radiation years earlier after a lumpectomy of the same breast. He knew my case history, didn't he? Did he just take my case when Dr. Dorman referred me to him and file the folder away never bothering to look at the medical information? Why did he not order CAT Scans (or whatever) back when I complained about that pulling? If the discovery of that aggressive sarcoma growing in my chest wall would have occurred sooner would I have had to lose the five ribs? Would the cancer have grown to almost stage IV? Could it have been caught early enough that the outcome would have been much different? Would I be suffering this unforgiving chronic pain for all these years after that big surgery on Halloween night of 1997?

I trusted my oncologist. I never sought a second opinion. I was naïve. Yes, I was a lot older (57 by this time) and should have been more "savvy" as they say. You would think with all I had been through in my earlier life I would have learned something along the way.

Again, when I saw a lawyer, several different ones in fact, they told me that they believed me and what I had been through, but after they did their own thorough research of medical records, doctors' notes and hospitalization files they informed me that the case hinged on Dr. V. A careful review of his office notes revealed that he had never written down my concerns about that pulling sensation. It was a case of "he said, she said." I could say I told him but I had to prove it. How? If he never wrote it down, it was a case of my word against his. He could deny it, and there was no way to prove he was lying.

Medical negligence cases are tough and long and a good, experienced law firm cannot afford to gamble on a case that might not be won. They take these cases on a contingency basis and put up all the money to get the case to trial. They told me it would be a minimum of $100,000. With everything hanging on "he said, she said," they just couldn't gamble on it. All of the different lawyers I consulted with told me the same thing.

Again, I ask myself, why I didn't insist that doctor write down everything I discussed with him at each office visit. Why didn't I insist on having a copy of his notes right then and there, every time I went in for a check-up? If only I had someone with me during just one of those office visits where I brought this concern up, I would have a witness to what was discussed. If, why and if only yet again.

*   *   *

My advice to all who read this book is as follows: Don't be afraid to gamble. Gamble on what you know in your heart is right. Gamble on what your gut tells you. Gamble on your instincts.

Next, money can be your worst enemy. Lack of it will stop you from following your gut. Don't let the lack of money stop you. So what if you have to take a second mortgage to do what you know you need to do. You just put more water in the soup to pay that second mortgage. Wish I would have done it instead of settling for less than what was right. I should have practiced what I preached, "where there is a will there is a way."

Next, don't be so trusting of professionals and those you think know more than you do. In important matters such as your health, be sure to have a good solid paper trail of everything that happens including office notes from the doctor you are seeing. Make sure he is competent; don't assume he is. Have someone accompany you to doctor office visits. Seek second opinions, even third opinions, in critical matters of your health.

Next, when someone asks for permission to perform a special or distasteful thing (like an autopsy, for example), think with your brain and not with your heart. Don't let your emotions cloud your judgment. Finally, learn from your mistakes—sooner rather than later. I sure didn't when it comes to me and the law. It was only after much later reflection that I was able to see my mistakes in all three "cases."

Now I sure do hope I have learned from all my mistakes of the past. The only case I want to win now is the one on Judgment Day. I certainly don't want to lose that case because of *naïveté*. My record for winning cases has not been great so far. I must be prepared to present my case to St. Peter, the gate keeper, so that it is winnable. God will be my judge, and St. Peter will surely be there as the prosecutor bringing up all my life's transgressions. I better have more on the plus side so I'd better get my act together. I do know that no one can win this case for me. I have to do it myself.

PART V

CHAPTER 43

I do believe in the benevolent care of a higher power, God. I must write some about my strong faith.

No Man Is an Island, a poem by John Dunne, has stayed with me throughout my life. It reminds me that we do not live our lives just for ourselves, isolated from others. Our life affects others' lives as others' lives affect ours. We are all connected.

If you have never read the poem *For Everything There is a Season*, please do. That particular poem reminds me there would have been no Melissa without Russell. There would never have been Jerry, Larry and Roger without Bob. The strength to survive would not have been there had not the foundation stones of that strength been subtly laid down in those childhood and pre-adulthood formation years. Living through all that "fate and destiny" was possible because of faith especially and also with that precious gift of my sense of humor. I've already given you a few examples of that sense of humor.

Now about my faith; I do firmly believe that everything does happen for a reason. Only God knows all the reasons. Only God has answers to all of our questions. As many times as we get discouraged and doubt and get angry with Him, in the end we have to turn it around and trust in His infinite wisdom, His love for us and His unending mercy. Then, we must ask His forgiveness for not always totally and instantly accepting all the little crosses He sends to us and even the big, roller coaster-type crosses that many of us get to bear.

"Ask and you shall receive," He told us. Sometimes we ask for something that is not good for us in His total knowledge of the plan for our life, and we think our prayers go unanswered. I do believe prayers get answered, but not always in the way we want them to be answered. If God says *no* to our prayer request, it is not because He's angry with us, or is stingy. He has something else in mind for us. Kids, remember me saying that whenever God shuts a door, He leaves a window open? When He does shut a particular door (in not answering a prayer), He does leave a window open, because He has something else lined up for us in answer to that prayer.

He is a generous, loving God who knows what's best for us at all times. It's our imperfect human nature that causes all the problems. We all have to continue to strive to trust in Him, completely and without hesitation. I personally have come a long way toward achieving that goal but, I admit, I am not totally there yet. On bad days, I still wonder why He lets me suffer this chronic pain. What I have to constantly remind myself of is that He doesn't send us any cross too heavy to bear in this journey called life. He, alone, knows the reason for our individual crosses, and He does give us the strength to endure the burden of those crosses.

CHAPTER 44

I have reached the final chapter of my book. I began my story with my thoughts about having to accomplish the mission in life that God assigned to me. Before I end my story, I ask myself again what that mission in life is that I must complete.

As I previously wrote, I thought I had to write this story down for my grandsons, to give them hope and courage to go on when they ride their own individual roller coaster rides of life. I thought that all the examples of "fate and destiny" could possibly help them sometime in the future when they are adults and they, too, realize that "Life is just a bowl of cherries, pits and all." I'm finishing up with my story right now. It's almost done.

With further thought on that question, I realize that the other part of the answer must be that I need to totally, without a mini-second of doubt, reach the point where I trust God completely, without ever taking one step back or hesitating. I must be able to truly say *Thy Will be Done* and mean it with unwavering faith, never asking for an answer to the old questions I have about why He let this or that happen. I now feel that is partly what fulfilling my mission in life means. I'm working on this too, but it's so hard. I keep falling off that path of total abandonment to the will of God.

I still continue to hope this final roller coaster ride I'm on, the chronic unrelenting PAIN one, does end soon. It is NOT going fast enough for me. I wish I could grease the wheels of this roller coaster ride to make it go faster and faster resulting in a great big roller coaster crash that would destroy the roller-coaster-track rides of my life once and for all. I would then be eternally free from any more rides and from this nasty, chronic pain. I know that hope is not in accordance with that total abandonment to God's will.

It very well could be that when my story is finished and I no longer fall off that path leading to total submission to God's will, my mission will have been completed and this last, downhill and PAINFUL roller coaster ride will finally end. Amen to that! It's that part concerning total abandon to the will of God that will surely hold things up. It is what is not allowing that roller coaster ride to come to its final stop.

I guess I must still have a long way to go to get to that point as God continues to leave me here on earth. I'm not getting any signs that I will receive a call soon. I still picture God and St. Peter in their daily conferences discussing me yet again. I'm guessing their conclusion as to my fate, so far, has not changed. It still must be, "Let's leave her down there a bit longer. Let them on earth deal with her. She has too many questions and still can be a bit of a pain in the butt. We don't really want her up here yet, do we?" (I know I'm putting words in God's mouth here, but it's just how I imagine it and is yet another example of my sense of humor.)

So, I must continue on the last roller coaster ride of my life which has slowed down but not stopped. I know there are no more big hills to climb. It's surely all downhill from now on. My consolation is in knowing that this final ride will end eventually. As they say, nothing is forever. Only eternity is forever. I often say to my children that, with my luck, I'll probably live to be 100. Well, I sure do hope my luck runs out because that would mean another thirty years. I pray the Lord is merciful and that does not happen but if it is His will that I do live that long, I trust that He will be with me, making those later years' coaster rides more like the enjoyable, idyllic rides of my childhood.

I do know that my ride, or rides, will end when God says so, period, and only after I have finally stopped being that "bit of a troublemaker with so many questions." I have sometimes been lax in being faithful to my prayers and in continuing in my spiritual growth. I know this is the key to reaching that point of total surrender to God's will. Oh how often I forget Monsignor Hamel's words during his Kennedy Street visits to me after Bob passed away, especially his words about fervent prayer. I will strive to be more attentive to that from now on.

I have so many inspirational books along with many inspirational and prayer tapes. Those should be revisited more often. The *Angels* magazine received as a gift subscription from Tom and Anna (Walter's brother and his wife) has to be read more carefully and the inspirational stories savored more deeply. I have all those cards sent to me at the hospital and over the years. As I said before (and I know I repeat myself a lot), some are so beautifully inspiring. Those should all be placed in a scrapbook with notations besides the extra special ones of my thoughts on how that particular card helped me, boosted me up or sustained me along the way during that horrible hospital experience. Adding my thoughts about the kind person who sent it to me would be nice too and would also remind me of all the caring, loving people God placed in my life. See, yet another project not completed. I'd better get a move on.

The cards and my thoughts could be read by my grandsons and, possibly, the generations that follow them. Just maybe it will come to pass that one of those cards and notations will be the "help" that a grandson, great-grandson, or great-great-grandson needs at a particularly trying time in his life. (Somewhere in the future this will change to a great-granddaughter, I suppose.)

I once told my dear *Tante* Jacqueline in Canada that I had one thousand questions for God when and if I ever get there, and I expect God to answer each and every one of them, no matter how long it takes HIM. She ever-so-wisely said that I will not have to ask questions when I reach heaven, as they will all be instantly answered when I gaze upon the face of God. I just have to trust and be PATIENT. That patient part is really tough for me.

Aunt Jacqueline didn't say, "*When and if I get there*", I did. She has told me I will get there. *Tante* Léa encourages me with the little inspirational Bible verse cards she includes in all the letters and cards she sends to me. One, in particular, is: *JE VAIS TE PORTER REMÈDE, GUÉRIR TES PLAIES*—(Jr.30, 17). Translated, this means: I will bring you relief and heal your wounds. They, and all of my other dear aunts and uncles, feel I have accepted the cross God chose for me and that I carry it well. That's because they haven't seen me on my bad days since all of them are in Canada. Being so far away they were all spared those "snippy days." They are all certain there is a special place in heaven for me. I hope they are right. I'll settle for just plain "a place in heaven" period. I am happy to forfeit the special part.

I sometimes do fear going to hell because my friend Judy had said if we both ended up there, she would probably be standing on my shoulders being as I was the bigger sinner. She was right, I am, but I wouldn't admit it to her. Judy weighed more than I did and I would be crushed into the bottom of the fire pit, surely making me the "crispiest" one in hell. (That's my sense of humor again,) I do know Judy has gone to heaven. Surely I have a decent shot at getting there because of my strong faith and hope. If I do, Judy will be sitting by "Jabberjaws" side trying to get a word in edgewise and certainly not standing on my shoulders. Thank the Lord!

Don't get me wrong. I am not a perfect, holier-than-thou, little 'ole lady. I never meant to give anyone that impression. I don't presume I WILL get to Heaven. I HOPE that I do. I admit to many faults, some of which I mentioned earlier, but in the end I do have hope and faith in our most merciful God and His promises. I have committed many offenses against God, as all humans do, and I still continue to offend God. I do, however, ask for forgiveness when I recall those transgressions. Jesus did say, "Ask and you shall receive." That's what He meant. Just ask for God's forgiveness, pick yourself up, try to do better and never repeat that particular sin. He wasn't talking about asking to win the million dollar lottery.

The key word there is "try." He knows we will continue to fall and to repeat our transgressions because of our human nature. He also knows in His infinite Wisdom that if we cooperate with Him and the abundant graces He sends each of us, trying to do better, always asking for His forgiveness, He will never abandon us. Rather, He will send us extra strength, extra courage and whatever else it is we need to continue on the individual roller coaster rides of the life He chose for each of us. When that final roller coaster ride does come to a full stop, having been successfully completed, we will all pass through the gates of heaven and dwell with Him forever. Passing through the gates of Heaven can't come soon enough for me. I know that's when I will finally be rid of this PAIN.

Since I really never found a prayer that fit my unique needs I made one up myself. Hey, we're allowed to do that. Prayer, after all, is just talking to God. Who says we have to only talk to God in formal, approved prayers? After reading my prayer it will be instantly clear to you why I have not reached that state of total abandon I speak about.

My Prayer

Lord, show me the way—the way to atone for my past sins and to complete whatever it was that you assigned to me as my "mission in life" on the day You created me. Show me the way to have complete trust in You.

I hope that when You feel that I have earned eternal life You will come for me. Please tell me or show me what I have to do to get to that point. Please give me some hints. I'm desperate and impatient as You well know.

I thank you Lord for all Your past Blessings and for Your continued Blessings. I hunger for the anticipated final Blessing of eternal life with You. While I await Your call to bring me home to you, I do offer up all this pain, all my days and especially all my bad days in expiation of my sins, for the sins of the whole world and particularly for the most forgotten soul in Purgatory.

P.S. Lord, the sooner I get that call, the better, okay?

Amen!

Notice the last line of my prayer <u>with the question mark</u>. See, I still try to coax God into doing it my way by asking Him for that call. This sure isn't total abandon to His will. I have to totally accept the fact that He will make that call only when He is ready to. Knowing myself almost as much the Lord does, I WILL probably live to be 100. Possibly, it will take that long for me to let go, no longer ending my made-up prayer with that postscript and a question mark, and finally letting God do it His way and according to the plan He had for me from the day I was born.

Until I try to stop asking questions, my journey on this last loop of this last roller coaster ride will not end. In the meantime I know what has reached THE END. It's this, the story of my life. Honestly, it has been a "wild ride" and yes, I CAN say that it was, in spite of everything, "pits and all," an enjoyable one too!

PART VI

AUTHOR'S NOTE

Truly God weaves the tapestries of each of our lives in such unique ways. When I wrote the final chapter of my life story, I did believe I was done with it. Now, I know that wasn't so.

Thinking that perhaps I had accomplished my mission in life, I hinted to the Lord that I was eagerly awaiting His "call" with that "P.S." and a question mark at the end of my prayer. Now, I have to petition Him to delay calling me home, as I have discovered I do have some unfinished work to do. Mainly, I realize that my children still need me. I won't go into all the details, but will say that one truly needed me to unravel the mess he found himself in. Other gifts from the Lord re-surfaced at this time. My sleuthing as "Gertie" and my bookkeeping skills were a big help in unraveling his messy situation. It's going to be a long haul, but he'll get through this and come out ahead a better and much wiser man as a result of all that has happened.

And so it came to pass. Larry's divorce from Mary was granted in June 2009.

Roger's ongoing battle against alcoholism is another reason I must remain here on earth for a while. He is alone, unmarried, and I am truly his only best friend. I need to be around to encourage him with his ongoing struggle to control this terrible disease. I have learned over the years that "tough love" is what he needs from me and that I must never be an enabler. I have done much research on the Internet on alcoholism and have also spoken to many people from various organizations that deal with the problems of this terrible disease. As I did with the problem of finding that missing puzzle piece where Larry's education was concerned, which took ten years, I will never give up on Roger. My prayers will get answered when God proceeds with His plan for Roger's life journey. Of course, Roger must cooperate with God's plan.

I must also continue to spread the word on faith and especially on the benefits of devotion to St. Gertrude, my patron saint, who received a directive from Our

Lord to say a special prayer and that each time it was said He would release 1,000 souls from purgatory. That prayer is:

Eternal Father, I offer Thee the Most Precious Blood of Thy Divine Son, Jesus, in union with the Masses said throughout the world today, for all the holy souls in purgatory. Amen.

As some day I may be the most forgotten soul in purgatory, I ask that all who read this say the prayer often. You may be the one that releases my sorry soul to join those already in heaven. My renewed devotion to her is also my way to make up for disliking my middle name all these years. For years, I truly disliked that name, Gertrude, but now I cherish it. After having read the story of her life I realized she is the only female saint given the title of "great." I used to tell everyone my middle initial of "G" stood for *gorgeous*. Now I'm proud to say it's "Gertrude the Great". (chuckle)

If I can leave my children and grandsons with just one quarter of the faith I have, perhaps the Lord will say, "Job well done" on the day He hopefully calls me home. That's another reason I am sure He leaves me here on earth—to pass on my faith. I also have too many projects to finish yet and He surely knows that I am not a quitter, leaving things undone so, truthfully, I'm not quite ready to go. How wise He is.

I have come to realize that the greatest factor in "Letting Go and Letting God" is to see with the eyes of faith that God permits, if He does not will, all that happens in our lives for a reason. That's why that poem *The Tapestry of My Life* is so precious to me. If we look at the days of our lives as stepping stones to our eternity with Him, we can cope with the heartaches, disappointments and yes, even the pain, offering it all up to the Lord and through these offerings, in the end, we shall profit in this life and in the life to come. You can bank on God. So, let go, let God. I am working on doing that 100% of the time.

Singer Patti LaBelle once said, "I do know I got it going on. You know what I got? I got Jesus. I got myself. I have a wonderful family. I have honesty." I ditto that one. Oprah Winfrey quoted Anthony Brandt in the December 2007 issue of *O Magazine*. His quote: "Other things may change us, but we start and end with family." I ditto that one too.

I would never trade any phase of my life, my loving family, or my amazing and faithful friends for less gray hair or even less pain. They all have made my life worth living in spite of all those scary roller coaster rides. Honestly, in retrospect, I realize the good parts of my life as well as the good people in my life far outnumber the not-so-good parts.

APOLOGIES

Until after this book was finished and after my daughter was in the process of editing it, I did not fully realize the true emotional pain, or the true count of actual tears, I had caused my children during the months and YEARS following my battle against the big "C." To have said that they rode that big mother-of-all-roller-coaster ride with me is definitely an understatement. While I may have many scars from the surgeries, they have many more emotional *wounds* as their reminders of that ride and the years that followed.

In the course of writing this book, I would often ask my children what they remembered about that ride. They were honest in their responses, but they never totally revealed how really nasty and downright mean I had been. When the editing phase began and Melissa suggested that I add more in some areas, I had to ask them for more help in recalling those difficult hospital days. I don't have full recall of many days as I was always so heavily medicated. My children then felt they could finally be totally honest in telling me what a true witch I had been.

My oldest son just recently told me about often leaving my hospital room and crying in the hallway because I had been so mean to him. My daughter recounted similar incidents of my cruel, mean and nasty behavior towards her and others.

They all did tell me that after a few weeks they concluded that the strong pain medication protocol I was on was the cause of that behavior. In spite of that realization, they continued to experience the pain inflicted by my sharp tongue. I believe it was they who finally told the doctor he had to change my meds, after the infection had been brought under control, because those meds had created a real life monster. *But four weeks had already elapsed before this happened.* I believe my daughter described me as a true Dr. Jekyll/Mr. Hyde. She is too kind to me with that remark. I was worse than that.

While I was so heavily medicated, I truly do not recall those incidents or days. I recollect some things about my doctors, nurses, medical procedures, bits and pieces of some days, some visitors, some phone calls, but not all. I was able to relate much of what happened by reading the doctors' operating notes, and all other files I have that relate to my medical course. I have concluded that whatever else I do recall is possible because these were the times when I was in between doses of the morphine or other strong meds. When they were wearing off and up until I received my next dose and it kicked in again big time, vague but often incomplete recollections were possible. In hindsight, these times that I do recollect a bit of were just small windows of total consciousness and alertness—I was then Dr. Jekyll. The majority of the time I was deep in la-la-land, and as I related earlier in my story, I was nasty, mean and cruel, belligerent, vitriolic and on the very edge of paranoia—a true Mrs. Hyde.

I wrote in an earlier chapter about the change in my behavior after they did take me off those strong doses of morphine. One of the nurses told me a few things about the "before" period when I was heavily medicated and the exasperations of the nursing staff. She remarked that I was a different person after I had been taken off those massive doses of pain meds. I don't even recall if I apologized to all of the staff after she told me that.

Here I will apologize to anyone I may have hurt and caused to cry during those times and later during the tough years that followed—and especially say to my loving kids, my dear sister Lulu and my dearest friend Annette: "I am so sorry." I am sure if I could recall everyone I hurt and wrote their names down the list would be so DANG long.

Now, whenever I recite the "Our Father" and come to that last part, "and forgive us our trespasses as we forgive those who trespass against us," I will especially remember the countless hurts I cruelly inflicted on everyone. I'm sure I will have to say that I am sorry many more times in future years. I promise to work on this so it happens less and less from now on. You all deserve that promise from me and so much more.

Finally, I have a very special thank you for you, Melissa. When I was rewriting some parts of the book somewhere along the line I realized that writing this book had truly been my therapy. I also concluded that when you first planted the seed for the book back in 2000, you had an ulterior motive. I bet you thought if I would try to write the book it would keep me busy and take my mind off my pain and all you children would then maybe get a much needed break from my nastiness. I rejected your suggestion. I recall saying to you: "Are you out of your cotton-picking mind? I can't write a book." I bet you also silently said to yourself: "No Mom, I'm not out of my cotton-picking mind but you are because you are driving us all nuts with your depressive attitude and tongue lashings."

In 2005, a full five years after you had planted that seed about writing a book, I called you and said I had decided to give your suggestion a try. You told me then that you knew I would come around to your way of thinking eventually, but you didn't think it would take so long. It had been five years. For almost all of those years I continued to be snippy and hurt you with my "poor me" attitude and my frustrations at never getting anywhere in my endless search for relief from this chronic pain. Had I listened to you back in 2000 and started the book then I may have spared you all years of dealing with my state of mind. I think you will agree that my change of attitude in regard to my chronic pain condition did gradually begin to change not too long after I took you up on your idea. How wise and smart you are. Now besides telling everyone you are my daughter, my best friend, my precious pearl, my mentor, my teacher, my editor, I can add you are my very own personal therapist. You are a true treasure to me.

When I gave Melissa the files that contained the chapters of my book, I told her I knew I had told her never to "come home with a package." Then I told her that now I was, indeed, *sending her home with a package*, a precious package . . . the fruit of all my labor in writing this dang book. I asked her to be kind to me in critiquing my humble attempt and to remember I am just an amateur when it comes to book writing. She WAS kind and, even more, she was ever so PATIENT with me when I would change something yet again, after I had originally told her I was finished with that particular chapter having made the revisions or additions she had suggested. I hope you have forgiven me for messing up your "clean files." You sure opened up a can of worms (for me and for you) when you planted that seed for a book way back then.

Thank you all for everything. I love you all so very much and, again, I'm sorry.

APPENDIX

SPECIAL AND FAVORITE INSPIRATIONAL BOOKS

Footprints, Scripture with reflections
> By: Margaret Fishback Powers—author of that best-loved poem by the same name (*Hey, my dear grandsons, do you remember that Indian grandmother story I told you earlier in this story? Take note here of the author's name: Fishback.*

Everyday Blessings
> By: Max Lucado

Grace for the Moment (Vol. I and Vol. II)
> By: Max Lucado

Meditations for Women Who Do Too Much by Anne Wilson Schaef

The Seat of the Soul by Gary Zukav

The One Year Book of Personal Prayer
> Prayers and quotes compiled by Daniel Partner
> Published by Tynedale House Publishers

Chicken Soup for the Surviving Soul (for cancer survivors)
> By: Jack Canfield, Mark Victor Hansen, Patty Aubrey and
> Nancy Mitchell, R.N.

Laughter, Silence & Shouting—an anthology of women's prayers
> By: Kathy Keay

20-Minute Retreats—Revive your spirits in just minutes a day
> By: Rachel Harris, Ph.D.

Living a Sacred Life
> By: Robin Heerens Lysne

The Healing Power of Faith
    By: Harold G. Koenig, M.D.

The Tapestry of Life—From the Salesian Missions collection
    Compiled and edited by: Sara Tarascio
    Published by the Salesian Missions

Sing His Praises—From the Salesian Missions collection
    Compiled and edited by Jennifer Grinaldi

*   *   *

FAVORITE POEMS AND PASSAGES

The Easy Way Out, anonymous

Easy looks for a short-cut to Blessings. Easy settles for something less than the best. Easy is being soft on priorities. Easy lacks convictions. Easy requires no sacrifices and does not want to endure. Easy stops short of the goal and wants no hardship. Easy has no permanence and few rewards. Easy will not get the job done.

Definition of Success, a quote from Ralph Waldo Emerson

To laugh often and much;
To win the respect of intelligent people
And the affection of children;
To earn the appreciation of honest critics
And endure the betrayal of false friends;
To appreciate beauty;
To find the best in others;
To leave the world a bit better—whether by a healthy child, a garden patch or a redeemed social situation;
To know that even one life breathed easier because you lived;
This is to have success.

Believe in Yourself—*A variation of an original poem,* author unknown

Set your standards high, you deserve the best.
Try for what you want, and never settle for less.
Believe in yourself no matter what you choose.
Keep a winning attitude and you can never lose.

Think about your destination, but don't worry if you stray.
'Cause the most important thing is, what you've learned along the way.
Take all that you've become, to be all that you can be,
Soar above the clouds, and let your dreams set you free.

Man in the Glass, author unknown

When you get what you want in your struggle for self
And the world makes you King for a day,
Just go to the mirror and look at yourself
And see what that man has to say.

For it isn't your father or mother or wife,
Whose judgment upon you must pass.
The fellow whose verdict counts most in your life
Is the one staring back from the glass.

Some people may think you a straight-shooting chum
And call you a wonderful guy,
But the man in the glass says you are only a bum,
If you can't look him straight in the eye.

He's the fellow to please, never mind all the rest,
For he's with you clear up to the end.
And you've passed your most dangerous, difficult test,
If the man in the glass is your friend.

You may fool the whole world down the pathway of years
And get pats on the back as you pass,
But the final reward will be heartaches and tears
If you have cheated the man in the glass.

POEM—By Lorraine Dube (*I bet you didn't know your Mémère was a poet, too!*)

Surprises and disappointments make up a life;
Endless joy or cruel pain, sometimes sharp as a knife.
Surprises are most always welcomed you'll agree;
Disappointments received with negatives you see.

But there are always two sides of a coin to choose;
So if you just turn it around, how can you lose?
Success is failure turned inside out, so true and wise;
And disappointments are sometimes blessings in disguise.

One has to accept and say it's just meant to be
And down the road the reasons become plain to see.
So when things don't go your way and you're hardest hit,
Hang in there and the coin will flip in just a bit!

When funds are tight, you put more water in the soup
And if plans go wrong, don't let it throw you for a loop.
Plans can be changed and revised once you look at another side,
And things do turn around . . . from the ebb and to the tide!

DON'T QUIT, author unknown

When things go wrong, as they sometimes will,
When the road you're traveling seems all uphill,
When the funds are low and the debts are high,
And you want to smile but you have to sigh,
When care is pressing you down a bit,
Rest if you must, but don't ever quit.

Life's race is full of twists and turns
As every one of us eventually learns,
And many a failure turns about,
When one might have won had one stuck it out;
Don't give up though the pace seems slow,
You may succeed if you give it a go.

Success is failure turned inside out,
The silver tint of the clouds of doubt.
You can never tell how the race will end,
A victory may be just around the next bend.
So stay the course when you're hardest hit,
It's when things seem worse that you must not quit.

My dear grandsons, if you recall I began my book (Foreword) with a passage on "The Tapestry of Life" and here I have added two more versions of it because I do so love it. My hope is that it will become a favorite of yours, too. I further hope that it will remind you that the Lord is the Alpha and the Omega and after first and always turning to Him for your needs, reading the "Tapestry of Life" passages and poems should be your next step in dealing with life's foul balls.

THE TAPESTRY OF MY LIFE, author unknown

My life is but a weaving
Between my Lord and me.
I cannot choose the colors
He works so steadily.

Oft times He weaves in sorrow
And I, in foolish pride
Forget He sees the upper
And I, the underside.

Not till the loom is silent
And the shuttles cease to fly,
Will God unroll the tapestry
And explain the reason why.

The dark threads are as needed
In the Weaver's skillful hand,
As the threads of gold and silver
In the pattern He has planned.

Additional version of The Tapestry of my Life (author unknown)

I wonder what the other side will be when I have finished weaving all my thread. I do not know the pattern or the end of this great piece of work which is for me. I only know that I must weave with care, day by day, the colors that are given me, and make of them a fabric firm and true, which will be of service to my fellow man.

Sometimes those colors are so dark and gray I doubt if there will be one line or trace of beauty there. But all at once there comes a thread of gold or rose so deep that there will always be that one bright spot to cherish or to keep and maybe against it's ground of darker hue it will be beautiful!

The warp is held in place by the Master's hand. The Master's mind made that design for me; if I but weave the shuttle to and fro and blend the colors just the best I know, perhaps when it is finished, He will say, "'Tis good," and lay it on the footstool of His feet.

I hope that last one, especially, will always serve to remind you (my grandsons and the generations to follow) that God is in charge of your life and believe me He knows what He's doing. Trust in Him!

Hop Aboard!
By: Lorraine Dube Barnes

Don't be afraid . . . just hop aboard;
Put all your trust in the Lord!
If the coaster rides of life give you a scare,
Don't fret and worry, because He will be there!

When those loop-da-loops keep facing you,
Resolve to totally trust HIM anew!
You will always survive a scary ride,
Because He is there . . . always right by your side!

My love forever and throughout eternity,

Your *Mémère*

*   *   *

A Final Word

I know I repeated myself numerous times all through my book, which most likely became annoying. There was a method to my madness, as they say. I wanted to drill you on remembering certain phrases such as, "Where there is a will, there is a way" and, "Never say never." If I succeeded, and if other readers remember them, too, I will have accomplished something—a double play, so to speak. Don't forget to pass them on and to pay them forward! Love, *MEM!*

Edwards Brothers Inc.
Blue Ridge Summit, PA. USA
April 13, 2011